RELIGION
AND THE SOCIOLOGY OF
KNOWLEDGE

Modernization and Pluralism in
Christian Thought and Structure

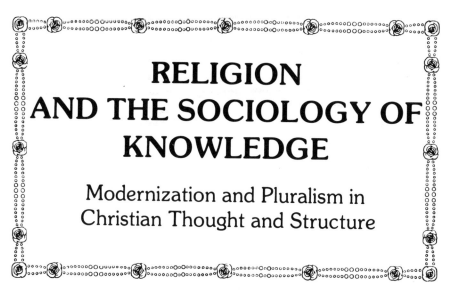

RELIGION AND THE SOCIOLOGY OF KNOWLEDGE

Modernization and Pluralism in Christian Thought and Structure

Edited by
BARBARA HARGROVE

Studies in Religion and Society
Volume 8

The Edwin Mellen Press
New York and Toronto

Library of Congress Cataloging in Publication Data

Religion and the sociology of knowledge.

   (Studies in religion and society ; v. 8)
   Includes bibliographical references.
   1. Sociology, Christian--Addresses, essays, lectures.
2. Religion and sociology--Addresses, essays, lectures.
3. Knowledge, Sociology of--Addresses, essays, lectures.
I. Hargrove, Barbara. II. Series: Studies in religion
and society (New York, N.Y.) ; v. 8.
BT738.R44 1984   306'.6   83-22149
ISBN 0-88946-872-9

Studies in Religion and Society
Series ISBN 0-88946-863-X

The Edwin Mellen Press
P.O. Box 450
Lewiston, New York 14092

Printed in the United States of America

STUDIES IN RELIGION AND SOCIETY

TABLE OF CONTENTS

PREFACE

The genesis of this book was a seminar in "The Sociology of Knowledge and The Sociology of Religion," held at The Iliff School of Theology in the Spring of 1982. Its first glimmerings arose in response to the clearly publishable quality of some of the papers being presented. Moreover, part of the excitement of the seminar came from the variety of backgrounds and interests of those present, which made the discussion itself an exercise in the sociology of knowledge. Participants represented the fields of sociology, theology, biblical studies, American religion and culture, and psychology and counseling. Many occupational and professional roles were represented, and many denominational backgrounds.

This volume contains the best of the papers presented at that seminar, a sampling of classics in the field that sparked the discussions, and additional contributions that increase the diversity as well as filling out the subject matter. Most readers, whatever their field of expertise, may find that some of these papers will be outside their usual range of consideration. I highly recommend reading them all anyway, for the perspectives they bring really make the point of the book: one's particular place in society shapes the ways in which one learns, thinks, and responds, even concerning the eternal verities of religion.

Although I must bear responsibility for its final form, plans for the book began in discussions of participants in the seminar. Without that group process it probably would never have happened. I must also thank Dean H. Edward Everding, Jr. and The Iliff School of Theology for providing for the typing of the manuscript;

Melanie Downs, Margaret Manion, and Alberta Smith for
actually creating the camera-ready copy. Patricia Edwards-
DeLancey deserves a special word for taking charge of the
many details that arose, particularly after I disappeared
from the campus to spend a leave in my mountain retreat.

But, most of all, I wish to thank the contributors,
who have put up with my editorial fussiness and have
responded, often on time, to my demands. It was their
creativity that sparked the project, and it continues to
do so.

Barbara Hargrove

Poudre City, Colorado
June, 1983

ACKNOWLEDGEMENTS

The diagram of the "Pastoral Circle" is reproduced from *Social Analysis: Linking Faith and Justice*, by Joe Holland and Peter Henriot, and published by Orbis Books of Maryknoll, New York, 1983, by permission of the authors.

"Concerning the Sociology of Religion," from *Problems of a Sociology of Knowledge*, by Max Scheler, translated by Manfred W. Frings, edited and with an introduction by Kenneth W. Stikkers, copyright © 1980, is reprinted by permission of Routledge & Kegan Paul, Publishers, London, Boston, and Henley.

"Charismatic Authority and Its Routinization," from *The Theory of Social and Economic Organization*, by Max Weber, edited and translated by A. M. Henderson and Talcott Parsons, copyright © 1975, by Talcott Parsons, is reprinted from the 1964 edition by permission of The Free Press of Glencoe, a Division of the MacMillan Company, Publishers, New York.

"Toward a Critique of Modernity," from *Facing up to Modernity: Excursions in Society, Politics, and Religion*, by Peter L. Berger, copyright © 1977 by Peter L. Berger, is reprinted by permission of Basic Books, Inc., Publishers, New York.

"Sociology of Knowledge and the Study of Early Christianity," by Harold E. Remus, was previously published in *Studies in Religion: Sciences Religieuses* 11:1, Winter, 1982.

PART I

INTRODUCTION

RELIGION AND THE SOCIOLOGY OF KNOWLEDGE
AN INTRODUCTION

Barbara Hargrove

The subdiscipline known as the sociology of knowledge occupies a rather lowly position in American sociological circles. There is no special section of the American Sociological Association designated for it. In a recent survey of the special areas of interest of professional sociologists, the sociology of knowledge was lumped together with cultural sociology and the sociologies of education; leisure, sports and recreation; marriage and family; religion, art and leisure; language and social linguistics; and sex roles; in a category titled "Normative Institutions," in which some one-sixth of the respondents indicated a major interest.[1] Given an equal share of that mixed bag (which may be optimistic), that would indicate that a little less than 2% indicated a major interest in the area, with about an equal number noting a secondary interest. Similarly, major sociological journals devote a very small amount of space to articles in this area. One would definitely not see the sociology of knowledge as a dominant force in contemporary American sociology.

By contrast, in many of the areas of religious study the sociology of knowledge has a status uncomfortably close to that of a fad. Theologians, biblical scholars, even those involved in the more applied areas of ethics or practice, are calling on the sociology of knowledge to help them understand the nature of religion and religious institutions in the modern world. What then, is the

sociology of knowledge, and why does it seem so pertinent
in the field of religion?

Although there are enough variations on the theme to
lead to disagreements as to an exact definition of the
field, I think most sociologists of knowledge would agree
that its core deals with the ways in which persons' and
groups' position in a society shapes their perception of
the world, and consequently, their responses to that world.
If this sounds like the Marxist critique of ideology as
the "false consciousness" attached to the vested interests
of groups differently related to the means of production,
it must be noted that those emphases of Marxism *are* part
of the sociology of knowledge. However, for many in the
field the Marxist perspective is at best partial, representing its own foundation in the European society of
Marx's time. For those whose experience of differences in
world view has been based more on status characteristics
such as race or sex, the purely economic categories seem
inadequate. What does seem to be the case is that just
as there are in the world many societies with different
cultures that provide a different perspective on the world
for their people, so in any one society there are different classes, regions, and groups that also create different social worlds for their members. And just as it is
the case in the world at large that some societies, some
cultures, tend to be dominant, and to have a tendency to
make their world view the normative one for everyone with
whom they come into contact, so in any given society, certain dominant groups control the normative definitions of
the world. For those whose experience is different, that
normative definition may be experienced as oppression.
For those who deliberately choose a different view of the
world, the reigning definitions may be defined as corrupt,
sinful, or outmoded.

The particular relevance of religion for the sociology of knowledge is that, in the long run, socially shaped understandings of the nature and meaning of human life are grounded in some vision of the cosmic frame in which it is experienced. Thus to ignore religion, at least in its broadest definition, is to miss the deepest dimensions of any human world view. Again, while this is less evident in modern society than in earlier or less pluralistic cultures, it is still true that some of the deepest currents of human meaning and action have been carried by religious institutions. The student of human knowledge ignores those institutions at his or her peril.

The relevance of the sociology of knowledge to religion will be made abundantly clear in the chapters that follow. Suffice it to say here, in theological language, that students of religion are finding that human understandings of the divine are incarnated in the experience of life in human society. It is only through the lens given by our experience as social beings that we view any transcendent realm that may exist. Given this fact, persons deeply immersed in quite different religious traditions sometimes find themselves joining together to investigate the sources of their world views and value systems, often meeting in their search other serious students who profess no religious faith at all, at least in traditional terms.

The study of the relation between religion and the sociology of knowledge can begin with the religious tradition—in Western society, with theology and scripture. It can begin with religious institutions and the currents of thought they propound or to which they respond. It can begin with movements in the society that are not—or not yet—institutionalized, but which demonstrate the human demand for cosmic meaning, which can be defined as religious. Since we understand the scriptures and theolo-

gies of various religious groups to reflect the history
and thought of previous movements of this type, we are
brought back to the study of tradition.

And so it is with this book: its structure is really
circular. Any portion of it could have been chosen to be
the beginning. But to create a book out of a circular
pattern, it must be snipped somewhere and laid out flat.
The reader who does not like our choice may start reading
at any section, read to the end, and go back to the beginning to reach his or her own starting point without losing
any of our sense of meaning.

The circularity reflects two different theoretical
sources, one dealing with how things come to be the way
they are, the other with how human beings may take action
to change them. The first is the paradigm of the sociology of knowledge given by Berger and Luckmann in *The Social
Construction of Reality*.[2] Their approach is to begin with
the nature of humankind, with the reality that we are of
necessity born into social situations. That necessity is
not only physical, based on the obvious need of infants
and young children for nurture from other adults, but also
psychological. That is, the data of sense experience from
our everyday lives are too numerous, too varied to be able
to comprehend unless they are organized into some kind of
meaningful patterns. Part of adult nurture of the young
in human society is the provision of those patterns from
the culture into which they are born, and the patterns
are maintained in daily conversation with others in the
society who share that culture. Without such patterns,
reality would dissolve into chaos.

We experience the world, then, within patterns that
have been created by the society in which we are born.
While these have been created by a process of *externalization*, through *objectification*, they are made to seem

factual to us. Then, through *internalization* they are
taken into our understanding of ourselves and the world
and become a part not only of external reality but of our
internal understandings. The circle is closed as we then
externalize these understandings to create an outside world
that becomes objectively real, and on and on. If one were
to portray their concept graphically, it might look like
this:

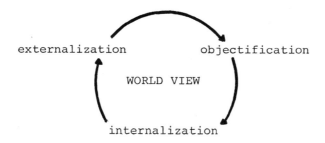

externalization   objectification

WORLD VIEW

internalization

The second source of our circular reasoning comes
from Joe Holland and Peter Henriot's *Social Analysis:
Linking Faith with Justice*, which contrasts the "academic"
approach to social analysis with what they call the
"pastoral" approach, "analysis in the service of action for
justice." They see a circular pattern in the relations
between what they call four "mediations of experience":
insertion, social analysis, theological reflection, and
pastoral planning. This pattern, which they call the
"Pastoral Circle," is diagrammed in this manner:[3]

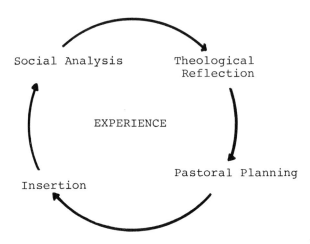

In this model, the issue is found in the ongoing process
of experience, where one inserts oneself into the process
for the purposes of pastoral action. Social analysis is
to be based upon that experience, theological reflection
on the analysis, and pastoral planning based on the reflection, with, of course, new experiences then evolving
which lead to new analysis, etc.

The place of the sociology of knowledge in this model
is clear, and is made clearer as the authors note questions that must be asked at each stage. For example, at
the point of insertion one may ask just where one places
oneself, whose point of view and experience are being considered. At the point of social analysis, the question is
that of the analytic tradition that is being used, and the
ideological factors implicit in it. Again, theological
reflection requires the same kind of questioning: What is
the theological tradition which is being used, and what
are the constraints its assumptions impose upon the reflection? Finally, in pastoral planning, one must ask
who it is who is doing the planning, and what are the

processes by which it is done. All of these are questions in the sociology of knowledge, and all revolve
around a process that is circular.

The sociology of knowledge, then, can never concern
itself only with the internal structures of human views
of the world, but rather must see that those structures
rest upon and reflect the forms of the social institutions
in which they are imbedded. We must see the reciprocal
effects of structures of consciousness and of institutions,
particularly structures of religious consciousness and of
religious institutions. For example, note the words of
Episcopal bishop John Shelby Spong, on the occasion of a
gathering of Episcopal and Lutheran worshippers around a
shared communion table which they held to represent future
union of those denominations:

> The church of the future will have to learn
> to embrace relativity as a virtue and to dismiss
> certainty as a vice. Christian survival may well
> require that our clergy, our laity and our theo-
> logians be encouraged to walk out onto the edges
> of faith, to explore terrain on which the
> Christians of the past have seemed loath to
> walk. Radical challenges to our traditional
> approaches will force open a theology that has
> bound us to literal creeds, literal Bibles, and
> infallible understandings of God. This gener-
> ation of Christians is being asked to cease
> judging one another, to accept the fact that
> all of us are pilgrims on a journey into the
> pluralism of truth, and none of us has the
> final answer. That is the fear implicit in
> the ecumenical movement--and that fear, when
> it becomes conscious, can be paralyzing.[4]

While the fear may become paralyzing, there is also a
hope involved in such an attitude toward the future. It
is the task of the sociology of knowledge, as shown by
Steven Stall and Kerry Edwards, to make more explicit the
sources of both that fear and that hope, that persons may
find ways or methods of theology and sociology, and ways
in which they inform or confuse one another, particularly
in the light of the collapse of the so-called "detente"
between religion and the social sciences, based on what is
now seen to be a false dichotomy between their two spheres.
Harold Remus traces some of the uses given to the sociology
of knowledge in biblical studies, using as an example the
study of miracle stories in scripture. John Stanley adds
to the discussion of further uses of the discipline, then
moves out to attempt new applications for texts of the
Christian religion. To some extent, this dealing with the
tradition parallels Berger and Luckmann's concept of externalization, of the human act of putting meaning on the
world.

The next section, then, is in the realm of Berger and
Luckmann's concept of objectification, where we see the
religious insights hardened into institutional form. The
opening excerpt from Max Weber is an example of the way in
which he formulated the process by which new breakthroughs
led by prophets or other charismatic leaders become institutionalized by their followers. The papers which
follow discuss this in terms of the forms of religious
institutions most common in our society at the present time.
The particular way in which institutions in our society
have made routine the charismatic religious institutions,
no less than other institutions of modern society, not only
develop a bureaucratic structure but also move to the
establishment of professionalization within their ranks.
In Part III of this volume, then, we begin with two studies

of religious institutions that attempt to maintain the
charismatic or traditional structures of the religious
community in the face of a modernizing world. Peter
Beyer, in his systems approach to the study of religious
institutions, relates the reaction of the Roman Catholic
Church to modernization, particularly in the setting of
Quebec, in which its relative success in maintaining the
older order has contributed to the separation of French
Canadian Catholics from much of the rest of the culture of
the country. Nancy Ammerman reports on a fundamentalist
Protestant church that has carved its own niche in a
modern city, acting in some ways remarkably like the
process described by Beyer. Howard Fuller, on the other
hand, in an empirical social-psychological study of West
Coast suburban Protestantism, shows how the local culture
has influenced and is carried by mainline churches. Ken
Merrick-Webb then turns to a comparison of the methods of
mainline and evangelical churches and their relation to
the modernizing impulse, showing how ideological opposition to modernization may be subverted by the methods used
to promote the ideology.

    We have said the modernization includes professional-
ization. In the chapters by Jan Sumner and Kady Cone we
see two facets of what that means in the modern church.
Jan's discussion of the socialization of professional
ministers is given additional poignancy in its focus on
women now entering the ministry, whose traditional roles
have been most removed from modernizing influences, and
for whom, then, the professionalization of the clergy may
represent a particular problem. Kady, thoroughly accepting the specializations of roles within the modern church,
turns her attention to the way in which the sociology of
knowledge can inform the specialization in which she finds
herself, that of pastoral therapist. Her chapter can also

be seen as a bridge to Part IV, in that many of the problems for which therapy is sought tend to be created by facets of modernization in society to which new movements have addressed themselves.

Part IV moves on to a discussion of movements that may be seen as responses to modernization which are in their own way religious, but with relations with the institutional churches as they now exist that are ambivalent at best. It begins with a short article by Peter Berger, one of the oft-quoted writers in this volume, pointing up some of the problems as well as some of the characteristics of modernization. Marilyn Hauck looks at the movements of the 1960s as a possible foray into the post-modern future, while Sheila Davaney discusses the relevance to newly emerging patterns of religion and living contained in such social movements as feminism and those carried out in the name of liberation.

And so we come full circle, for some of the papers in the first section reflect upon some of the constructive theology in which Davaney is engaged. Whatever else this volume may portend, its very structure indicates what I think all of us suspect--that the relation of the sociology of knowledge to religion is a lively and unfinished one, one which will go through many more stages before it settles into predictable patterns.

NOTES

1. Bettina Huber, "Sociological Practitioners: Their Characteristics and Role in the Profession," American Sociological Association *Footnotes* 11:5 (May, 1983), p. 8.

2. Peter L. Berger and Thomas Luckmann, *The Social Construction of Reality* (Garden City, NY: Doubleday Anchor Books, 1967).

3. Joe Holland and Peter Henriot, *Social Analysis: Linking Faith with Justice* ((Maryknoll, NY: Orbis Books, 1983), p. 8. Their discussion of the model occurs on pp. 7 through 10.

4. John Shelby Spong, "Hope and Fear in Ecumenical Union," *Christian Century* 110:19 (June 8-15, 1983), p. 581.

IN CANDID CONVERSATION: THEOLOGY
AND SOCIOLOGY OF KNOWLEDGE

Elizabeth Schmidt

OF KNOWING AND SPEAKING:
THE SOCIOLOGY OF KNOWLEDGE
AND ITS IMPORT FOR GOD-TALK

The sociology of knowledge, one of the most significant developments of modern thought, is predicated on the
recognition of the social foundation and character of all
knowing. Although the scope and aims of this recently
emergent discipline are undergoing definition (and re-
definition), and although the thinkers gathered under this
"umbrella" are divergent in their claims, the shared central tenets of the sociology of knowledge have already
issued forth profound and far-reaching implications.

The theological enterprise is in no way immune to
these effects. In the twentieth century, the content,
task, and method of theological reflection is being re-
articulated by various voices in conversation with social
theories of knowing. Sociologically derived insights
increasingly inform the verbs and very grounds of God-
talk. The intentions of this paper are threefold: first,
to set forth in a brief historical survey several of the
major assertions of sociology of knowledge; second, to
illustrate the manner in which social theories of knowing
have been appropriated in several contemporary theological
strands; and third, to discuss the theological "meta-
issues" raised by the ramifications of sociology of knowledge, particularly the problem of religious relativism

and pluralism. With this introduction, it is to the
history and main claims of sociology of knowledge that I
now turn.

SOCIOLOGY OF KNOWLEDGE: ROOTS,
RENDERINGS, AND REJOINDERS

   Roots of the sociology of knowledge may be traced
back at least as early as the seventeenth century, when
Blaise Pascal astutely observed that what is true on one
side of the Pyrenees is error on the other.[1] Over two-
hundred years later, French sociologist Emile Durkheim
(1858-1917), in his *Elementary Forms of the Religious
Life*, speculated that the fundamental categories of human thought were religious and therefore social in origin. Durkheim, who defined religion as a socially
grounded system of rites and beliefs related to the sacred, held that religion is a cosmology reflective of
social reality. Concepts of time and space, for instance, express conceptual reflections of social structures. Durkheim's contemporary, German sociologist Max
Weber (1864-1920), examined the relationship between
religious ideas and socio-economic development. In his
Sociology of Religion, Weber theorized that religious
ideas could be the impetus for charismatic "breakthroughs" which changed society into more complex social
forms, becoming institutionalized through the process of
rationalization.
   Yet study of the relationship between human thought
and its social context was not christened "sociology of
knowledge" until the 1920's, when the term was coined by
German philosopher Max Scheler. The intellectual climate of Scheler's Germany was preceded and influenced by
Marx, Nietzsche, and the historicist perspective.[2] For

Marx, human consciousness is determined by social being
(which Marx interpreted primarily in economic terms).
Sociology of knowledge inherited from Marx the notion of
the social determination of consciousness, as well as
the key concept of "ideology." For Nietzsche, human
ideas are closely aligned to the struggle for power.
While not directly incorporated into sociology of knowledge, Nietzsche's perspective helped shape the milieu
from which it arose, and his terms "resentment" and
"false consciousness" were re-articulated by social
knowledge theorists. The historicist perspective was
characterized by an overwhelming sense that all of human knowledge is historical through and through, bound
to time and place. The possibilities for what and how
one knows are relative to and determined by history.

Out of this mood came the philosophy of Max Scheler
(1874-1928), who rejected economic reductionism and
sought a perspective that would transcend the relativity
of socially and historically conditioned viewpoints.
Scheler's rendering of sociology of knowledge focused on
the manner in which "real factors" (familial, political,
and economic) determined the stages (but not the content) of "ideal factors" (moral and intellectual values).
The resulting pyramid of factors bears resemblance to
personality theorist Abraham Maslow's hierarchy of human
needs, which maintains that fundamental physiological
needs must be met before higher psychological needs can
be fulfilled. With a universal hierarchy of value-
stages, socially determined in sequence but not in content, Scheler hoped to circumvent full-fledged relativism. Scheler's work became known as "value sociology,"
because of his insistence that facts and knowledge are
determined by the socially-regnant axiology, the living

system of positive and negative value-rankings which he
called an *"ordo amoris."*[3]

Also responding to the Marxist challenge was Karl
Mannheim (1893-1947). Mannheim incorporated Marx's notion of "ideology" into a tool of general analysis, and
directed its use to the diagnosis of distorted visions
of reality. Rather than lamenting that "everything is
relative," Mannheim used the term "relationism" to emphasize that knowledge is always related to, and cannot be
understood apart from, its social context. Rather than
acquiescing in the inability to be totally free from
ideological influences, Mannheim hoped to mitigate the
situation by accumulating different perspectives and appealing to the "socially unattached intelligentsia"[4]--
the socially marginal persons whose perspectives he hoped
would be unhindered by vested interests.

Responding to Mannheim, Werner Stark in *The Sociology
of Knowledge* (1958) distinguished clearly between the
study of the *political* element in thought (Mannheim's
"ideology") and the systematic investigation of the
social conditions of knowledge as such, which is, in
Stark's estimation, the *real* task of sociology of knowledge. Inheriting the critical epistemology of Kant,
Stark called attention to the *"social a priori"* of
thought, a given system of values which forms the perceptual grid through which and in which humans encounter
reality. Without such prior judgments, such a perceptual screen, humans would be capable of only a blurred and
indistinguishable focus, and their attention would "roam
helplessly and hopelessly over the boundless plains of
history and human geography, coming to rest nowhere, receiving no tangible or definite impressions anywhere."[5]

The loudest rejoinder of all was the duet offered by
Peter Berger and Thomas Luckmann, whose joint opus *The*

Social Construction of Reality (1966) reconceived the
discipline of sociology of knowledge. Citing Durkheim's
assertion that society possesses objective facticity, and
Weber's view that society is constructed of activity that
expresses subjective meanings, Berger and Luckmann addressed the dual character of society. How does subjective meaning become objective facticities? How is social
reality constructed? *This*, they claim, is the question
to be answered by sociology of knowledge.

Berger and Luckmann were the first to articulate systematically the dialectical relationship between knowledge and society, which was only intimated (and often,
only one-sidedly) by earlier thinkers. Society is a human product, produced for the welfare of "biologically
unfinished" offspring for whom instinct alone would guarantee neither individual nor species survival. Society,
including language, roles, institutions, and plausibility
structures all incorporated into a "symbolic universe,"
takes on an aura of objective facticity. This objective
reality is internalized in the process of socialization;
thus humans are social products. In other words, humans
create the reality which creates them in turn. To forget
or deny that reality is a social construction is to reify
social reality, and overlook half of the dialectic, in a
moment of "false consciousness."

Many of these themes are echoed in Clifford Geertz's
Toward an Interpretation of Cultures (1973). Coming
from an anthropological perspective, Geertz believes with
Weber that humans are suspended in "webs of significance"
that they themselves have spun.[6] "Incomplete animals" at
birth, humans develop the symbolic capacity which creates
culture. Culture, in turn, is not given in the DNA or in
some way an accessory feature of the human organism--but
is ingredient in its very completion and humaneness. For

Geertz, to be human is to find oneself suspended in a
symbolic universe. Without this culturally-created and
given symbolic network with which to encounter reality,
humans would not know or understand anything, and would
indeed be less than human. Humans are creatures and creators of culture, whose society and culture is constitu-
tive of their very being and knowing.

As this succinct survey illustrates, a diverse group
of thinkers and a varied assortment of theories fall
under the rubric of sociology of knowledge. Underlying
the diversity are several primary premises which would
evoke affirmation from most of these theorists. Foundational is the assertion that human knowledge of reality
never takes place in a vacuum, or from an objective or
value-free perspective. Rather, humans are social and
cultural beings whose experience, action, and thought is
mediated through and screened by a web of symbolic meanings and values. What is considered knowledge, and how
it is known, is dependent upon the axiological grid
through which any given society encounters reality. This
social *a priori*, which selects and orders perceptions, is
conditioned and specified by that given society. In other
words, human knowledge is always socially created and
socially given.

By implication, then, there can be neither isolated
individual knowledge, for no human exists totally apart
from society and culture, nor can there be universal
knowledge[7] (although Mannheim for one would like to make
exception for mathematics and parts of the natural sciences). Rather, knowledge is always filtered through a
system of social values and commitments, a social *a priori*, and "*ordo amoris*." These social values emerge from
social realities, and function to support what is apprehended; thus, socially constructed reality takes on a

quality of objective facticity. In dialectical development, a given social form issues forth the basic and underlying systems of values, which, in turn, provide the
social *a priori* through which reality is perceived, and
tend to uphold what is perceived--the very social structures from which they arose. In sum, no knowledge is
unconditioned by its social context. On the contrary,
the only knowledge available to humans reflects and depends upon socially prior value commitments which are
bound to and defined by time, place, and social realities.
Knowledge is inherently socially grounded.

THEOLOGICAL INTERFACE: CONSEQUENCES
FOR CONTENT, SOURCES, AND METHOD

Talk about God, no less than any other form of human
conversation, is shaped and mediated by the values inherent in a social matrix. Again, by implication, there
can be no absolutely private talk about God--nor any universal theological discussion either. The mouthpiece of
theology is intrinsically social, thus the language of
theology is always interested and contextual. A given
social order gives rise to a particular theological
framework and religious symbolism, which turns to under-
pin these very social structures. Talk about God both
reflects and instigates changes in social realities.
These assertions have received theological appropriation
by liberationist, feminist, and constructivist perspectives, in varying and overlapping degrees. In order to
assess systematically these forms of appropriation, I set
forth as categories the content, sources, and method of
theological endeavor.

The content of theology has been radically recast
in light of the insights adopted by feminist, Black, and

Latin American liberation theologians. Drawing heavily
on sociology of knowledge to analyze the dynamics of oppression and ideology, these thinkers transform theology
into a vehicle for the liberation of oppressed persons.
The bottom line is that, in social situations of unequal
and unjust distribution of power, the dominant group controls not only political and economic conditions but the
very interpretation of reality, including religious symbolism as well.[8] The idea of God, with its supporting
theological scaffold, rises out of and reflects societal
structures, which it serves to sanction and legitimate in
turn. This relationship has been unmasked most clearly
in situations of oppression by liberation theologians
who argue that a perverse and distorted society is mirrored in a similarly distorted image of God. As Juan
Luis Segundo writes, "Our unjust society and our pervert-
ed idea of God are in close and terrible alliance."[9]

Because dominant powers employ distorted religious
symbolism on their own behalf, liberation movements seek
not only the transformation of structures and institutions, but a spiritual revolution, a new vision in light
of which to encounter and redeem reality.[10] For Black
and Latin American theologians, this perspective is
yielded in the dynamic, dialectical encounter between
their experience of oppression, and scripture. Interpreting the one in light of the other, the ideology of
the oppressors is unmasked, and the content of scripture
is the imperative of Christ the Liberator, the story of
God's action on behalf of the oppressed. Because the
oppressors' vision of reality is distorted to serve their
unjust interests, theology done from their perspective is
"ideology."

Liberation thinkers grant that their own perspective
is interested and partial, *but*, they would argue, the

value-laden viewpoint of the oppressed is less distorted
than that of the oppressors whose vision propagates the
interests of the powerful at the expense of the weak.
Appealing as did Mannheim to the element of marginality,
these thinkers claim that it is only from the vantage
point of the oppressed that the dynamic of oppression can
be clearly apprehended. This is, in the words of Latin
American theologian Hugo Assman, "the epistemological
privilege of the poor."[11]

In all of this, both Black and Latin American liberationists appeal to divine revelation in scripture as a
privileged authority which transcends historical relativ-
ities. Because of its transcendent quality, scripture
safeguards against liberationist ideology and provides
an unshakeable foundation for hope. In recognition of
the contextual character of knowing, however, how can
these thinkers make exception for the ideas of God contained in scripture? In so doing, they seem to ignore
the implications of the insights that enable them to un-
mask their oppressor's distorted views of reality and
God. Here radical feminists part company with Black and
Latin American theologians, holding that the very *sources*
of theological reflection merit critical evaluation in
light of social theories of knowing.[12]

The claim of radical feminists is that the idea of
God as developed throughout Judeo-Christian history reflects, through and through, the ongoing dominance of men
over women, because women have not had access to positions of power in the social settings from which the idea
of God emerged. According to Mary Daly, to exist humanly is "to name the self, the world, and God,"[13] and
women have been denied the power of "naming." The resultant idea of God is a male idea, grounded in and supportive of male interests and power. Scripture is in no

way "above" this analysis, for it as well is a product
of male-dominated societies. The traditional ideas and
authoritative sources for theological reflection, rather
than providing foundations for liberation, function as
available sanctions for oppression of women because, as
Daly states, when "God is male, the male is God."[14]

At this point the implications for theological *method*
come up for consideration. When certain feminists, who
reject male-saturated sources derived from a male-dominated history, seek to create more appropriate imagery
for the deity by drawing on women's experience and traditions, they are employing a new, constructivist methodology. Theologian Gordon Kaufman's distinction between
hermeneutical, correlational, and constructivist methodologies is helpful here.[15] Hermeneutical theology assumes a given, unquestionable authority such as revelation in scripture or tradition, and seeks to interpret
it. Correlational theology incorporates hermeneutical
theology, recognizing a given authority and correlating
between that source and an additional authority, human
experience. Black and Latin American liberation theologians belong to this camp. But when sociology of knowledge illumines the contextual, partial, and in some cases
oppressively distorted nature of the authorities formerly
seen as absolute givens, theology can no longer be done
in a hermeneutical or correlational mode. In the absence
of absolute, transcendent authorities, the alternative
methodology is constructivist (which may be, in light of
Berger and Luckmann, a self-conscious and straight forward admission of what has been happening all along).

In the constructivist perspective, as articulated by
Kaufman, theological reflection is understood as imaginative creation of the idea of God, a construct which has
evolved with human history. Kaufman traces the develop-

ment of the idea of God in the biblical record, from a
jealous tribal war god to a universally salvitic diety.
He claims that God is not a "reified being," but a human-
ly-constructed symbol, a product of human attempts to
focus, order, and structure their life in the world. In
his own words, Kaufman has become convinced that "theology is (and always has been) essentially a constructive
work of the human imagination, an expression of the imagination's activity helping to provide orientation for
human life through developing a symbolical 'picture' of
the world roundabout and of the human place within that
world."[16]

The task of theology is thus reconceived as the "imaginative construction of the image/concept of God," as inherited from the languages and traditions of the West.
The endeavor begins with criticism of available traditions,
followed by imaginative reconstruction of a more adequate
idea of God. When no source is elevated and absolutized
as an (the) ultimate and final authority, the field of
available resources opens up to include all information,
encompassing and surpassing scripture and theological
tradition, as available for evaluation and imaginative
integration. The final test of human theological constructions is then a field test--that is, does it make
sense of human experience and serve to order and orient
fulfilled human life in the world? The task is never
completed once for all time, for talk about God demands
reconstruction in light of changing social situations.

Kaufman's position seems to appropriate to the full-
est extent. the far-reaching implications of sociology of
knowledge--implications which necessitate a re-visioning
of not only the content and sources but the very methodology of the theological undertaking.

META-MUSINGS: RELATIVISM
AND A THEOLOGY OF PLURALISM

As we have seen, awareness of the social and hence
partial and relative character of all theological discourse has raised profound questions about the foundational assumptions of the discipline itself. The eternal
and universal truth-claims which the "queen of the sciences" once claimed to articulate systematically are now
revealed to reflect many of the characteristics of the
social setting from which they arose. Nor can it ever
be assumed that conversation about God is common parlance
throughout the generations and cultures of the human race.
As Kaufman has pointed out, the idea of God is primarily
a Western construct, not a universally-shared attribute
or artifact. Some, venturing further along the lines of
Feuerbach, have wondered whether God-talk is anything more
than the product of sustained and somewhat distorted reflection on the reflection in the mirror, on the part of
particular persons in particular social settings. Acknowledgement of the sociality, temporality, and relative
particularity of human constructs has effectively erased
the notion of universal truth for all people, for all time.
The only "universal" of which to safely speak is that
humans, in the language of Berger and Luckmann, share the
common task of creating "symbolic universes" which impart
order and meaning to their lives.

The recognition that these social constructions are
always partial and perspectival, having no privileged
position from which to make absolute truth-claims, functions beneficently to protect against the idolatry to
which humans are all too prone. Remembering the perspectival character of our claims helps to keep them in
perspective. In this sense, critical theory functions

as a "critical principle" which relativizes and calls
into question all perspectives. At the same time, however, it denies any absolute axiology with which to dis-
criminate and evaluate the value-claims of others. From
a relative and limited perspective, how can one person
call another into question, or make judgments about a
different symbolic universe? The "abstract" question
comes all too close to home when families and friends find
that a loved one has become a disciple of the Rev. Sun
Myung Moon, for instance.

Of course, humans do make judgments and evaluate each
other's perspectives, but often in so doing we do not
assume our views are merely relative or "relational"--
which may explain why our criticisms are sometimes neither
heard nor heeded. Being self-conscious about our socially-
relative constructions of value and meaning need not, however, bid us be silent in face of what looks like evil
from where we sit. Rather, in the spirit of Mannheim, we
do the best we can in the light of our values and commitments, accompanied by a healthy dose of humility. In constructing towards evaluative criteria for making "inter-
perspectival" judgments, one might examine, first, whether
the view in question bears the same contours as objective
reality. For instance, parents might deny the reality of
illness, and refuse medical attention for a sick and dying
child. Second, can the consequences of the construction
be judged as destructive of human persons? Although any
criterion for judgment is in some sense relative, criteria
can at least be grounded in shared ideas about objective
reality and what is helpful or harmful to human persons.

The discussion is, on another level, the problem of
religious pluralism and interfaith dialogue. Concomitant
with the recognition of relativism is the problem of
pluralism. How can theology approach, interpret, even

incorporate, the situation of pluralism? One possible
alternative is grounded in the recognition and affirmation of all world-views as unique, partial, and relative;
meaningful and important only in relation to their respective contexts. The concern is to allow various traditions to affirm their own particular heritages and maintain their identities and integrities, hence prosyletism
is taboo. The attitude may be phrased summarily as "live
and let live." The net result is that no one has to--or
is *able* to--take anyone else seriously.

Another approach also begins with the recognition of
all human religions as partial and perspectival, yet
moves beyond to recognize their universal import: All
are contributions to a greater cumulative understanding,
all are pieces of a larger puzzle which, when completed,
will give a satisfactory representation of the whole.
The mood is more than ecumenical. And in its worst extreme, this approach may be caricatured as a sort of
casual eclecticism, a shopping-bag tourist consumerism.
The disregard for the integrity and uniqueness of individual religions presents a problem. And like the above
approach, it fails to offer a basis for critical evaluation. Yet in recognition of religious relativism, from
whence come such criteria?

A third option has been articulated by Gordon Kaufman.[17] In full recognition of religious relativism, he
asks whether there might be a theology which is universally appropriate, based on a concern for common human-
ization. Citing the growing imperative to reconstruct
the present global order into a world that is more humane
for all its inhabitants before it is too late, Kaufman
names as criterion for assessing theology whatever is
necessary or required to build a more humane order.

It is appropriate to ask whether there is a universal and definitive understanding of what it means to be fully human, which seems to be presupposed in this way of proceeding. Western notions of the self, for instance, differ profoundly from those of eastern cultures, and the more specific vision of the free, fulfilled self varies further with its social context. If theology is human constructive activity, grounded in common language and culture, is it limited to the limits of those commonalities? Must we become a global village before we can do global theology, or can a common anthropological base be assumed in a world of pluralism?

Social theories of knowing, while not claiming to do definitive anthropology, have suggested that humans are socio-symbolic beings whose constructions of reality are value-laden and socially defined. The sociology of knowledge may offer tools for articulating how a particular perspective understands itself, its sources, and its situation, as well as tools for facing the constructive task which confronts us all. Perhaps humans will soon be able to enter into interfaith dialogue on issues of global justice, using their common humanity as a common court of appeal. For although humans may not agree on a definition of what it means to be human (or divine), they can agree that some actions are more humane, more just and compassionate, than others. May this meta-musing metamorphise into a metaphysical reality.

In closing, it is simply reiterated that the original insights of sociology of knowledge can no longer be denied or avoided in theological reflection. Rather, the content of what is said about God, the sources upon which it is based, and the very manner in which it is spoken stand revised in light of sociology of knowledge. God-

talk does not take place in a vacuum. Talk about God reflects the social setting of the speaker, and may serve
either to sanction or transform the social order. Visions
of God change with changing social situations, illumining
the inevitable involvement of imagination, and issuing
the imperative for self-conscious and responsible theological construction. In the final analysis, the fulfillment or destruction of the entire human society is
intimately and profoundly related to the gods we create.

NOTES

1. Werner Stark, *The Sociology of Knowledge: An Essay in Aid of a Deeper Understanding of the History of Ideas* (London: Routledge and Kegan Paul, 1977), p. 178.

2. Peter Berger and Thomas Luckmann, *The Social Construction of Reality* (New York: Doubleday and Co., Inc., 1966), pp. 5-7.

3. Kenneth W. Stikkers, in his Introduction to Max Scheler's *Problems of a Sociology of Knowledge*, tr. by Manfred S. Frings (Boston: Routledge and Kegan Paul, 1980), p. 14.

4. Karl Mannheim, *Ideology and Utopia* (New York: Harcourt, Brace and Co., 1940), p. 137.

5. Stark, p. 16.

6. Clifford Geertz, *The Interpretation of Cultures* (New York: Basic Books, Inc., 1973), p. 5.

7. Sheila Greeve Davaney, "Social Theories of Knowing: Liberationist Appropriation and Feminist Rejoinder" (unpublished manuscript), p. 3.

8. In this discussion of liberationist and feminist appropriation of sociology of knowledge I am drawing on the claims set forth by Dr. Sheila Greeve Davaney in her unpublished paper, "Social Theories of Knowing: Liberationist Appropriation and Feminist Rejoinder."

9. Juan Luis Segundo, *Our Idea of God* (Maryknoll, New York: Orbis Press, 1974), p. 8.

10. Davaney, p. 6.

11. Hugo Assman, quoted in Robert McAfee Brown, *Theology in a New Key* (Philadelphia: Westminster Press, 1978), p. 61.

12. Davaney, pp. 13-14.

13. Mary Daly, *Beyond God the Father* (Boston: Beacon Press, 1973), p. 8.

14. Ibid., p. 14.

15.   Gordon D. Kaufman, introductory lecture "The Question of God and the Question of Theological Method," presented on 29 June 1982 in the course, "Constructing the Concept of God." Iliff School of Theology, Summer School, 1982.

16.   Gordon D. Kaufman, *The Theological Imagination* (Philadelphia: Westminster Press, 1981), p. 11.

17.   Ibid., Ch. 7.

PART II

SOCIOLOGY OF KNOWLEDGE AND THE
RELIGIOUS TRADITION

CONCERNING THE SOCIOLOGY OF RELIGION

Max Scheler

In the sphere of *religion* those religions based on the
person of a "founder" are always *preceded* by a religious
and anonymous group-consciousness that binds souls together,
i.e. a genealogical-tribal-*folk-religion*.[1] Religious unity
and the unity of cults and rites appear to be attached
everywhere to *genealogical bonds and bonds of blood*, rather
than to economic, political, commercial, or learned communities. Only when, in a *political era*, there appears an
exceptionally "charismatic" *"homo religiosus"*--i.e. someone
in whom there is unconditional but non-rational faith in
regards to his personal and extraordinary links with the
deity--be he a prophet, or a war hero who has founded his
authority on religious grounds, or a magician, or a conscious
"founder", can religion detach itself from its original
blood ties. A sorcerer or a shaman[2] is not at all yet a
"homo religiosus." He is a technician endowed with supernatural "powers". And a "priest", i.e. an official cult-
technician, always is dependent upon a *"homo religiosus"*
above him.

The transition toward *religions of founders* is indirectly enhanced by the already completed transition of the predominant forms of genealogical units into the large *political*
and mostly monarchic ruling units. The latter grow in
strict opposition to the genealogical and family units with
their patriarchal leaderships, and they grow from the
perennially emerging groups of war lords; they break up

the *religious* authorities of the patriarchal-genealogical
units and tend to dissolve larger genealogical family-
groups into smaller families. It is for this reason that
religions based upon founders and all religious movements
and groups tied together by a *person* never appear *prior to*
this stage of societal development, which W. Wundt termed
"the political society". The political society is the
beginning of the formation of classes and the beginning of
large-scale suppression of animistic, matriarchal cults and
womanhood.[3] Religions of founders are of express *male* and
mental origins.

The *sources* of religious knowledge are to be seen neither in animism nor ancestry cults--as has long been sug-
gested--nor in metaphysical judgments of reason. Rather,
they are to be seen in a *believed experiential contact,*
accepted by the group, that eminent persons have with a
supra-powerful, holy person himself. And such experiential
contact is attested through certain rites and actions and
proves itself to be true through belief in "miracles". The
first bearers of these "charismatic" qualities, prior to
the appearance of a founder-religion, are the patriarchal
leaders of a blood-community. The first bearers of the
higher religions of founders comprise a lasting priesthood
"inaugurated" [*eingesetzt*] by the founder, and its membership is drawn without regard to lineage.

The source of ideas of the divine appear in various
combinations. (1) They are to be seen in the flexible
traditions of the prominent genealogical groups of families
and clans (folk-religion). (2) They are seen in the *living
visions of the divine* gained by *charismatic "homines religiosi"* with the rich ramifications of their "holy words",
deeds, teachings, and advice that have come down only by
oral tradition or by so-called "holy scriptures" (book-
religion). (3) These sources are to be seen, furthermore,

in new experiences gained *during the performances of cults
and rites* pertaining to the divine and its functioning.
This experiential source represents a one-sided technicality
in the history of religion: it often tended to make itself
the only source for religious knowledge. But it always has
been only one factor that modifies this knowledge and not a
source for the genuine formation of religious knowledge.
(4) The sources of the ideas of the divine pertain, finally,
to those ideas of salvation and God that come from metaphysics (for example, Plato's and Aristotle's philosophies
as origins of Christian theology). When those metaphysical
origins lose their service or modifying functions to become
primary functions with respect to religious knowledge, they
tend to destroy positive folk-religion and the authority of
the *"homines religiosi"* proper (as is the case in all forms
of "gnosticism" from Plato to Ekkehart and Hegel). It is
only when we have large institutions of salvation which
claim to be of universal validity that a *formula* of faith
in the name of the founder can be found. This is the so-
called *"dogma"*. A dogma develops by means of *"via nega-
tionis"* against "heresies" which seek to destroy the unity
of a church.[4] But it is only when there are such dogmas
that something like *"theology"* can exist. Theology is the
most derivative and most rational form of religious knowledge. However, the proper *sociological condition* for
religious knowledge by no means comes uniformly from these
four sources, but first of all from family-, clan-, town-,
and folk-*traditions* and occupational-technical *cults*. The
latter sources are in sharp contrast to the four former
sources. And it is through these latter two sources that
the *division of classes, occupations, estates, and castes*,
with their divisions of labor, are mirrored most sharply
in the pantheon and pandemonium of the world of religious
objects (functional gods)--not through the ideas of the

divine belonging to *"homines religiosi"* or concepts of the
divine in metaphysics. For the latter are much *less* conditioned sociologically.[5]

    Revealed religion in Jewish and, even more so, in
Western Christian religions, as societal and historical
factors, has a tremendous predominance over the pure or
semi-religious *metaphysics of self-knowledge* and of spontaneous self-revelation--a predominance which stands in
contrast to almost all of *Asian* and the *ancient* world's
religions, which were without churches and dogmas. This
predominance is very likely to be based upon *sociological*
conditions and upon the character of the peoples concerned.
It is the desire of those peoples to transform the surface
of the earth and to expand power politically, technologically, and economically, a process which entails consoli-
dations of their masses by actively questioning the ultimate
grounds of existence, and which entails the systematic
pacification of those masses and providing them with final
securities by answering such questions. Such can happen
only in the highly personalistic-theistic religions of
revelation and, in the political age, through "ecclesiastical" organizations, which are always copied from the
state. Peoples who think about the metaphysical sense of
life on their own and who seek to find it *actively by them-*
selves cannot devote their thinking and will as exclusively
to earthly affairs and things as can peoples whose revelation, authorities, dogmas, and universal institutions of
mass-salvation provide them already with *final* and *absolute*
solutions to such questions.

    Ever since the Roman Church succeeded in doing away
with neo-Platonism and gnostic sects[6] this predominance of
revealed religion over the self-active metaphysical mind
has become extremely powerful in the *West*. And it is no
surprise how little social and historical effect spontaneous

metaphysical thought has had in the West! Only Cartesian
metaphysics, German classical philosophy up to and especially in the case of Hegel, and later Marxism has had temporary
mass-effects.[7] In my judgment, it was Descartes, alone
among the great philosophers, who was able to change the
categorial structure of thinking among learned people--his
doctrines were, in general, *"la nouvelle philosophie"* during
the seventeenth and eighteenth centuries.[8] But this, too,
had only small effects on ecclesiastical institutions! In
addition to this, the Western development of sects and
churches after the Reformation followed a general law of
direction whereby revelation and grace became *increasingly*
significant for religious knowledge, and man's free activity
became *more restricted* in regards to the Divine and rational
cognition (and with this the metaphysical spirit in general)
the more *earthly* activities *increased* through work, technology, occupation, economy, and power politics. In also considering this fact one sees even more sharply, since the
origin of Christianity, the very same law of direction
underlying the development of the relationship between religion and metaphysics in the West: present-day numbness of
religious consciousness among believers, the utter helpless-
ness and anarchy among non-believers, the increasing sociological power of the most *consolidated* churches during the
rise of democracy, and the increasing determination of
social aims which those churches enjoy during the economic
age, all have their primary reason in the *suffocation of
metaphysical knowledge* and *free religious speculation,* which
resulted from the growing seclusion of revealed religion and
positive science. This makes understandable why people like
Wilhelm Dilthey, Max Weber, and Karl Jaspers agree with the
older positivists that objective metaphysics in general has
been overcome and is nothing "but a historical category" of
human thought--a category that would have to be elicited

psychologically and historically, only in its various forms
and ideal typifications. Yet, these same researchers hold,
in contrast to the old positivists, that religion is an
essential category of the human mind.[9] But *we* are con-
vinced--for I speak not only as a philosopher but also as
a sociologist--that all who think in such a way are victims
of a great deception which the not-so-distant future will
correct.

But the most consequential process in the history of
founder religions, a process which is thoroughly and only
sociologically conditioned--the process which alone makes
possible the formation of a true church with its claims of
absolute authority in matters of salvation[10]--appear to me
to be *the same* wherever such structures have appeared: it
is the *objective,* more or less penetrating *deification of
the founder,* as expressed in various formulations. More
precisely: his change in status from a *"subject"* of relig-
ion--with whom one spiritually *"identifies",* whom one
practically and theoretically *follows by cooperating* with
his personal acts, whose advice and divine teachings one
follows and believes, and who, as essentially a *"model
person",* is a model of man's inner and practical ways to
God--into an *object* of worship, an object of religion, is
assigned a special ontological origin from the Godhead.
The *cult of the elevated Christ,* which first came into full
force and expanded with Paul, is the root for the Christian
Church in the same way that the subsequent deification of
Buddha transformed what was originally Buddhism's metaphysical theory of salvation and ethics into a "religion".[11]
This process of deification, wherever it has taken place,
has always been demonically ambiguous. On the one hand it
elevates a founder *essentially* above all other men and
obtains, in this manner, a special relationship to the
Godhead; the founder's authority becomes *"absolute"* and

can only become absolute in this way. On the other hand
this process *eases* and *relieves* a community, especially
the *masses*, from the harsh pressures of the founder's
demands and advice precisely because a common person can
no longer compare himself with a person whose origin is
ontologically in God or who is, at least, of other dis-
tinctly divine origins. The deification of a founder is,
therefore, always *distantiation* and inner alienation. It
is *great relief* from the *responsibility* which so easily
flatters human nature and which, *prior* to the process of
deification, the founder, as *subject* of religion and *model
person* of his community, bestowed upon his followers.[12]
The process of deification is tantamount to the victory of
the *pressures of the masses* and their leaders over the
higher and purer forms of spiritual religiosity. All other
objectifications and materializations in any specific
"ecclesiastical" development are only consequences of this
one basic process. Such consequences we find, for example,
in the development of personal faith into the *"fides quae
creditur"*, in the development from the founder's deeds and
actions which commanded following to an *"opus operandum"*
(i.e. to a "merited" capital of objective salvation and
grace which the church gives to believers according to
rule), and the development of the charismatic priesthood
of the person into an objective, sacramental, and legal
dignity or office.[13]

I have excluded from this essay a treatment of the
sociology of the inner structure of religious knowledge.
Instead, I wish to mention some typical influences of religion and churches that either *further or curb* the development of *science and philosophy*. I consider this subject
to be indispensible for an objective and penetrating treatment of our subject here.

Friends and foes of religion and churches have thus far only onesidedly described, by enumerating historical *facts*, the furthering and curbing elements existing between religions and churches, on the one hand, and the development of other forms of knowledge, on the other. A systematic investigation of the *laws of typical relations* between religion and other forms of knowledge has only rarely been made in terms of a comparative sociological methodology. The relations concerned do not all come to the fore when one merely looks at such historical facts alone, for instance, the fact that the Christian churches and monasteries in the West preserved the treasure of ancient writings, the fact that scholastic theology and philosophy created an excellent exercise in and culture of thinking and making distinctions, which secondarily became fruitful for positive science and whose loss such an excellent scholar as R. Virchow deplored, and the fact that there had been men of faith in all forms of knowledge. The laws of said relations cannot come to the fore either when one looks at the church as a place of superstition and witches or as the source of terrible prohibitions of doubt concerning questions in philosophy and natural and human sciences which touch upon questions of dogma, or when one enumerates all those "cases" where ecclesiastical authorities fell into the hands of philosophy and science (Galileo, Giordano Bruno, Vanini, Serveto; gospel criticism; comparative religion). By such a method one can never get beyond *partisan* standpoints and there will always be a point and counterpoint. It is only by comparing the larger totalities of cultures that we can trace *unities of style* between religious systems and systems of knowledge. These interconnections are far above such historical "cases" and partisan world-views. What is needed here is a macroscopic, not microscopic, art of consideration. Furthermore, the *types*

of knowledge must be distinguished precisely from one another.

First of all, one must abandon the commonly held and
erroneous idea that *positive science* and its progress--as
long as it stays within its proper domains--can affect religion in any way. Whether such a position is held by
believers or non-believers, it is equally false. On the
contrary, whenever an objective area, in the sociological
sense of a general phenomenon, is to become "free" for
metaphysical and scientific study, religion is subject to
a spontaneous change within its *own* domain. This is because, first, religion is not a preliminary form of metaphysics and science, nor does it come after them; rather
it possesses its own *autonomous* evolution.[14] And, second,
in every instance positive religion has already filled out
the group-soul and group-mind of men when a metaphysics or
science comes on the scene. What alone can shake a religion
is not a science but the *dying* of its faith and living
ethos, i.e. when a "dead" faith and "dead" ethos replace a
"living" faith and ethos, and, above all, when a *new* religious consciousness, and perhaps also a new metaphysics that
wins over the masses, begins to replace the old religion.
Taboos, which religions have imposed upon human cognition
in all areas by declaring certain things as "holy" or as a
"matter of faith", must lose their character as taboos,
always on the basis of their *own* religious or metaphysical
motives, should they become objects of science. Only when
a "sacred" scripture has lost its quality of salvation, on
the basis of religious or metaphysical motives, can it be
"scientifically" investigated like any other historical
source. Or, as long as nature is filled out by personal,
volitional, and godlike, or demonic, powers for a group,
it remains "taboo" for scientific exploration. Only when
a religious step is made into a more spiritual, less

biomorphic, and, by necessity, more or less monotheistic
idea of God--as it appears in the vast *political monarchies
of the East,* along with their monarchical societies--can
religion raise itself above blood ties and genealogical
communities and can the idea of God become more spiritual-
ized and less vitalized. Religion can then make the parts
of nature growingly deprived of religion's activities and
make the objective, "inanimate" nature *free for scientific
investigation.* He who holds the stars for invisible gods
is not yet mature enough to have a scientific astronomy.[15]

The Judeo-Christian monotheism of a Creator and its
victory over the religions and metaphysics of the ancient
world has undoubtedly been the *basic* factor that made possible the West's systematic exploration of nature. This
monotheism freed nature for science to such a degree that
it perhaps surpasses everything that has happened in the
West up to this time. Its spiritual God of *Will, Work,*
and *Creation,* unknown to the Greeks and Romans, Plato and
Aristotle--no matter whether His assumption is true or
false--has been the greatest *sanctification of work and
domination* over subhuman nature. And simultaneously it
effected the *greatest de-animation,* deadening, distancing,
and rationalization of *nature* that has ever happened in
comparison to Asian cultures and the ancient world. Work
and Science, however, belong *intimately* to one another, as
we shall see.

The main phases of accepted and believed *relationships
between "faith and knowledge"* in the *Christian West* are of
less significance. The direction of this development is
completely clear: it begins with a vague admixture of faith
and knowledge (from the Church fathers to Augustine there
were hardly any distinctions between truth of faith and
truth of reason, religion and metaphysics) and moves toward
a sharp division between them while, however, retaining

their harmony (*"gratia perficit, non negat rationem"*, says
Thomas Aquinas); from this the development moves toward a
growing *dualism*, which necessarily is one of Will and Reason in God and man, progressing into nominalism (Scottish
and Franciscan natural philosophy), and then moving towards
the *co-original* opposition between the abrupt Reformationist
teachings of grace, which reject all rational metaphysics,
and *rational deism*, for which God is nothing but the al-
mighty engineer of the world-machine (Herbert of Cherbury,
who is also the point of departure for the freemasons).
This development then continues on through the moderate
English and German Enlightenment to the radical romantic
Enlightenment which comes to an end with positivism as its
highest product (d'Alembert, Condorcet, A. Comte, etc.).
Following Max Weber's and Ernst Troeltsch's methodology, P.
Honigsheim showed[16] that this development *reflected the
struggles among estates and classes* and that it reflected
the abolition of feudal and contemplative (close-knit)
upper estates by political, sovereign powers, united with
cities, burghers, and religious separatism against the
Emperor and the Pope. Honigsheim also showed how the various rejections of *"causae secundae"* (Cartesianism, Male-
branche, Jansenism, Gallicanism, Calvinism, and the theory
of sovereignty of Bodin, Machiavelli, and Thomas Hobbes)
reflect *absolutism and individualism* in the growing *democracy* and *"nation"*. And he showed how the connection between religious ways of thinking and social structure had
been disintegrated by the mutual victory of independent,
liberal, middle-class democracy and the industrialization
of economy, technology, and science over the "absolute"
states. The elimination of *mediating* causes and powers
(i.e. the *causae secundae* in the metaphysical world-view
and the independent [*eigenmachtigen*] estates within the
state) until Bossuet's *"un dieu, un maitre"* and the

abolition of absolute central power (materialism--French
Revolution) are processes of the same *logical sense and
belong together*.

Concerning the complex questions pertaining to the
relationship between religion and science [*Wissenschaft*],
both the positivist sociology of knowledge and Marxist
sociology have thus far held only *partisan* opinions on the
subject. It would not be surprising if they were faced
with a series of new romantic movements which they considered to be "reactionary" and which would prove *their* opinions of development to be wrong. For the wholly Roman
Catholic Comte, for instance, religion coincides with the
Catholic Church as it does for the French *traditionalists;*
i.e. he conceives the Catholic Church wholly as a *medieval
institution*. And, furthermore, "metaphysics", in general,
coincides, for Comte, with the Aristotelian theory of forms
held throughout Scholasticism. Comte saw no value in modern metaphysics regarding its sociological function. But
if these *Western* relationships between religion, metaphysics,
and science are seen from the vantage point of an Asian
culture, even from a Russian vantage point, one immediately
notices a *unity of style* that encompasses all these conflicts. Already the Slavophiles, for example, who initially
were more religious, tended to see in medieval high Scholasticism and its "syllogistic" rationalism the *beginning* of
the "Western European" counter-religious *Enlightenment*.
Kirijewski sees the development from Thomas Aquinas to
Voltaire as *one and the same* line of Western "disintegration
of belief"![17] Dostoyevsky's "Legend of the Grand Inquisi-
tor" has the same meaning. And I would like to add that
in Germany E. v. Hartmann foresaw, in what he called the
immanent union of a "socially eudemonistic Jesuit Church"
and a socially eudemonistic social-democracy, many things
that for us today appear to be almost reality.

A second fundamental point concerning the relationship between religion and other types of knowledge that has often been ignored in discussions of particular items within the subject is the fact that points of either agreement or disagreement over this relationship emerge only when religion, understood as an object and major premise for the "science of faith", or "theology", is nothing but formalized *dogma*, when knowledge *is genuinely metaphysical*, or when scientific knowledge unjustifiably transgresses the limits of its province by raising its own results to *metaphysical levels*. In the case of the Church's condemnation of Galileo, for example, the point at issue was not the scientific content of Copernicanism and Galileo's dynamics. The Church directed its thrust against the "metaphysician of Copernicanism", against Giordano Bruno, and against *metaphysical vestiges* in Galileo's theories, as P. Duhem and H. Poincaré clearly showed to be the case in the correspondence between Galileo and the Cardinal who presided over the suit (vestiges which have no foundation for present-day physicists and which have been wiped out by the theory of relativity). In the preface to his work on the motion of stars, dedicated to Pope Paul III, Copernicus refers to the *"lex parsimoniae"* in support of his theory, and he made a distinction between his principle and "philosophical truth" about absolutes. And in a letter to Galileo the Cardinal advised him to do exactly the same. The fact that Galileo did *not* do so and put forward *metaphysical* assumptions in a wrong place was the factor that decided that case against him. But a large number of other obstructions that the Church incurred upon scientific progress had hardly any influence upon the positive effect that it *indirectly* did have on the development of the *exact sciences*--even by its suppressions of philosophical and metaphysical thought and of free religious speculation.

(This can be seen when one compares this state of affairs
with Asian cultures where such suppressions did not occur
and where *incomparably more energy* from human thought flowed
into *metaphysical* thinking and spontaneous *self*-redemption.)
Of direct benefit to the sciences also was the intense
struggle between the Church and the growing rationalism of
its clergy against myth, saga, legend, popular types of
devotion, "superstition", free mysticism, and belief in
miracles. In these cases genuine metaphysics also benefitted because *all* higher types of knowledge form a *united*
front against types of knowledge that are *organismic and
psychic* in their nature. It is precisely because revealed
religions increasingly delineate a "supranatural" area of
faith and assert it to be absolutely perfect and unchange-
able that they have become indirect pioneers of scientific
rationalism. In this way human energy to think is diverted
in the direction of *exact* investigation; and this path is
at the same time that of *technical-pragmatic* thinking. It
is no wonder, therefore, that there exists a mutual understanding between positivists hostile to metaphysics and
ecclesiastical philosophers in the politics of choosing a
professor to occupy a philosophy chair, and when it is
important to keep proper and serious philosophy away from
the universities.[18]

Factors that are also beneficial to science are religious *ascetism*, which, as Nietzsche already saw clearly,
helps to increase the *scientific knowledge of truth which
itself is ascetic*, and censorship by ecclesiastic adminis-
trations, which helps bring about responsibility for possible assertions and leads to refinements of and precautions
in style and choice of words, to the avoidance of rash
generalizations, to increased carefulness in thinking, to
criticism, and to an attitude above an odd and befuddled
"spirit of the time", hypnotized by a few ideas. It is

not the Church, therefore, that obstructs science, but the
presumptuous pathos of "a scientific church" (E. Mach),
which soon will also reject science itself. The history
of Darwinism, which collapsed with the rise of the hereditary theories of exact science, is a clear illustration of
this proposition. It may be true that the area of conflict
between religion and the *human* sciences is much wider, but
here also in conflict with dogmatic religion is the historically and culturally *philosophical* understanding of historical facts and not so much the critical investigations
into sources (which goes back even to Benedictine monks who
were followers of St. Maurus).

Yet, the conflicts proper between religion and knowledge of the world are to be found whenever we are concerned
with *metaphysical knowledge*. It is here, no doubt, that
ecclesiastical dogma and the church are the *most powerful
and inborn enemies of any independent development*. And
this is all the more so when the church, either in full
awareness or unconsciously, has aligned itself with a
metaphysical system of the past by way of its own theology
or even through dogmas. If, for example, the dogmas *themselves* contain metaphysical principles from a past philosophical system, as is undoubtedly the case in Roman Cathol-
icism--for example, in the dogma of the transubstantiation,
which contains the material principle of Aristotle (*materia
prima*), in the Thomistic theory of the soul, dogmatized
with tooth and nail at the Council of Vienne, and in the
"proofs for the existence of God"[19] and the theory of free
will as freedom of choice--metaphysics is utterly and completely fixed.

Perhaps the most important *peculiarity* in the formation of Western knowledge is the fact that the powers of
revealed religion, of exact science, and of technology
have almost always won their common struggle against a

spontaneous metaphysical spirit. Their common victory is
rooted in the practical, Roman *spirit of domination*. It
is a victory over the more contemplative and purely theoretical attitude of the mind which has its own ways of
"investigating". By contrast, in all Asian cultures it
was *the "sage"* and a *metaphysical* mind that won over religion as well as science. This, it appears to me, is the
*most significant difference between Western and Eastern
cultures*. In the East metaphysics is *self*-cognition and
self-redemption, and in this sense it is not primarily
Buddhism but the "religion" of the Brahmans that was a
first metaphysics. For this reason also we find in the
beliefs of the peoples of China, India, and even Japan,
the predominance of the *ideal of the sage*[20] in contrast to
the Western *ideals of heroes and saints* and their model
persons--which, from the time of Benedictus until Ignatius's
overcoming of the proper monkhood, became more and more
practical, eudemonistic, and social. This also explains
the typical Asian "tolerance" concerning membership in a
religion or more than one religion; and it explains, too,
the absence in Asia of both rational science and specialization, industrial technology of production, and hierarchical, ecclesiastical institutions with stringent dogmatics
of an imperial form. The Asian metaphysical idea of self-
redemption also explains the widespread conviction, which
to us Westerners looks so curious, that the emperor, sov-
ereigns, and supreme leaders are responsible for everything
that happens in the world, including natural events such as
floods, destruction of harvests, etc. The exclusion of any
traces of magic techniques by the Reformation equally elimi-
nated from Protestant culture all tensions between techniques
of *magic* and *positive* technology. But also for Catholicism,
which preserved a few traces of magic techniques--for example, meteorological techniques ("weather"-pilgrimages),

medical techniques (exorcism; final unction), etc.--such
magic techniques had little importance for the progress of
positive technology.

The most *devastating weapon* against metaphysics in the
hands of the dogmatic churches, however, is the *prohibition
of any doubt* in tenets and things relevant to faith. This
principle holds that all but merely "methodological doubt"
is "sinful"--in conjunction with the identification of the
Platonic-Aristotelian systems, i.e. systems of specific
historical metaphysics belonging only to Greek culture,
with a so-called *"philosophia perennis"*, or "the" doctrine
of "sound mind" and "universal" human reason. Not only
does it suppress all development of metaphysical knowledge
and misunderstands its historical and factual development,
which reveals elements that are worlds apart (for example,
the connection between Aristotle's God as the first mover
or "the thinking of thinking", νοησυς, νοησεως, and the
Judeo-Christian idea of God), but this principle also *dogma-
tizes* and *petrifies* a *specific* metaphysics. Aristotle's
theory of God as first mover cannot be disconnected from
his logic, from his astronomy, and from the basic spirit
of Greek religion, which is wholly different from the Judaic
idea of God as God of Will and Creation. Also, Aristotle's
logic[21] is not separable, except in some formalist games,
from his metaphysics of "form" and "matter" and their applications in nature. The whole system cannot be disconnected from the intercontainedness of positive science and
metaphysics, which as a *form* of knowledge, has been completely lost in modern times; it cannot be disconnected
either from Greek slavery, which allowed a small contemplative elite to venerate and admire the world as a realm
of meaningful, teleological "forms" of regulation rather
than to attack and work with the forms in practice; nor
can it be disconnected from the *biomorphic* type of thinking

in that community, which had not yet discovered the peculiar
nature and laws prevailing in *inanimate* nature and had no
knowledge of mathematical applications in nature and technology, and which, as a whole, was characterized by workmen
and the use of tools. When such a *historical system* becomes
inflated into a so-called *"philosophia perennis"* it must
empty out its living, clear, and concrete contents. A so-
called *"scholastic"*[22] method must arise whose nature it is
to be a philosophico-historical interpretation of a philosophical authority and, *at the same time*, a systematic
comprehension of things and states of affairs--i.e. to be
a *twofold source of deception* for all historical interpretation *and* the understanding of states of affairs. But
historical interpretation and understanding of states of
affairs [*Sacherfassung*] have to be *distinguished* from one
another. What happens here is the following: a specific
and strictly historical stage of metaphysical thought, out
of the anxiety of a new metaphysics which could be perilous
to theology is artifically conserved in an age whose lines
of thinking are completely different and can--if properly
understood--only exist as an anachronism. Positivism,
especially through the authority of Comte, openly or tacit-
ly accepted this idea of scholastic philosophy that the
metaphysics of timeless forms and essences, such as the
Platonic-Aristotelian system, would coincide with metaphysics *as a whole*. And it was in this fashion that metaphysics *became nothing but* an atavistic phenomenon because,
as Comte clearly saw, the Platonic-Aristotelian systems are
tied, indeed, to the present-day thinking of a modern society to which they are wholly alien.

One cannot be too surprised today about the growing
popularity of the churches, especially the Roman Catholic
Church and all parts of its philosophy (natural right,
social philosophy), when one examines the exact powers that

are sworn against any independent metaphysical activities
and free, speculative activity in religion, powers which
in hiding or openly work together.

    As A. von Harnack often emphasized, it is the ideo-
logical indifference of the *masses* that is the strongest
basis for the oldest and most inflexible conservative
powers; they are the strongest preservers of things past.
Blind churchgoers belong to this, and this "rotten wood
on Christ's vine" is not likely to be rejected by the
churches while the churches direct more of their attention
to *mass-guidance* in regard to social welfare problems, and
the more--as they have learned to do since the French
Revolution--they bring themselves in contact with democracy
and the right wing of socialism. Positive *science*, as we
saw, cannot do anything about this because it cannot enter
into competition with the churches, which seek to solve
the eternal needs of knowledge. But scientistic and positivistic currents, as well as all metaphysical "agnosticism"--all of which, it is true, are anti-ecclesiastical--
do help the churches in this (although hiddenly) because
they also tend to suppress metaphysics on the grounds of
their own epistemological and sociological errors. The
motto here is: "Foes of my greatest enemy are my friends".
Messianic *Marxism's* substitution for religion, the "future
state", pays, however, for its role in this. Where Marxism
holds sway, as in Russian Bolshevism, there is a pure reversal of the cultural politics of the Roman Church, as shown
by the Bolshevik censorship of books, the new *"index libro-
rum prohibitorum"* (including the Bible, the Koran, the
Talmud, and all Western philosophers from Aristotle to
Fichte). Also the *mysticism* of modern circles, sects, and
other groups is sworn against genuine metaphysics. Expanded *democracy*, however--which once had been an ally of free
research and philosophy in a struggle against ecclesiastic

supremacy--slowly turns out to be one of the greatest dangers to spiritual freedom.[23]   There is *another* type of
democracy--not the type that goes hand-in-hand with free
research as was the case at the times of our youth--*the*
type of democracy, which, in Athens, Socrates and Anaxagoras
rejected and which in modern Japan opposed all acceptance
of Western methods in technology and science, begins to
win ground again in the West and perhaps also in North
America. Only the struggling and predominantly *liberal*
democracy of a relatively "small elite", as the facts already show us today, is an ally of science and philosophy.
The prevailing democracy, expanded to include women and
half-grown children, is no friend but rather an enemy of
reason and science [*Wissenschaft*].   In Germany this process has begun with professorships for those holding ecclesiastic world-views, with "punitive professorships" for
social democrats, and with pressures being placed on lesser
State authorities by Parliament in all questions pertaining
to filling vacancies of academic chairs.   But this process
will continue!   The new *relativist theory of "Weltanschauung"*--as it has been introduced by W. Dilthey, M. Weber,
K. Jaspers, and G. Radbruch even in the philosophy of law--
is a theoretical reflection of this democratic parliamentarism that reaches into *Weltanschauung*.   In this parliamentarism one discusses all possible opinions without
making assertions and negotiates without coming to decisions;
and one abandons mutual convictions based upon knowledge in
the manner which parliamentarism, at its peak, always presupposed.[24]

NOTES

1. Concerning the definition of "folk-religion", see the introduction to the book by A. Dieterich, *Mutter Erde*, 2nd ed. (Leipzig, 1905). Concerning the division among religions in general and the structure of the history of religions, see the rewarding essay by J. Wach, *Religionswissenschaft* (Leipzig, 1924).

2. In this regard see Fritz Graebner, Ibid. [*Das Weltbild der Primitiven* (Munich, 1924)].

3. Concerning Greek religion, see Bachofen, *Das Mutterecht* (1861) [vols. 2 and 3 of the *Gesammelte Werke* (Basel: B. Schwabe, 1948)]; also C.A. Bernoulli's rich new (aforementioned) work on Bachofen [*J.J. Bachofen und das Natursymbol* (1925)], which, however, requires a sharp critique.

4. Very relevant in this regard is E. LeRoy, *Dogme et critique* (Paris, 1907). E. Troeltsch has so thoroughly investigated the various forms of religious communities in Christian-Western culture (church, sect, and mystical community are his main concepts) that we need not discuss them further here.

5. Max Weber, in his *Religionssoziologie,* has provided us with a large number of examples concerning the reciprocal relationship between class structure and the religious object-world; still more examples can be found. The sociology of religion must avoid a causal interpretation of these corresponding relationship, whether they be made in terms of an economic or any other conception of history. [Scheler is referring here either to Weber's *Gesammelte Aufsätze zur Religionssoziologie*, 3 vols (Tübingen: J. C. B. Mohr [P. Siebeck], 1920-1), or to his "Religionssoziologie: Typen der religiösen Vergemeinschaftung", bk. II, ch. IV of Wirtschaft und Gesellschaft (Tübingen: J. C. B. Mohr [Paul Siebeck], 1922), part III of the series *Grundriss der Sozialökonomik*. In the fourth edition (1956) this essay appears as part II, ch. V, pp. 245-381, and bears the title "Typen der religiösen Vergemeinschaftung (Religionssoziologie)". "Religious groups (the sociology of religion)", trans. Ephraim Fischoff, in *Economy and Society*, vol. II, pp. 399-634; also published separately as *The Sociology of Religion* (Boston: Beacon Press, 1963).]

6. See also A. v. Harnack's excellent work on the gnostic Marcion, *Marcion: Das Evangelium vom Fremden Gott* (Leipzig, 1921).

7. Similarly, Positivism temporarily became, at the time of [Emile] Combes [1835-1921], a philosophy of the *state* both in Brazil and in France, as did Hegel's philosophy in Prussia under the ministry of Altenstein. In Soviet Russia, Marxism is the state philosophy.

8. R. Eucken, *Geschichte der philosophischen Terminologie* (1879).

9. In this regard, see W. Dilthey, *Die geistige Welt*, vol. 5 of the *Gesammelte Schriften* [Leipzig: B.G. Teubner] (1924), pp. 339 ff. "Das Wesen der Philosophie" (1907) is a most highly instructive essay for the sociology of knowledge.

10. On these points I must retract a judgment I made in my necrology of E. Troeltsch; see ["Ernst Troeltsch als Soziologe"] *Kölner Vierteljahrshefte für Sozialwissenschaften* III, no. 1 (1923-24): 7-21.

11. Shortly before the downfall of the last Manchu dynasty, which had ruled since 1644, Kung was deified (1907) by an imperial decree. Laotse has been deified in Taoism for 2,000 years. Similarly Buddha, Akbar, and Ali have been deified. See my essay on the "Soziologie der Vergottung" [unpublished manuscript].

12. One reads in R. Rolland's book, *Mahatma Gandhi* (German translation, Zurich, 1923) [*Mahatma Gandhi: The Man Who Became One with Universal Being*, trans. Caroline D. Groth (New York and London: Century; London: Swarthmore Press, 1924)], about the anxiety and fear that the great Indian religious revolutionary leader had even before the tendency began here and there in India to deify him. He knew: if he were deified his whole movement would be *practically* and politically *dead*.

13. R. Sohm has shown everything essential here in his admirable works on the origin of ecclesiastical law.

14. In this regard, see my "Probleme der Religion" in *Vom Ewigen im Menschen* [1921]; also, H. Scholz, *Religionsphilosophie* (1921); R. Otto, *Das Heilige* (1920) [*The Idea of the Holy: An Inquiry into the Non-Rational Factor in the Idea of the Divines and Its Relation to the Rational*, trans.

John W. Harvey (London: Humphrey Milford, Oxford University
Press, 1923)]; J. Wach, *Religionswissenschaft* (1924).

15. But how slowly was this biomorphic-theological
conception of the heavens abandoned! For Aristotle his
"nous" and "spirits of the spheres" are still "astronomical
hypotheses" (see in this regard W. Jaeger's recent work on
Aristotle [*Aristoteles: Grundlegung einer Geschichte seiner
Entwicklung* (Berlin: Weidmann, 1923); *Aristotle: Fundamen-
tals of the History of His Development*, trans. Richard
Robinson (Oxford: Clarendon Press, 1934)]). Even Kepler
originally introduced, in his work *De harmonice mundi*,
spirits of spheres, which are supposed to act according to
his three laws of planetary motion. Newton was the first
to displace completely this conception with his own law of
masses. But his "gravity" still retained something thoroughly magical, as Mach pointedly said (see *Geschichte der
Mechanik*), despite his explanation that he wished "to establish no hypotheses", because it retained a timeless,
distant effect and conspiration of the masses in absolute,
yet demonstrable, space. [Scheler is probably referring
here to Mach's *Die Mechanik in ihrer Entwicklung: Historisch-
kritisch dargestellt* (Leipzig: F.A. Brockhaus, 1883); *The
Science of Mechanics*, trans. T.J. McCormack (Chicago: Open
Court; London: Watts, 1893).] One can say that Einstein
was the first to eliminate these last remnants of "magic"
from our image of nature through his general theory of
relativity.

16. See, above all, his valuable work on Jansenism
[*Die Staats- und Soziallehren der französischen Jansenisten
im 17. Jahrhundert*] (1914); furthermore, the contribution
in the writings in memory of Max Weber (1925) [Scheler is
probably referring to Honigsheim's "Zur Soziologie der mit-
telalterlichen Scholastik (Die soziologische Bedeutung der
nominalistischen Philosophie)," in *Hauptprobleme der Soziologie: Erinnerungsausgabe für Max Weber*, ed. Melchoir Palyi
(Munich and Leipzig: Verlag von Duncker & Humbolt, 1923)
vol. II, pp. 173-238], as well as his contributions to my
anthology, *Versuche zu einer Soziologie des Wissens* (Munich,
1924).

17. J.W. Kirijewski [Ivan V. Kiréevskii], *Drei Essays*
[translated from Russian to German by Harold von Hoerschel-
mann] (Munich, 1921).

18. Those knowledgeable in the internal politics of
German universities know that professorships tied to the
Church strive to fill the chairs of philosophy with experi-
mental psychologists or with researchers who only subsequently

seek to synthesize positive-scientific results, i.e. with
persons who are harmless to the teachings of the Church.
The more the churches and their representatives join in
the techniques of guiding and directing their masses and
the more pragmatic they become, the closer becomes their
cooperation with the world of work, technology, industry,
and positive science. For this reason they represent today
a ten-times stronger bastion against the mystical tendencies
of the times (against the bad tendencies, for example,
anthroposophy, as well as the good tendencies) than science.

19. Concerning the "proofs for God", what the Jesuit
P.H. Lennertz says about the contradiction contained in my
theory of the cognition of God ["Probleme der Religion"]
in respect to the teachings of the Catholic Church, is
thoroughly correct. It was--as I had to learn only slowly
and painfully--a complete mistake of all "modernistic"
theology to regard the Thomistic philosophy as *separable*
from the ecclesiastic dogmatics. For the ontological
validity of the principle of causality itself is *dogma*
today--and it is not only the "that" but also the *method*
of metaphysics and the cognition of God by causal conclusions. See P.H. Lennertz, *Schelers Konformitätssystem
und die Lehre der katholischen Kirche*, (Cologne, 1924).

20. Concerning the primacy of the ideal of the wise
man in China as opposed to the Western ideal of the hero,
see the interesting remarks by R. Wilhelm in *Chinische
Lebensweisheit* (Darmstadt, 1922).

21. See the recent outstanding work (already cited)
by Jaeger, *Aristoteles* (Berlin, 1923), on the genesis of
the Aristotelean system.

22. In this formal meaning of scholasticism there is,
however, also a Protestant "scholasticism". It is a twofold one: it is the still strong Aristotelean Scholasticism
introduced by Melanchthon, which ends up in Wolffianism,
and it is the Protestant scholasticism of the nineteenth
century, the Kantian scholasticism, which likewise reveals
the above-mentioned mark of "scholasticism in general".

23. The present movement of fundamentalism shows that
this applies not only to Europe but also to the United
States of America. This movement would make it law that
nothing may be taught in any state school (and even the
universities!) that contradicts the Bible, especially any
form of the theory of evolution (!).

24. I have shown already in my above-cited essay,
"Weltanschauungslehre, Soziologie und Weltanschauungsset-
zung", how much I recognize as necessary a theory of
Weltanschauung and consider it especially practically
applicable for adult education and, on the other side,
how much I regard a pure theory of *Weltanschauung* as a
precondition for posited philosophy. But this discipline
must not attempt to replace metaphysics--just as the science of religious studies must not replace theology.

SOCIOLOGY OF KNOWLEDGE, RELATIVISM,
AND THEOLOGY

Steven W. Stall

RELATIVISM

Alfred North Whitehead in *Adventures of Ideas*
suggests at one point that new ideas tend to be inclusive.
That is, they tend to dominate scholarly work in all
fields. All scholars pay homage to the novel and attempt
either to weave it into their existing pattern or to use
it as a new pattern on which to base their work. Carl
Raschke has put the point more succinctly and more color-
fully, as well as more caustically: "All new theories
are imperialistic." Sociology of knowledge, rather than
contradicting this assertion, may well be a paradigm case.
It is a current vogue of history, psychology, anthropology,
philosophy, and theology to invoke sociology of knowledge.
It is either the salvation of the discipline (e.g. liberation theology) or the bane of its existence (e.g., dogmatic theology). In any event it seems that all claims
must be tested by sociology of knowledge and judgment
passed based upon this testing. The "imperialism" of
the discipline should be obvious to all. Regardless of
the merits of such testing, sociology of knowledge seems
to rule the roost.

The tragedy of the contemporary empire is that it is
not sociology of knowledge, per se, which rules but rather
one of its major consequences: relativism. While rela-

tivism is clearly one of the implications of the social
sources of knowledge, it is not an entirely new claim.
Many nineteenth century historians and theologians were
well aware of this claim, at least in its historical expression. Modern biblical criticism played heavily upon
this idea as did the movement in quest of the historical
Jesus. The shortcoming of much of the work of the nineteenth century was the failure of the scholar to see the
relativity of his/her own position. The twentieth century reaction of Karl Barth and Neo-orthodoxy was, in
part, against the relativism of the previous century.
Barth, of course, accepted many of the claims of relativism. He sought, however, to protect theology from
these claims by invoking Kierkegaard's "absolute quali-
tative distinction between time and eternity (i.e. humanity and God)." In the same era H.R. Niebuhr, while
opposed to Barth at numerous points, also affirmed the
cultural relativity of humanity and the absolute nature
of God. In *Radical Monotheism and Western Culture* he
identified the problem as one of humans placing ultimate
trust in and loyalty to penultimate or relative spheres
of value. The solution is radical monotheistic faith in
the One Beyond the Many, i.e. in the absolute sphere of
value.

   However, it has not been the humanities which have
emphasized and popularized the idea of relativity. For
that one must look to the sciences, and particularly to
Albert Einstein. Einstein's theory of relativity received much more attention in both scholarly and popular
circles than did the work of any historian, philosopher,
or sociologist. The vast scientific and technological
accomplishments made possible by Einstein led to relativity becoming a widely known theory and an even more

widely used word (even when people were ignorant of the
theory). It is no surprise that sociology of knowledge
has been utilized with relativity and relativism in mind.
It is my contention that: there is a misuse of the word
as Einstein intended it; there is a misuse of the word as
intended in sociology of knowledge; and there are aspects
of sociology of knowledge which have been largely ignored.

In order to provide some initial support for my
claims I wish to invoke three sociologists on the task of
sociology of knowledge, Werner Stark, Peter Berger, and
Thomas Luckmann. Stark writes, "The Sociology of Knowledge is concerned in the first place with the origin of
ideas, and not with their validity."[1] In a similar vein
Berger and Luckmann write, "There has been general agreement to the effect that the sociology of knowledge is
concerned with the relationship between human thought and
the social context within which it arises."[2] The point
here is twofold. One, the work of sociology of knowledge
goes well beyond the simple idea of relativism. Sociology of knowledge seeks to make the connections between
society and knowledge explicit. The discipline cannot be
reduced to an investigation of the principle of relativity within and among cultures. To do so would be to assert the imperialism of the principle of relativity. Two,
the sociology of knowledge is uninterested in the truth
or falsity of the knowledge it investigates. It is not
the purpose of the discipline to falsify all claims or to
deny the idea of truth. Indeed, if that were the case it
would falsify its own efforts. Certainly the sociology
of knowledge claims that its descriptive and analytical
efforts are accurate, although also conditioned by their
own social experience. If not, then the whole edifice
and all that is built upon it collapses of its own weight.

The use of sociology of knowledge and the claims of
relativism for theology are most clearly seen in contemporary liberation theology. In an unpublished manuscript
Sheila Greeve Davaney identifies two basic claims. One,
there is no bare objective knowledge. All knowledge is
within a socially defined context. This allows social
self-consciousness as well as giving us only a perspective that is socially defined. Knowledge is not individual; knowledge is not universal; knowledge is bounded by
time and space in a specific manner. Two, all perspectives are value-defined, never neutral (i.e. objective).
Social systems are value systems which form a legitimating
circle. "There is no universal or so-called objective
knowledge. There is only particular, concrete, context-
ually-defined and thereby provisional, partial, and relative knowledge."[3] Oppression occurs because the holders
of power control the social perspective which is seen as
reality, not simply as one vision among many. Reality
thus defined becomes a legitimating principle for whites,
males, and the rich. Since theological symbols emerge
from the same social context, they also become part of
the legitimating system.

It is along these lines that James Cone writes, "What
people think about God, Jesus Christ, and the Church cannot be separated from their own social and political status in a given society."[4] Likewise Juan Luis Segundo
writes, "Our God is fashioned partly in the image and
likeness of the social reality to which we apply two ad-
jectives: Western and Christian."[5] On the basis of such
statements Cone and Segundo make scathing denunciations
of white and North American theology respectively.
These theologies serve to legitimate the existing power
structure. They are self-serving, self-aggrandizing, and
self-legitimating. As such they serve to oppress those

who do not share the power. So far, so good. However, a
curious thing happens. On this basis these theologies
and views of reality are not considered partial, relative
views or one view among many, but as distorted, false
views, and are labeled ideology, as if ideology were a
dirty word. They are, of course, ideologies in the sense
in which Karl Mannheim uses the word (*Ideology and Utopia*.)
But Mannheim's sense does not carry the connotation of
evil that some might want to associate with the word. At
the same time both Cone and Segundo want to claim that
the perspective from which they work is somehow absolute,
not relative. It is claimed that the experience of oppression allows one to have a comprehensive view that
safeguards one from the dangers of relativism. Cone does
acknowledge that black theology will be criticized as ideology unless its authenticity can be shown to be "pointing to the divine One whose presence is not restricted to
any historical manifestation."[6] In other words there is
a claim of divine transcendence and divine revelation
available only to the oppressed. This seems suspiciously
like the claim of divine revelation available only to the
church or to the faithful or to those gifted by the Holy
Spirit, etc. Other liberation theologies which do not
appeal to divine revelation nevertheless claim an ontological superiority for the experience of oppression and
the experiences of those whom they represent.

In any event it seems clear that one is still dealing
with a socially constructed perspective that is subject
to the same criticisms to which the dominant view is subject. It is true that a subordinant segment of a society
is in a position to criticize the dominant segment in a
unique way. Members of minority groups are in a marginal
situation. They must learn not only their own social system but that of the dominant society as well. However,

it is an untenable position to claim that the subordinant
community is in the dominant ontological position. When
such a claim is made those making it have fallen into the
same trap that Mannheim accuses Karl Marx of having fall-
en into, namely that of calling everyone else's position
ideology (i.e. relative, partial, and socially conditioned) but failing to recognize that one's own position is
ideology as well.

This leads into an analysis of the two types of relativism identified by some scholars. Such an analysis may
help to clear up the situation. Stark calls one type
radical relativism, and the other may be termed moderate
relativism. In a similar analysis Van Harvey calls the
two types hard perspectivism and soft perspectivism. (It
should be pointed out that Harvey is working as an historian; however, the analysis is still apropos.) In the
hard or radical type, true and false are declared to be
inappropriate categories. All views, all knowledge, all
perspectives are just that: perspectives. Whatever
claims that are made are value laden and self-serving.
There can be no general or universal knowledge. Whatever
is true is true only for a certain context. There can be
no adjudication of conflicting truth claims. Harvey
writes, "Hard Relativism assumes that selection [of details and facts] always involves distortion, that interest and purposes are necessarily antithetical to object-
ivity."[7] Compare this statement with that of Cone in his
criticism of the dominant theologies of history, "Theology is not universal language; it is *interested* language
and thus is always a reflection of the goals and aspirations of a particular people in a definite social setting."[8] The emphasis in the two sentences is on "necessarily" and "always" respectively.

Hard relativism smacks of social determinism. It
denies humans any ability to transcend their own context
in order to look at any issue from a fresh or different
perspective. It claims that all world views are purely
legitimating and can be nothing else. It holds no hope
of going beyond the conflicts of cultures except by brute
force. Hard relativism eventually shipwrecks on its own
rocky coast. The only possible result is despair and nihilism. Having seen the futility of our efforts, we can
only give up.

On the other hand, soft relativism provides hope
rather than despair. The problem is not relativism but
hard relativism. Indeed, Stark finds soft relativism liberating. It frees humans from dogmatism and intolerance
of all kinds. "It is not the least valuable service which
the sociology of knowledge has to render that it can teach
all men humility and charity, both of which are not only
virtues of the heart, but potentially also virtues of the
intellect."[9] It must be affirmed that there is a distinction between social determinism and the social context
which allows for certain developments. "Copernican astronomy was correct even before Copernicus; it was merely not
yet known."[10] Stark and Harvey agree as to the root of the
problem. It is not that knowledge is not possible, or that
true and false are inappropriate categories but that in
the search for truth (i.e. absolutes and certainties) the
part is elevated to the dignity of the whole.[11] Or in
Harvey's words, distortion comes when "exhaustive significance is claimed for a selective answer" not when an answer is selected.[12] All knowledge is, by definition, selective. It is improper to criticize knowledge for not
being exhaustive. To be exhaustive is to be omniscient, a
desirable but unavailable position. Knowledge kept to its
proper sphere as partial and selective is still knowledge.

Soft relativism, then, does not deny that some selective judgments are better than others. It, in fact, asserts this position. Further, it asserts that all perspectives or world views can make contributions to the larger project of truth. For Stark the project of knowledge is ecumenical--that is, all cultures, societies, and perspectives must be included. Hard relativism denies the possibility of getting past the values and perspectives which cause us to raise the part to the significance of the whole. Stark disagrees; he believes we can transcend these limitations.

The liberation theology of Cone and others like him wish to deny both forms of relativism. Soft relativism is clearly antithetical because it allows for whites or others to contribute to the cause, to have something of value to say. Cone denies this possibility, or at least Cone denies the possibility of whites contributing from their position of whiteness. Neither can Cone embrace hard relativism. To do so would deny the ontological status he has granted to his own position. Again he would have no more claim to truth than would any other world view. He could only validate it by mustering enough power to impose his view upon others. Cone instead wishes to create a hybrid form of relativism which supports his own world view. Sociology of knowledge understands this move but cannot allow it to be made in the name of sociology of knowledge.

It must be quickly added that this criticism does not negate the analysis of oppression. Neither does it deny that the current power structure has elevated its particular view of that of the whole. Those in power do define reality for the rest of society. What is being denied in this approach is a special status to the world view of

liberation theology. This denial holds whether the view
comes from revelation as Cone and Segundo claim or if it
comes through existential and cultural analysis as Mary
Daly and others claim.

Before moving to a discussion of the task of theology
in light of sociology of knowledge I would like to offer
a few final words about relativity in popular thought,
its use and abuse. "Relative" has come to mean, for most
people, arbitrary, anything goes, one thing is as good as
another. Religion, value systems, morality, and political systems are all arbitrary. Whether they come about
through conscious choice, random chance, or are simply
delivered to a society or an individual, they all are on
equal footing. There is no reason to place any institution above or below any other institution. Expressions
of this use of the word relative are rampant. For example, "All religions are equal and are striving for the
same thing (or nothing)." "All sexual lifestyles are
equal." "All political systems and ideologies are equal
(including Hitler's Nazism)." At this point there is no
ground from which to criticize any institution, society,
or individual. All are equally arbitrary; all are morally equal. This is obviously a development of hard perspectivism.

The problem is that this is a misuse of the word relative. A relative is someone who is related to someone
else. An event or an object which is relative is related
to other events or objects. The idea of arbitrary does
not belong to that of relative. Better terms, due to
current abuse of relative, are related, relatedness, relational, and relationalism. These both maintain the intent of relative and make its intent more explicit. To
say that an institution is relational simply means that
it does not stand apart from the society in which it

exists, but rather it is related to and rooted in that society. The institution cannot exist as it is apart from the society, and the society would not be the same without the institution.

Relationalism salvages the possibility of moral judgments, value judgments, and the pursuit of truth. We must recognize that value systems are also relational, but we need not capitulate to the pressure to reduce all such systems to zero. We need not sanction Hitler because Nazi Germany had an equally valid and arbitrary system. We can say that Hitler was wrong. At the same time we must submit our value system to a thorough and ongoing critique.

A switch in terminology also preserves the meaning intended by Einstein and others pursuing relativity physics. Never in Einstein's wildest dreams did he suppose that his theories of relativity meant that the cosmos was arbitrary. "God does not shoot dice with the universe." Instead, his emphasis was one of relatedness. Mass, size, etc., of an object are all related to the velocity of the object with respect to an observer at a specific place and time.

The use of relational rather than relative also militates against the idea of social determinism. That knowledge is related to culture means that it is conditioned, not determined, by society. While the social vector is very strong and most likely overcome from within only consciously, it is not omnipotent.

THEOLOGY

For the greater part of history philosophy has been the search for truth, and not only truth but Absolute

Truth. Whether the method was rational, empirical, existential, or some other method or combination of methods,
the task has remained the same. Underlying this search
have been two assumptions: 1) that there was an Absolute
Truth to be had, and 2) humans were capable of knowing
this Truth. Theology has had a parallel history. Whether the method was confessional or philosophical, whether
the source was special revelation or natural revelation,
the task was the same as philosophy: seek and find Truth.
The same assumptions held here as in philosophy with one
addition, God equals Truth, or at least Truth is contained in the mind of God. Sociology of knowledge, along
with historical relativism and theoretical physics, has
laid this idea of theology to rest for large numbers of
people. No longer do most theologians seek after Truth
as if it had a separate and reified existence. Truth and
knowledge of truth are relative, or better, related to
human culture in its various forms. Whatever is meant by
God, it cannot mean a being or an existence which can be
known apart from the world and apart from humanity. On
this basis it must follow that all access to the divine
must be through the world and through humanity. More
than ever before, today theology is anthropology.

The idea that theology is anthropology is, of course,
not new. Feuerbach explicity made the statement in the
last century. But even before Feuerbach (who has a very
specific meaning for the phrase), many theological debates centered not on the nature of God but on the nature
of humanity, e.g. Original Sin and its transmission, the
resurrection of the body, law and freedom, determinism;
even the christological debates were largely anthropological. It is also appropriate to recognize various movements towards incarnational theology which claim that the
significance of the Christ event is to make explicit the

idea that we only come to know God through our being human. The difference is the unabashed nature of theology as anthropology today and the free use of God as an integrating anthropological symbol rather than the name of a being "out there" somehow separated from humanity.

With this in mind I have identified six pairs of concepts which spring either directly or indirectly from sociology of knowledge and which have application to theology as anthropology. The six pairs are: ideology--utopia, priestly function--prophetic function, fragmented--whole, hard relativism--soft relativism, absolute truth--related truth, and social determinism--social freedom. It is my contention that the first member of each of the six pairs form a set, albeit incomplete, while the second members form an opposing set.

Ideology	Utopia
Priest	Prophet
Fragmentation	Wholeness
Hard Relativism	Soft Relativism
Absolute Truth	Related Truth
Determinism	Freedom

Further, it is my contention that the second set characterizes theology as it ought to be done while the first set characterizes theology as it is too often done.

Ideology and utopia are obviously borrowed from Karl Mannheim. Ideology was used in the first part of this paper in connection with James Cone's liberation response to the dominant white theology. Cone, of course, uses it to condemn those he opposes without fully recognizing the ideological dangers of his own position. The sad part is that Cone's analysis of other theologies is virtually 100% correct. The dominant tendency has always been to use theology as one of the legitimating mechanisms of society, a la Berger and Luckmann.[13] That sociology of

knowledge has uncovered this legitimating tendency for us
can prove to be a liberating movement. The task must be
to actualize the opposite pole. Instead of being ideological, theology must now strive to be utopian.

Such a constructive task must contain at least four
points. First, it must be clearly anthropological. It
must analyze the status of human beings, all human beings,
and their relationships to one another and to the cosmos.
God talk, when used, must be humanizing (i.e. supportive
of humanity, human goals, and human aspirations) and integrating. God talk in ideological theology tends to be
de-humanizing as it legitimates one view over another.
Second, it must be visionary. It must seek after a new
order, a new vision of reality. It must see the maintenance of the status quo or the movement back to any
historical expression of reality as demonic. Such movements are ideological, not utopian. It must be pointed
out that progress is not guaranteed, and surely change
simply for change's sake is not divine. However, gain is
not possible from a stationary position. Third, it must
be self-criticizing. Utopian theology must realize that
it is always in danger of becoming ideological. Indeed,
Mannheim states that the distance between any social
state and its utopia is continually shrinking, due presumably to the modification of one or the other or both.
Not only must utopian theology be self-criticizing, it
must seek criticism and continually stand under criticism.
It is always provisional; it will never be able to write
its own *Church Dogmatics*. Fourth, it must be ecumenical,
as Werner Stark suggests. It must draw not only from all
academic disciplines, it must draw from all societies,
cultures, and subcultures. It must be free of the criticism that the rich are telling the poor what is good for
them or that whites are defining reality for blacks.

Such a utopian methodology could be truly liberating. If it is successful it must expect to be assailed on all sides by those who do ideological theology, for it will seek to radically change that which ideology seeks to maintain. Total tranquility is a sure sign that utopian theology has been reduced to ideology.

The second pair, priestly function--prophetic function, clearly go with ideology and utopia, respectively. What is needed for utopian theology is the prophet. The prophet is not a soothsayer or a fortune teller, but is rather one who speaks a word of judgment, one who questions, one who muddies the waters, one who rocks the boat, one who prods, prompts, and urges. All this is done, of course, out of love and concern for the well-being of the ones who are addressed, not out of malice. The priest, too, is concerned with the well-being of the institution being represented. There is necessarily an ideological responsibility; one hand washes the other. The prophet, on the other hand, sees no institution as sacrosanct.

The third pair are fragmentedness and wholeness. It is the analysis of Berger, Berger, and Kellner (The Homeless Mind) that modern consciousness is characterized, in part, by componentiality or fragmented lives. We see the different aspects of our lives and of our society as components which may be separated from one another or discarded and replaced. It is interesting that David Bohm, operating out of the sphere of theoretical physics, comes to much the same conclusion (Wholeness and the Implicate Order). However, Bohm sees the root of the problem with Democritus and the atomic theory.[14] The problem began as soon as the world was conceived of as an indeterminate number of discrete particles which could be combined or broken down at will. The theology of ideology promotes

the fragmentariness of reality. It pits ideology against
ideology and society against society. Each sees itself
as ultimate; each declares what reality is. The acute
observer, however, sees these competing claims as a primary source which denies the wholeness of reality. Utopian theology must presume that reality is a whole, that
somehow all the pieces fit together. If they do not, then
various ideologies are legitimate and can never be transcended. While the wholeness of reality can never be
demonstrated, we must proceed as if it were so. The alternative is nihilism.

    Enough was said of hard relativism and soft relativism
in the first section. It should be clear that hard relativism and arbitrariness are divisive and lend themselves both to fragmenting reality and to promoting ideology. The opposite is true of soft relativism and relationalism. It is assumed that truth is manifold and is
contained in the whole of reality, not just in segments.
The ecumenical tendencies of soft relativism lend themselves well to the construction of utopian visions.

    The contribution of the pair absolute truth--related
truth should, by now, be somewhat transparent. The claim
of absolute truth is an imperialistic claim, the claim of
ideology. It opposes all else and tends to fragment
reality. On the other hand, related truth has an ecumenical, wholistic, healing tendency. Related truth is compatible with utopian theology and the other concepts;
absolute truth is not. Note that truth is not here being
placed in opposition to any thing else. It is absolute
and related which are in opposition.

    Finally, we come to social determinism and social
freedom. As was stated earlier, hard relativity is cloak-
ed determinism. In a deterministic schema ideology cannot be transcended; fragmented existence must follow.

On the other hand, if freedom of some magnitude is assumed then the possibility of going beyond ideology to
utopia will always be present; the possibility of pulling
the fragments together into a whole will always be present. It should be noted that there is no claim here for
absolute or total freedom. Freedom is relative or related just as are knowledge and truth.

There is no way to prove freedom, to prove that
truth is related, to prove soft relativism, or to prove
that reality is a whole any more than there is a way to
prove the existence of God. Utopian prophetic theology
will operate with these as assumptions, as if they are
the case. The alternative is to assume determinism,
absolute truth, hard relativism, and fragmented existence, that is, to assume an ideological position. The
result must be nihilism and despair; there can be no
hope. In such a case the only appropriate philosophical
position is hedonism. This is not a viable alternative.

An obvious question concerns the survivability of a
utopian stance. Lasting ideas tend to become institutionalized. Can prophecy, wholeness, soft relativism, related truth, and freedom survive institutionalization? Can
they survive without it? The answer to both questions
is probably "No." The process of institutionalization
could be fatal for utopian theology. The tendency in
institutionalization is for the ideas of the prophet to
become the sacraments of the priest. Such a movement
from a fluid to a static position promotes a fragmented,
ideological situation. The related truth of the prophet
becomes the absolute truth of the next generation. At
the same time the complete lack of institutionalization
would assure the death of any utopian theology. Utopian
theology must somehow avoid both pitfalls. Its only hope

is to remain on the fringes of society in a marginal status. Further, it must take on the character of a series of movements with successive developments only loosely related to one another. From this point it may be able to function as a small lump of leaven, hidden and unnoticed, but with great potential for effecting change.

I wish to close with a gratuitous remark. As illuminating as aspects of sociology of knowledge are for theology and philosophy, it would be foolish to think that the last word has been uttered. Such an assumption would violate sociology of knowledge itself. For example, several sociologists of knowledge criticize Immanuel Kant for assuming that his categories of thought were absolute and universal. This criticism has just cause. However, by modifying Kant slightly and invoking contemporary physiological research one can see that there are common, universal mechanisms through which humans perceive their world and gather knowledge about it. An analysis of these mechanisms and the parameters they set is in order. This is physiology, not sociology of knowledge. It could be claimed that the research must have a sociological basis and the knowledge gained has a social character; however, a total reduction of physiology to sociology is stretching the point. It seems very like the medieval attempt to reduce all other disciplines to theology. Another example might be existentialism. How much of what is expressed socially is due not to society but to being a human individual is not fully known. What is the full relationship between individuals and society? The work goes on. Certainly humans are social beings; that cannot be explained away. However, humans are also individual, finite, existential beings as well. In any event the imperialism of any discipline must be resisted in favor of an ecumenism of all disciplines.

NOTES

1. Werner Stark, *The Sociology of Knowledge: An Essay in Aid of a Deeper Understanding of the History of Ideas* (Glencoe, Illinois: The Free Press, 1958), p. 152.

2. Peter L. Berger and Thomas Luckmann, *The Social Construction of Reality: A Treatise in the Sociology of Knowledge* (Garden City, New York: Doubleday & Co., Inc., 1966), p. 4.

3. Sheila Greeve Davaney, "Social Theories of Knowing: Liberationist Appropriation and Feminist Rejoinder," unpublished manuscript.

4. James Cone, *God of the Oppressed* (New York: The Seabury Press, 1975), p. 45.

5. Juan Luis Segundo, *Our Idea of God* (Maryknoll, New York: Orbis Books, 1974), p. 8.

6. Cone, p. 39.

7. Van Austin Harvey, *The Historian and the Believer: The Morality of Historical Knowledge and Christian Belief* (New York: The Macmillan Company, 1966), p. 209.

8. Cone, p. 39.

9. Stark, p. 159.

10. Ibid., p. 169.

11. Ibid., p. 156.

12. Harvey, p. 210.

13. Berger and Luckmann, pp. 92-128.

14. David Bohm, *Wholeness and the Implicate Order* (London: Routledge & Kegan Paul, 1980), p. 8.

SOCIOLOGICAL AND THEOLOGICAL METHOD

Kerry Edwards

Marx, in a pun on the German meaning of the name
Feuerbach, once said that anyone doing serious
philosophy in that time would first have to pass
through the "fiery brook" of Feuerbach's thought.
Today the sociological perspective constitutes
the "fiery brook" through which the theologian
must pass--or, perhaps more accurately ought to
pass. It is sociological thought, and most
acutely the sociology of knowledge, that offers
the specifically contemporary challenge to
theology.[1]

Berger is quite right. Like it or not, the contemporary
theologian is faced with the encroachment of sociology on
theology. I use the word encroachment with its negative
connotations because it sometimes appears that sociological analysis of religious belief is some kind of usurpation
of the theological task. But it will be my contention in
this essay that insofar as sociology, particularly the
sociology of knowledge, has true insight into the nature
of human existence, the theologian needs to integrate
this into his or her understanding and execution of the
theological task. In other words, the theologian must
consciously enter the circle which Barbara Hargrove has
described in the introduction to this volume.

For many years there was a detente between the disciplines of sociology and theology. The grounds for this
detente were twofold. On the part of the sociologists

the detente began when they realized that the indictments
of religion as illusion by earlier sociologists like Marx,
Comte, and Spencer were unscientific.[2] On the theological side detente was made possible by the Barthian separation of religion and faith, which posited two different philosophical foundations for religion and faith.
Religion could be examined by the sciences, but Christianity called for faith which was unexaminable by scientific
method.[3]

The breakdown of this detente is rooted in two
changes. On the theological side it does not take a very
philosophically adept person to realize that the Barthian
position is an obvious example of special pleading reinforced by piety. On the sociological side, sociologists
became aware either that it was virtually impossible to
establish a value-free sociology, or that if it was possible, then such a sociology would only deal with trivi-
alities. If this is the case then dialogue is desirable
with theologians who have traditionally been concerned
with value. Robert Friedrichs comments:

> What I will contend is that, though the scien-
> tific study of religion does indeed precipitate
> images of man and elicit behavior upon the part
> of those engaged in such research which screen
> out and/or contradict an image and an ethic to
> which the theologian has traditionally spoken,
> *neither the scientific study of religion, nor*
> *theology is able (whatever one's ontic pre-*
> *dilections may be) to carry out the task it has*
> *assigned itself without intimate, and to this*
> *point, relatively unwitting, dialogue with the*
> *other.*[4]

This end to detente does not come without serious
risk for both parties. Robin Gill notes that the theologian could be disturbed by the kind of causal explanations
that sociology will give for theological belief.[5] I would
add that it is equally likely that the sociologist may be
subject to distress. The theologian may provide arguments
for some kind of transcendent value, that could be dis-
turbing to a sociologist used to working within an empirical, sometimes positivistic discipline.

Because historically sociology has been reductionistic
in dealing with religion, I think the most appropriate
issue to begin discussion is whether the breakdown in
detente means that theology is overwhelmed by sociology.
Robert A. Segal apparently thinks that it could be.[6]
Whenever sociologists or psychologists have claimed to
undermine the truth of religion by pointing to the origin
of belief in society or psychological development, theologians have always had a strong defense in the form of the
genetic fallacy. The genetic fallacy is committed when
one tries to invalidate some truth by pointing to its
origin. For instance, if I say that I believe that the
Hudson River is in New York State because I had a vision
to that effect last night after taking LSD, that belief
cannot be invalidated by pointing to the fact that that
belief was a direct consequence of taking LSD. Whether
or not I came to that belief through taking LSD, the
statement remains true that the Hudson River is in New
York State. Therefore, for the sociologist to say that
belief in monotheism is a consequence of living in a
highly structured society does not imply anything about
the *truth* of that belief.

Segal, however, tries to show that even granted the
defense of the genetic fallacy, sociology still has a
legitimate claim to have explained away religion.

His argument is as follows: As he understands the social
sciences, he sees them considering whether the reasons
people say that they hold religious beliefs are truly the
reasons why they hold them.[7] Sociology presumes the error of religious explanations for religious belief and in
giving reasons other than the believer's for religious
beliefs the sociologist makes religious explanations
unnecessary:

> If no natural explanation of religious belief
> can make a supernatural explanation impossible,
> a sufficient natural explanation would make a
> supernatural one superflous. . . . By Ockham's razor
> the explanation would reduce a supernatural
> explanation to an unnecessary hypothesis. . . .
> Science refutes a supernatural explanation of
> the world not by directly refuting the exis-
> tence of God but by explaining the world with-
> out having to postulate his existence.[8]

He concluded consequently:

> Nineteenth century social scientists were simply
> not averse to clashing with believers. Twentieth
> century social scientists are. Doubtless nine-
> teenth century social scientists erred in assum-
> ing that their natural explanations of religious
> belief necessarily refuted the truth of religious
> belief, but twentieth century scientists err in
> assuming that their explanations necessarily do
> not.[9]

I think there are a number of reasons why this argument
does not work. The first is that despite Segal's assumption that "natural" explanations are simpler than
"supernatural", parsimony of explanation is an elusive
goal. Presumably he has in mind the formulation of
Ockham's razor which says: "Do not posit entities beyond

necessity." However what Ockham said was, "What can be done with fewer assumptions is done in vain with more."[10] Consequently, if belief in one additional entity, God, can do away with numerous other assumptions, then the most parsimonious explanation of religious belief would be to posit God as the source. A clear example of this would be the difference between divine creation and evolution. What is simpler, the theory of creation by divine fiat or the theory of evolution? I am not trying to argue either for divinity as the sole source of religious belief or for divine creation. I am simply pointing out that Segal's assumption that sociological explanation is simpler than what he calls "supernatural" explanation is clearly not the case.

Two further comments on this. As Segal himself realized, it is not at all clear that the social sciences have been able to give thoroughgoing explanations of religious belief. To use Tillich's analogy in reference to Feuerbach: one may be able to explain images of God as projections of human wishes, but what is the screen upon which these images are projected? Secondly, as theologians have always realized, there is a great deal of difference between what is called the context of discovery and the context of justification. For the most part it is foolish to appeal to the context of discovery to justify beliefs. After all, if someone asks you why you think the world is round, do you justify that belief by saying that your mother told you? You may have initially discovered the truth that way, but you justify the belief by other reasons. This is why there always have been and probably always will be arguments for the existence of God in some form or another. To the extent that one finds such arguments convincing, the reality of religious beliefs can be affirmed without appeal to their societal origins. I think that it is to this kind of justification

for his own religious beliefs that the sociologist of
religion Peter Berger, resorts in his book *Rumor of
Angels*.[11]

The upshot of this discussion is that if detente is
over, and sociology and theology dialogue, there is no
reason to assume that theology will be overcome by sociology.

If sociology does not overwhelm theology then does
theology have something to add to sociology? I think it
might have something to say to the issue of sociological
method. The issue that needs to be addressed is the
bracketing of the question of the truth of religious
belief by the sociologist. It is what Berger calls
methodological atheism:

> Within this frame of reference (of scientific
> theorizing), the religious projections can be
> dealt with only as such, as products of human
> activity and human consciousness, and rigorous
> brackets have to be placed around the question
> as to whether these projections may not *also*
> be something else than that (or, more accu-
> rately, *refer to* something else than the human
> world in which they empirically originate).
> In other words, every inquiry into religious
> matters that limits itself to the empirically
> available must necessarily be based on a
> "methodological atheism".[12]

In light of the fact that Berger later writes a book
arguing for the more than empirical reference of religious
beliefs and later also has some reservations about "methodological atheism" we can ask, why does Berger feel com-
pelled to assert a methodological atheism? Let me speculate. Sociology is the child of positivism. The founders

of the discipline were clearly impelled by the belief
that only that was real which was empirically available.
For them there was no transcendent reality, religion was
to be explained solely in terms of society. Durkheim
states:

> I believe that this idea--that social life must
> be explained, not by the notions of those who
> participate in it, but by more profound causes
> which are unperceived by consciousness--is
> fruitful; and I think also that these causes
> must be sought principally in the manner ac-
> cording to which the associated individuals are
> grouped. In this way--and in this way only--it
> seems to me, can history become a science, and
> sociology itself exist.[13]

As Segal pointed out, twentieth century sociology has
repudiated the allegedly unscientific claims of this
position and is willing to concede as Berger does that
perhaps religion has some validity beyond its social
construction. The problem is that although the explicit
formulations of positivism are rejected, the underlying
implications seem to hang on. The main reason for insisting on a sharp separation of the "empirical" and scientific from the non-empirical and unscientific is the assumption that empirical methodology is uncovering something
more true, something "more profound" than some other
methodology. The move has been from what is seen to be a
"prejudiced" positivism to an allegedly value-free empiricism. However, I think a value-free empiricism is not
only not possible, it is not even desirable. Twentieth
century sociologists have been quite right in seeing
that nineteenth century positivistic sociology was based
on an unjustified positivism, but they are negligent in
not seeing that the narrow investigations of empirical

science need a broader metaphysical framework into which
they fit. To the extent that nineteenth century sociologists provided such a framework in their positivist metaphysics, they need to be commended.

The lack of an explicit overarching framework may
have something to do with the fact that some people think
that methodological atheism extends beyond method. Ninian
Smart suspects that Berger is being imperialistic in his
methodological atheism.[14] Benton   Johnson comments:

> . . . much of Berger's work seems calculated to
> drive a wedge between the two domains (religion
> and social science).[15]

Keith Dixon, similarly:

> It is difficult to take this caveat (that he is
> not treating religion simply as alienation)
> seriously since what is clearly implied in his
> actual account of religious belief is that view
> that religion may be treated *merely* as an
> enclave of meaning for the purpose of the
> sociology of knowledge. Religion for all
> practical explanatory purpose *is* the pro-
> jection of this worldly alienation into a
> non-empirical sphere.[16]

It would not be fair to direct all this criticism against
Berger without recognizing that he is not the only one
who advocates a methodological atheism. Robin Gill, in
his book *The Social Context of Theology* argues for a
similar position calling it an "as if" methodology:

> A more fruitful account of the basis on which
> the sociologist in general and the sociologist
> of religion in particular, operates might be
> found in an "as if" methodology. Adopting such
> a methodology the sociologist would work "as if"
> there were social determinants for all human

 interaction--believing as an individual,
 though, that there may not be.[17]
The counterpart to this argument is that the theologian
must work in his or her discipline "as if" there were a
god or other transcendent realities. On this model we
end up with two neatly compartmentalized departments of
knowledge, and never the twain shall meet. As a matter
of fact, each department acts as if the other is false.
This is not much different from the notorious philosophical position of Averroes in the middle ages who insisted
that there were two realms of truth, the theological and
the philosophical, and they were free to contradict each
other. It seems to me that all three of these writers,
Berger, Averroes and Gill, fall into the same class of
perverting the idea of truth in order to avoid conflict
and unification of knowledge in a new synthesis.
They fail to see that the idea of truth is based on the
presupposition or postulate that there is some one state
of affairs that judges and mediates between our perceptions of it and is the reason for assuming that knowledge
can be whole. We are not satisfied in compartmentalizing
knowledge. Indeed, Berger, in advocating such a position,
is adding to the compartmentalization that he criticized
in his writing on secularization.

     Instead of this "methodological atheism" Berger would
have done better to speak of "methodological specificity."
Such a methodological statement would have enabled him to
analyze specific religious beliefs according to strict
criteria of scientific method while leaving open during
that investigation the question of the kind of reality to
which such beliefs refer. Perhaps we might call this
methodological agnosticism, but it leaves open the possibility for some kind of unification of sociology and
theology outside the realm of specific analysis.

Berger, however, apparently has come to understand
that all is not well with methodological atheism. He
expresses his doubts in an article entitled "Some Second
Thoughts on Substantive Versus Functional Definitions of
Religion." Here he still maintains that we must keep a
separate compartment for scientific knowledge that is
empirically verifiable.[18] This means that in the realm
of science transcendence must appear as immanence.[19]
However, he is suspicious of functional definitions of
religion:

> I have become more militant in my opposition to
> functional definitions. . . . The reason for my
> revised attitude is rather that I have become
> more aware of the *ideological uses of* function-
> al definitions of religion.[20]

This results in a reinforcement of secularization:

> The ideological interest that concerns me is
> much more basic: *It is the interest in quasi-*
> *scientific legitimation of the avoidance of*
> *transcendence.* My thesis is this: The func-
> tional approach to religion, whatever the
> theoretical intentions of its authors, serves
> to provide quasiscientific legitimations of a
> secularized world view.[21]

The consequence is:

> Religion is absorbed into a night in which all
> cats are grey. The greyness is the secular-
> ized view of reality in which any manifesta-
> tions of transcendence are, strictly speak-
> ing, meaningless, and *therefore* can only be
> dealt with in terms of social or psychological
> functions that can be understood without
> reference to transcendence.[22]

Berger's solution to this problem is still to maintain
the epistemological neutrality of science but insist that
the "methodological" in "methodological atheism" must be
stressed in order to avoid ideological use of methodology.

Berger has pointed to a very real problem. As I speculated earlier, the root of the problem lies in the fact
that sociology has positivistic roots and, barring any
sustained attempt to avoid these roots, methodological
atheism passes naturally into ideological atheism. I do
not think that Berger's solution will solve the problem.
The problem is more basic, and I think Segal pointed to
it. If religion can be adequately treated by sociology
by only considering its immanent aspects and ignoring its
transcendent aspects, then considering the possibility of
religion being in any way transcendent becomes superfluous.
In other words, if methodological atheism really works,
then there is no reason why it should not pass into ideological atheism. If on the other hand there is reason to
believe that methodological atheism does not adequately
deal with the phenomenon of religion (as Berger apparently
himself thinks, since he wrote *Rumor of Angels* and signed
the Hartford Appeal) then methodological atheism is not an
appropriate method, and apart from the need to bow the
knee to the powers of scientific empiricism there is no
need to assert an atheistic method.

If we are to be fair to the sociologist in arguing
that methodological bracketing is not adequate, the same
criticism must apply to the theologian. The theologian
cannot bracket sociological discoveries but must come
face to face with the issues and sort them out. The major
issue with which theology needs to come to grips in sociological thought is the sociology of knowledge. Some
think that if the possibility of absolute truth is denied
on the grounds that what counts as knowledge is culture-
related, theological discourse is jeopardized.

One way to integrate theology and sociology would be
to follow the method of Karl Mannheim. He tries to maintain an absolute perspective for himself while relativ-
izing most other knowledge by positing the existence of a
socially unattached intelligentsia, who, because they are
unattached, are able to have the true perspective on the
knowable. The theologian could do likewise. He or she
could argue that the theologian is socially unattached
and therefore capable of having some kind of absolute insight while recognizing that the socially attached do not
have an absolute perspective. This in fact may be a description of the theologian in our time who is becoming
less and less attached to a religious community and more
to an academic community. The problem with this kind of
integration is pointed out by Karl Popper in his comments
on Mannheim's intelligentsia.[23] He argues that Mannheim's
position is simply a case of special pleading. It is an
attempt to relativize everyone else's knowledge while
maintaining a privileged position for one's own. Besides,
a little historical study will show that theologians and
philosophers are as much a part of the cultural environment as everyone else. On this score it is interesting to
note that even Karl Barth, who wanted to separate "faith"
and the social sciences, traces the change in his own
thinking to the day his theological professors proclaimed
support for the war policy of Wilhelm II in August 1914.[24]

Another possibility of relating theology to sociology
would be to exclude each from the other as Berger and Gill
think sociology should do with theology. The problem with
this, as I already mentioned, is that unless we want to
live a compartmentalized life we must have a method which
allows unity.

An additional alternative would be what Kai Nielson
calls "Wittgensteinian Fideism".[25] This position would

interpret statements about transcendent reality into assertions about one's intent to live a certain kind of
life.[26] This is quite a plausible response. It does not
ignore sociological explanations of religious beliefs but
avoids the problem of having to justify statements about
transcendent reality. This is the position that D.Z.
Phillips takes in *Religion Without Explanation*. One
example that he gives of such an understanding of religious belief is that of belief in the last judgment.
Such a belief simply means that one lives one's life as
if there is a last judgment without being committed to
the idea that there actually will be one.[27] The same
applies to talk about the reality of God:

> To ask whether God exists is not to ask a
> theoretical question. If it is to mean any-
> thing at all, it is to wonder about praising
> and praying; it is to wonder whether there is
> anything in all that. This is why philosophy
> cannot answer the question "Does God exist?"
> with either an affirmative or a negative reply.
> For from whose mouth does the question come and
> how is it answered?[28]

I wonder if Gordon Kaufman has a similar idea in mind
when he says:

> Ordinary human speech about God is not abstract
> logical talk about an "ultimate limit" but
> rather talk about life and the world, about
> our deepest human problems, about catastrophe
> and triumph, about human misery and human
> glory. It is about what is really important
> in life, how we are to live, how comport
> ourselves, which styles of life are truly
> humane and which dehumanizing.[29]

One problem with this approach is that although it
avoids the problem of discerning transcendent reality,
it still faces the issue of the value and appropriateness
of different forms of life. It must be careful to assert
reasons for choosing one form of life over another, or
else it can fall victim to the supposition that a crimi-
nal form of life is as appropriate as one dutifully sub-
mitted to the categorical imperative. It must be cogni-
zant of the fact that although values are related to different cultural situations this does not necessarily make
values arbitrary.

Along with the danger of assuming that forms of life
are arbitrary goes the danger of neglecting dialogue because of the different cultural presuppositions underlying the form of life. Neglecting a dialogue degrades
the related knowledge that we do have and shortcircuits
the possibility of new insights that could be gained
through interaction.

Truth as consensus could be an additional theological
methodology uniting sociology of knowledge and theology.
A good example of this might be Bultmann's *Jesus Christ and
Mythology*.[30] In that book one finds numerous references to
what the "modern mind" now finds incredible, even though
it was credible in New Testament times. Since the "modern
mind" cannot believe these things any more, the same things
must be translated into statements about the meaning of
existence, instead of being statements about some supernatural realm. This approach squares with a sociology of
knowledge approach in that it first determines what the
"modern mind" can and cannot believe and then tailors
theological statements to their credibilities.

The method is faulty. First of all, as Gill points
out,[31] Bultmann and others like him make pronouncements
about what can and cannot be believed by the "modern mind"

without providing any sociological research to back up
their claim. We all know people who believe exactly what
Bultmann says they cannot believe. Secondly, the last
thing it does is to relativize or relationalize theology;
instead it absolutizes whatever is believed in the present. It is philosophical foolishness simply to find out
what people do and do not believe and then tailor one's
philosophical or theological opinions to the consensus of
belief. This is the worst form of truth as consensus.
Theology and philosophy have never operated on this model.
They have always relied on insight and wisdom on the part
of the individual seers and prophets. Can you imagine
Amos taking a poll to find out what prophecy the Hebrews
were willing to accept?

Bultmann could have avoided most of these problems if
he had avoided the appeal to the elusive "modern mind" and
instead focused in on what I suspect was really going on
all along. It was not that the "modern mind" could no
longer believe certain things, but that Rudolf Bultmann
could no longer believe those things. Once the discussion
is moved from the realm of the "modern mind" and into the
realm of the belief possibilities of the individual, that
individual can give reasons why he or she finds certain
things incredible. This change switches the criterion of
truth from the crude truth as consensus model which offers
no *reason* for truth, to the individual conscience which can
proffer grounds for acceptance and rejection. If one does
this the integrity of truth is not compromised while the
relational character of truth is recognized.

We could call this the historicist approach to theology. It recognizes that its suppositions and generalizations are related to the present social construction
of reality and that there is no indication that they will

always be acceptable; but on the other hand it does not
turn relativity into arbitrariness, but into relationalism, by insisting that there are grounds for belief which
can provide some discernment amongst possibilities and
provide some insight that is better than another.

The fact that we see that our understanding of reality
is always open to revision does not mean that we must
think that our understandings of reality are mistaken.
Indeed as Kaufman points out, we need to have the faith
that our interpretations do reflect reality itself:

Ultimately, this means that we must assume that
the presupposition on which our interpretations
are based conform with the structure of reality
itself. It is on these presuppositions--on this
faith which has been given to us--that we must
stake our lives, for no others are available
to us.[32]

The truth of a theological or metaphysical understanding
of reality can only be "proved," however, by its ability
to function as a paradigm over a period of time:

Though thought can be judged from within only
on the basis of coherence, its adequacy is finally judged not by coherence, but by its ability
to survive and to interpret and become a significant factor in the historical process. Its
final justification must be its "pragmatic"
power in the historical process, made possible
by its "correspondence" with the realities of
that process.[33]

One might suppose that since the necessarily limited perspective that we have cannot be proven to reflect reality
as it really is, that each separate social construction
becomes an isolated creation in itself, not sharing the

same presuppositions with other constructions and therefore incapable of dialoguing with it. Such an understanding I strenuously wish to avoid. I would avoid it by
understanding that absolute truth is the ideal goal
towards which all knowledge and belief aspire, and is the
ground for discussion between apparently contradictory
understandings of reality. Such a dialogue would take
seriously the *justifications* that each perspective has
for its understanding. Dialogue may end up by discovering
the basic presuppositions or primitive assertions of each
side and may conclude with disagreement on primitive assertions. On the other hand the parties may reflect on
their presuppositions and modify them. As Dixon argues,
this is the way to take human knowledge seriously:

> In seeking to give an account of why people
> come to hold the beliefs that they do one must
> pay serious attention to the *grounds* for their
> belief--viewed not merely as subjective partici-
> pant rationalization but as potentially object-
> ive judgment. Failure to do so leads to a
> self-defeating relativity that parodies the
> nature of human knowledge.[34]

There is no guarantee that this process will ever result in a unified human perception of the nature of reality. In fact, such a conclusion would be undesirable,
because it would rid the discussion of a need to pursue
truth any further. But the reason that such dialogue is
so important is that apart from it we end up in a position
like Gill's or Berger's, in which different paradigms live
alone in their own circle and knowledge that seeks the
whole cannot be pursued. Fences may good neighbors make,
but they do not make good theologians or philosophers.

In conclusion, let me summarize my argument. Detente
between sociologists and theologians is over, or at least
ought to be over. The grounds of detente were based on a
false compartmentalization of knowledge, which assumed
on the one hand a sociologically unexaminable faith and
on the other a value-free science. The consequence of
dialogue between the two disciplines for the sociologist
is that he or she cannot treat religion "as if" it were
illusory. If it is illusory it should be treated as illusory. If it is not illusory it should be treated as
not illusory. The theologian, on the other hand, must
take seriously the sociologists' claim of the culturally
influenced nature of knowledge. This means that absolute
truth claims are impossible, but does not imply that
truth rests on arbitrary foundations. This non-arbitrary
yet non-absolute idea of truth is the ground for the
dialogue between theology and sociology, and the ground
for discussion between theologians of different genus.
I do not think that this dialogue will result in a
universal cultural synthesis, because the world is too
culturally pluralistic. There would be too many factors
to integrate. But the attempt to do it is necessary as
long as human beings want to unify their knowledge, live
in harmony, and maintain some of the roles which the idea
of truth has played in our societies.

NOTES

1. Peter L. Berger, *A Rumor of Angels* (Garden City: Doubleday, 1969), p. 36.

2. Benton Johnson, "Sociological Theory and Religious Truth," *Sociological Analysis,* 38, no. 4,(1977), p. 370.

3. Robert Friedrichs, "Social Research and Theology: End of Detente?", *Review of Religious Research,* 15, no. 3, (Spring, 1974), pp. 116-117.

4. Friedrichs, p. 121 (His emphasis).

5. Robin Gill, *The Social Context of Theology* (London: Mowbrays, 1975), p. 26, see also Johnson, p. 386.

6. Robert A. Segal, "The Social Sciences and the Truth of Religious Belief," *Journal of the American Academy of Religion,* 48, no. 3, pp. 403-413.

7. Segal, p. 404.

8. Segal, p. 407.

9. Segal, pp. 410-411, see also Gill, p. 20.

10. Paul Edwards, ed. *The Encyclopedia of Philosophy* Vol. 8 (New York: Macmillan, 1967), p. 307.

11. Berger.

12. Berger, *The Sacred Canopy* (New York: Doubleday, 1967), p. 100.

13. Emile Durkheim, "Review of Labrola," *Essais sur la conception materialiste do l'histoire,* in *Revue Philosophique* 44, 1897, p. 648, quoted by John Bowker in *The Sense of God: Sociological, Anthropological and Psychological Approaches to the Origin of the Sense of God* (Oxford: Clarendon, 1973). p. 22.

14. Gill, p. 32.

15. Johnson, p. 382.

16. Keith Dixon, *The Sociology of Belief* (London: Routledge and Kegan Paul, 1980), p. 187.

98   RELIGION AND THE SOCIOLOGY OF KNOWLEDGE

17. Gill, p. 37.

18. Peter Berger, "Some Second Thoughts on Substantive versus Functional Definitions of Religion" in *Journal for the Scientific Study of Religion*, 13, no. 4, (June, 1974), p. 125.

19. Berger, "Second Thoughts", p. 127.

20. Ibid., p. 127, (His emphasis).

21. Ibid., p. 128.

22. Ibid., p. 129.

23. Karl Popper, "The Sociology of Knowledge" in James E. Curtis and John W. Peters eds. *The Sociology of Knowledge: A Reader* (New York: Praeger, 1970), p. 653, Reprinted from Popper, *Open Society and its Enemies* (Princeton: Princeton University Press, 1966).

24. Karl Barth, *The Humanity of God* (Richmond: John Knox Press, 1960), p. 14.

25. See Charles M. Wood, "On the Reality of God", in *The Iliff Review*, 39, no. 1, (Winter, 1982), pp. 3-9.

26. R.B. Braithwaite, *An Empiricist's View of the Nature of Religious Belief* (Cambridge: Cambridge University Press, 1955).

27. D.Z. Phillips, *Religion Without Explanation* (Oxford: Basil Blackwell, 1976), p. 167.

28. Phillips, p. 181.

29. Gordon Kaufman, *Theological Imagination* (Philadelphia: Westminster, 1981), p. 83.

30. Rudolf Bultmann, *Jesus Christ and Mythology* (New York: Scribner's, 1958).

31. Gill, Chapters 5 & 6.

32. Gordon Kaufman, *Relativism, Knowledge, and Faith* (Chicago: University of Chicago Press, 1960), p. 94.

33. Kaufman, *Relativism*, p. 94.

34. Dixon, p. 120.

SOCIOLOGY OF KNOWLEDGE AND THE STUDY
OF EARLY CHRISTIANITY

Harold E. Remus

Sociological study of biblical data, of ancient
Judaism, and of Christian origins is hardly new.[1] In
Canada, one of her most eminent biblical scholars, T.J.
Meek, many years ago took account of social factors in
delineating Israelite origins.[2] More recently, sociological interpretation has, for various reasons, come to
occupy a prominent place.[3] One compelling reason has
been that study of sociological dimensions and elements
of the much-studied texts of biblical studies often casts
them in a different, sometimes new light. In turn, however, these modern studies, as well as the data they seek
understanding of, are better understood if some of the
precursors of such study are noted. This essay will
focus on one area of sociological study--sociology of
knowledge--offering some examples of its application to
the study of early Christianity and then calling attention to some precursors.

SOCIOLOGY OF KNOWLEDGE

The sociology of knowledge investigates the relation
of thought to its social settings. The theoretical
foundations of the discipline were laid in the 1920s by
Max Scheler.[4] He and Karl Mannheim, another of the
earliest and most noted of the theoreticians, focused on
the history of ideas as these were formulated by the

thinkers in a society.[5] Some recent sociologists of
knowledge have defined "knowledge" more broadly to
include also the presuppositions and maxims of the day
to day, "what people 'know' as 'reality' in their everyday, non- or pre-theoretical lives. In other words, com-
mon-sense 'knowledge' that constitutes the fabric of
meanings without which no society could exist."[6]

This broader conception of the sociology of knowledge
is appropriate to first- and second-century Christianity,
where the socially and intellectually elite were a small
(though important) minority[7] and much of the literature
produced was popular.[8] At the same time it does not preclude taking account of the thinkers of that period, as
represented by the philosophical schools and those
Christians who were influenced by them.

Conversion, one of the phenomena discussed by Berger
and Luckmann,[9] illustrates some of the generalizations
and terminology of the sociology of knowledge and how
they may be applied to early Christian data. A.D. Nock
saw conversion (in contrast to adhesion) as characteristic of the way in which persons entered early Christianity.[10] The social processes involved, which he did not
attempt to spell out, may be outlined briefly. One begins with the convert before conversion. To the child,
social mores, values and institutions present themselves,
and are presented, as the only ones possible, that is,
as objective reality. Primary socialization takes place
in an emotionally charged atmosphere in which this "objective reality" is internalized.[11] Secondary socialization presupposes the primary and builds upon it but
is generally not as intense and emotionally charged.[12]
Viewed in these terms, conversion is an intensive resocialization that resembles primary socialization.

This is a necessary resemblance because the convert is urged to abandon or reinterpret many of the basic maxims and mores of his or her primary socialization, and these are generally not surrendered without a struggle. Many of the basic structural elements of primary socialization are requisite, therefore, especially a social setting in which the convert sees how the new premises and values are embodied and acted upon. Important to the setting are "significant others,"[13] that is, persons with whom the convert identifies and whom he or she imitates, thus replicating in some way and to some degree the emotional element of childhood rearing. Berger and Luckmann call this kind of social setting a "plausibility structure," a "laboratory" within which the convert internalizes the new reality, acquiring a new "symbolic universe."[14]

Many of the elements in this description can be found, without distortion, in early Christianity. There are the significant others--authority figures, such as Paul, with whom converts identify and whom they imitate and obey. In addressing his converts Paul employs language from the context of primary socialization: they are children and he is their father[15] who expects them to imitate or obey him or Christ.[16] It is a form of reality maintenance when Paul tells the Corinthians he has sent Timothy to remind them of his "ways in Christ, even as I teach everywhere in every church" (1 Cor. 4: 17). If they fail to heed Timothy, Paul himself will come and demonstrate the divine power (1 Cor. 4:18-19). Even at a distance, however, Paul is able to enforce the new reality, through the presence of his *pneuma* in the assembled community (1 Cor. 5:3-5). The importance of the community in giving credence to a new reality is evident in these texts. In this instance--a crisis in the community caused by a flagrant violation of the

morality Paul is seeking to inculcate--the reality maintenance requires the pain of expulsion from the community,
with the purpose of fitting the offender for the ultimate
telos of the community, its final deliverance by its
saviour. Such a situation is an example of "therapy,"[17]
a heightened form of reality maintenance in the time of
crisis for the purpose of retaining the integrity of the
community and of its members.

Observance of the social context of knowledge is important also in other areas of early Christianity. The community at worship, for example, is a powerful plausibility
structure in which the new reality is embodied.[18] Ethical
statements function not only logically--"love one another
as Christ loved you"--but also societally. ". . . 'Christ
loved you' is a shorthand way of referring to a whole pattern of discourse and memory, of symbol and story, of experience and reflection belonging to the lore of the community."[19] Turning to beliefs about miracle, the assertion
that "With God all things are possible" is prominent in
early Christianity.[20] But like the love command, it, too,
is a "shorthand way" of referring to symbolic universes of
various Christian communities. To distinguish such a statement from very similar assertions by pagans,[21] therefore,
requires reference to their communal settings, i.e., to
social data.

CONFLICT SITUATIONS AND SOCIOLOGY
OF KNOWLEDGE: PRECURSORS

Attention to social data is especially important when
studying conflict situations. One area of sharp conflict
within early Christianity, as well as between various
Christians and Jews or pagans, is the assessment of
"miracles"--wondrous interventions by the divine in the

cosmic order or in human affairs. Understanding of these
conflicts has often been blurred by neglect of their
social and cultural dimensions. That neglect is now being
redressed in a number of studies. A methodological caveat
is in order, however. It is common for proponents of a
new approach to find earlier practitioners of it on every
hand. As Albert Schweitzer once asked, "Whoever discovered a true principle without pressing its application too
far?"[22] Some distinctions put forward by Robert Merton
are useful therefore. Reviewing the history of theory in
various academic disciplines, Merton distinguishes between
prediscoveries, anticipations, and adumbrations.[23] A pre-
discovery is one that was forgotten and substantially re-
discovered later. An anticipation is an insight or a
finding which in its formulation overlaps later ones but
is not pursued further nor are the implications developed
or applied in a systematic and significant way. An adumbration vaguely approximates later findings, with practically none of the implications being developed.

These distinctions help to guard the proponent of a
new insight or methodology from claiming too much in the
way of antecedents by offering a way of weighting them
and their continuity or discontinuity with one's own
findings. One can be grateful to these predecessors for
sharpening one's perception of the data and for indicating
that one is not simply engaged in eisegesis: in an earlier time they made similar finds from the extant data.
It will be incumbent upon the investigator in the present day, however, to pursue his or her research more
systematically than they, to order findings in a coherent
way, and to provide a theoretical justification for the
manner in which he or she does so. Some examples from the
study of miracle will illustrate these remarks.

Falling in the category of adumbration is the awareness by a number of writers in the Western Catholic tradition that education and culture affect one's judgment of
extraordinary phenomena. Educated pagans were generally
distinguished from those of little or no schooling by
their knowledge of the causes of eclipses.[24] Augustine,
in a conflict situation, makes this awareness explicit
in order to debunk the belief that Romulus, by his divine
power, caused an eclipse of the sun: "the ignorant multitude [*imperita . . . multitudo*] . . . did not know that
it was brought about by the fixed law of the sun's
course."[25] Aquinas, in seeking to define *miraculum* according to its cause, must deal with the problem of
variance of judgment from one person to another in regard
to causes. An untutored person (*rusticus*), he observes,
will marvel at a solar eclipse whereas an astronomer will
not.[26] Neither Augustine nor Aquinas has any interest in
developing these insights, which both men employ incidentally in defense and exposition of Christian thought.
Similarly, today Karl Rahner and other modern Roman
Catholic thinkers argue for certain of the Gospel miracles
by singling out their cultural context as figuring de-
cisively in their acceptance or rejection.[27] By contrast,
thinkers in the Enlightenment tradition sometimes point
to the social conditioning of miracle claims in order to
discredit them or reduce their number: the more barbarous
and uncultured a people or social group, the greater the
number of miracle accounts.[28] Much of Hume's polemic
against uncritical acceptance of extraordinary phenomena
consists of keen observations on the effect of education
and culture on perception of such phenomena. His distinctions between various societies, or between urban and
rural peoples, or between ancient and "enlightened" times,

and his observations of the effect of geography or
religion on perceptions are suggestive of later historical and sociological study.[29]

Also falling in the category of adumbration is the
observation by J.B. Mozely and W. Herrmann that it is
not only persons trained in natural or historical science who find belief in miracles difficult; others do,
too, inasmuch as miracles go counter to everyday experience.[30] In his discussion of "present knowledge"
Van Harvey has explored the methodological implications
of insights like those of Mozely and Herrmann.[31]

Related to education and culture are social status,
power, and group loyalties, which played a role in
ancient assessments of extraordinary phenomena. Hume
drew attention to the biasing effect of political loyalties[32] while Kant noted how class and power operated to
allow for the possibility of miracles in the past but
not in the present for fear of upsetting the status quo.[33]
Neither made much of these insights, however, and these
factors have generally been neglected in discussions of
miracle.

One of the distinctions most commonly drawn by historians, including students of miracle, is between ancient
and modern presuppositions. After the natural sciences in
the modern period began to offer comprehensive explanations
of ordinary and extraordinary phenomena, such explanations
were commonly put forward as warrants for dissolutions of
ancient miracles. In the first flush of Newtonian physics,
"the laws of nature" were invoked as sanctions of such
dissolutions, a practice that has persisted down to the
present. Either polemically or matter-of-factly, the
ignorance of past ages has been contrasted with present
knowledge, which could be utilized to provide explanations
of ancient miracles that denied their divine reference or

called it in question.[34] Twentieth-century discussion
conversant with the natural sciences and aware of the
nature of scientific claims has been less categorical
about the causation and demarcation of extraordinary
phenomena.[35] The upshot of such discussion has been a
recognition of the role of a priori commitments in demarcation of certain extraordinary phenomena as "miracles,"
the same phenomena being adjudged miraculous or non-mira-
culous according to whether or not one approaches them
with belief in divine agency and causation of a kind that
manifests itself in miracle.[36] Though these observations
are not characterized by their authors as "sociological,"
they may not unjustly be assessed as adumbrating a sociological approach to miracle: judgments of extraordinary
phenomena are relative, differing from age to age as well
as within a particular age, depending on such factors as
social status, education, power, and group loyalties, and
are nurtured and transmitted within specific social
matrices.

It is on this point--socialization--that some rare
observations were made by H. S. Reimarus and D. F. Strauss
that anticipate certain insights of the sociology of
knowledge. Reimarus spells out at length how primary
socialization affects religious belief, including belief
in miracle. Against those who maintain that non-Christ-
ians may be led to Christianity through reasoned demonstration, Reimarus argues that both Christians and non-
Christians are strongly inclined to persist in the religion of their first nurturing.[37] Christians (in Germany)
sometimes decide already before marriage, through con-
tracts, in which Christian confession their children will
be reared; that is, the upbringing is consciously socially
determined.[38] For the children this species of religion
is the only religion they know; in Berger and Luckmann's

terminology, it is "reality."[39] Were children not taught
from early on to accept the historical veracity of the
Bible, on reaching adulthood they would read it as a novel,
a collection of ancient fables.[40] Accordingly, Reimarus
elsewhere asserts that a people accustomed to a general
belief in miracles will incline to belief in specific miracles or in the possibility of miracles.[41] Indeed, belief
in miracle may actually make extraordinary phenomena possible.[42] When such general belief was lacking, even Jesus
could work no miracles.[43] Conflicts between peoples with
differing miracle beliefs are inevitable, and unresolvable
by appeal to objective criteria, i.e., criteria mutually
agreed on by those peoples.[44]

As a professor of oriental languages, Reimarus had
some acquaintance with the sacred books of other religions.[45] He notes that Europeans had been in contact with
non-European peoples for two to three centuries.[46] Yet
this had not resulted in a general consciousness of the
relativity of religious commitments and their social and
cultural conditioning: Reimarus felt constrained to con-
fide his thoughts on this subject only to private man-
uscripts. In retrospect they may be seen as anticipating
the sociology of knowledge at a number of points, though
at times his judgments are too crude.[47]

David Friedrich Strauss's observations on how the presuppositions of different eras and of different peoples
within them affect assessment of extraordinary phenomena
mark him off as a competent and pioneering historian;[48]
they also belong to the genuine anticipations of the sociology of knowledge and its application to the study of
miracle. Against writers on the New Testament who, in
commenting on certain New Testament miracle accounts,
credited first-century Jews with holding modern explanations of psychic disorders, Strauss asks for the evidence,

maintaining that such judgments are anachronistic and that
persons from one era transported to another would still
assess such disorders from the standpoint of their own
era.[49] Strauss faults his contemporaries with failing
to perceive the effect of present knowledge on their
judgments of ancient phenomena.[50] Translated into the
language of sociology, Strauss is here drawing attention
to the effects of socialization and social contexts on
knowledge.

Strauss is generally keenly aware of the relativity
of thought and its social conditioning. He observes that
"what is ordinary and regular in our estimation" may
differ from "what was so in the ideas of the author whose
writings are to be explained," something the rationalists
of his day did not perceive.[51] Myths, that is, narratives
originating in and embodying ideas rather than historical
fact,[52] Strauss regards not as the inventions of individuals seeking to hoodwink their contemporaries, but
rather as expressions of the maxims and beliefs of groups,
within which "the one who invents the mythus is only obey-
ing the impulse which acts also upon the minds of his
hearers, he is but the mouth through which all speak, the
skillful interpreter who has the address first to give
form and expression to the thoughts of all."[53] The social
contexts of thought, Strauss notes, were not uniform within the Roman Empire but varied from people to people;
Reimarus and Hume had already observed this, as we have
seen, and Strauss carries these reflections further.[54]
Thus, one sees scattered in Strauss a variety of insights
anticipating sociology of knowledge and brought to bear
on the interpretation of miracles in a more systematic
way than heretofore, and, often, subsequently.

In the twentieth century, form criticism, with its
search for the typical social settings of ancient texts,

was explicitly formulated in the New Testament area as a
sociological method.[55] Dibelius especially offered significant leads for placing Christian miracle accounts in
typical life-situations in Christian communities. However,
this remains to be pursued in a more systematic way for
early non-canonical and pagan miracle stories. And as
Oscar Cullman noted long ago, the speculative impression
conveyed by much of New Testament form-critical work derives from its failure to offer adequate sociological
parallels to New Testament data.[56] A number of suggestive
parallels are to be found in current anthropological and
sociological literature. These offer concrete illustrations of how group settings can function as plausibility
structures of extraordinary phenomena, but investigation
of them goes beyond the scope of this essay.

CONCLUSION

     The approach to the study of miracle accounts in early
Christian and contemporaneous sources via sociology of
knowledge has some honourable precursors. It is not something new under the sun. At the same time, *systematic*
application of insights from the sociology of knowledge to
the study of miracle accounts, and especially to conflicts
over miracle, enhances understanding gained from other,
more traditional approaches. It puts in a new light
Geffcken's lament over the untidy polemic that resulted
because pagan and early Christian opponents often employed
the same weapons against each other while defending opposing positions,[57] or Harnack's puzzlement that two men
of such intellectual prowess as Celsus and Origen should
so mingle superstition and critical acumen in defending
the rival deities Asclepius and Christ,[58] or the now
familiar observation that a social group will designate

its thaumaturge as "saviour," "*theios aner*," or "son of God" and his or her wonders as "miracle" while outsiders will often label him or her a "magician" and denigrate the same wonders as "magic" and belief in them as "superstition."[59] Conflicts over miracle, also in early Christian texts, are better understood when they are seen, not simply as clashes of ideas, but also as reflections of rivalry between communities with competing symbolic universes, social structures, personnel, and worships.

NOTES

1. See, e.g., H. F. Hahn, *The Old Testament in Modern Research*, 2d ed., with a survey of recent literature by H.D. Hummel (Philadelphia: Fortress Press, 1966), ch. 5; L. Finkelstein, *The Pharisees: The Sociological Background of their Faith* (2d ed.; Philadelphia: Jewish Publication Society of America, 1940); A.J. Malherbe, *Social Aspects of Early Christianity* (Baton Rouge and London: Louisiana State University Press, 1977), 4-11.

2. T.J. Meek, *Hebrew Origins* (2d, rev. ed.; New York: Harper, and Toronto: University of Toronto Press, 1950); see, e.g., 112, 119-31, 148-49, 215 in the Harper Torchbook edition (1960). The second edition is a substantially revised version of the first edition (Harper, 1936), which represented the Haskell Lectures for 1933-34. It is worth noting that an article by Meek, "The Interpenetration of Cultures as Illustrated by the Character of the Old Testament Literature," which appeared in *Journal of Religion* 7 (1927), 244-62, was selected for inclusion in Wilson D. Wallis and Malcom M. Willey (eds.) *Readings in Sociology* (New York: Knopf, 1930), where it appeared (81-86) with the title "The Fusion of Traits through Contact."

3. See W.A. Meeks, "The Social World of Christianity," *The Council on the Study of Religion Bulletin* 6/1 (1975), 1, 4-5; J.Z. Smith, "The Social Description of Early Christianity," *Religious Studies Review* 1/1 (1975), 19-25.

4. Max Scheler, "Probleme einer Soziologie des Wissens," in M. Scheler (ed.), *Versuche zu einer Soziologie des Wissens*, Schriften des Forschungsinstitutes für Sozialwissenschaften in Köln, 2 (Munich: Duncker and Humblot, 1924); revised and expanded version in M. Scheler, *Die Wissensformen und die Gesellschaft* (Leipzig: Neue Geist-Verlag, 1926); reprinted in M. Scheler, *Gesammelte Werke*, Vol. 8, *Die Wissensformen und die Gesellschaft*, 2d ed. edited, with additions, by M. Scheler (Bern and Munich: Francke Verlag, 1960), 15-190.

5. K. Mannheim, *Ideology and Utopia: An Introduction to the Sociology of Knowledge*, trans. by L. Wirth and E. Shils (1936; reprinted, New York: Harcourt, Brace and World, n.d), esp. Part 5, "The Sociology of Knowledge." See also his articles "Das Problem einer Soziologie des

Wissens," *Archiv für Sozialwissenschaft und Sozialpolitik*
54 (1925), 577-652; "Wissenssoziologie," in A. Vierkandt
(ed.), *Handwörterbuch der Soziologie* (Stuttgart: F. Enke,
1931), 659-80; and the study by G.W. Remmling, *Wissenssoziologie und Gesellschaftsplanung: Das Werk Karl Mann-
heims*, Sozialwissenschaftliche Schriftenreihe, 6 (Dort-
mund: Ruhfus, 1968).

     6. Peter L. Berger and Thomas Luckmann, *The Social
Construction of Reality: A Treatise in the Sociology of
Knowledge* (Garden City, NY: Doubleday Anchor Books, 1967),
15.

     7. This is a view of long standing among students of
early Christianity; see the overview in H. Kreissig,
"Zur sozialen Zusammensetzung der frühchristlichen Gemein-
den im ersten Jahrhundert u. Z.," *Eirene* 6 (1967), 93-95,
and the literature cited in J.G. Gager, "Religion and
Social Class in the Early Roman Empire," in S. Benko and
J.J. O'Rourke (eds.), *The Catacombs and the Colosseum:
The Roman Empire as the Setting of Primitive Christianity*
(Valley Forge, PA: Judson Press, 1971), 119, n. 70.
Recent research has challenged simplistic statements of
this view in favour of a more nuanced interpretation that
takes fuller, more careful account of the presence in early
Christianity of influential members of the middle and upper
ranks of Greco-Roman society; see *inter alia* E.A. Judge,
*The Social Patterns of the Christian Groups in the First
Century: Some Prolegomena to the Study of New Testament
Ideas of Social Obligation* (London: Tyndale Press, 1960);
G. Theissen, "Soziale Schichtung in der korinthischen
Gemeinde: Ein Beitrag zur Soziologie des hellenistischen
Urchristentums," *Zeitschrift für die neutestamentliche
Wissenschaft* 65 (1974), 232-72; Malherbe, *Social Aspects
of Early Christianity* (see n. 1 above). In judging the
social constituency of early Christianity the distinction
between social class (in the Roman Empire, a legal classification) and social status (related to such matters as
wealth, education, and associates) is worth observing;
see, generally, L. Dubermann, *Social Inequality: Class
and Caste in America* (Philadelphia et al.: Lippincott,
1976), 84-85, 94-97, and for the Roman Empire of the first
two centuries John G. Gager's review of Malherbe, *Social
Aspects*, et al. in *Religious Studies Review* 5 (1979), 180.

     8. Though caveats regarding the incautious use of the
distinction between "epistle" and "letter" or the application of the term *Kleinliteratur* to early Christian
writings are in order (see, e.g. S.N. Neill, *The Interpretation of the New Testament 1861-1961: The Firth
Lectures, 1962* [London et al.: Oxford University Press,

1964],241; H. Conzelmann, *1 Corinthians: A Commentary on the First Epistle to the Corinthians*, trans. by J.W. Leitch,Hermeneia [Philadelphia: Fortress Press, 1975], 6), they do not call in question the basic distinction between literature produced for an educated, elite and exemplified by the Greek and Latin classics and more popular, occasional pieces intended for a broader spectrum of readers. Christian writings of the first two centuries fall largely in the latter category; see, recently, Malherbe, *Social Aspects*, 18-19, and ch. 2.

9.   *Social Construction*, 156-63.

10.   A.D. Nock, *Conversion: The Old and the New in Religion from Alexander the Great to Augustine of Hippo* (London: Oxford University Press, 1933).   G. Bardy's more recent, detailed study, *La conversion au christianisme durant les premiers siècles*, Théologie, 15 (Paris: Aubier, Editions Montaigne, 1949), affirms Nock's thesis.

11.   Berger and Luckmann, *Social Construction* (see n. 6 above), 60-61.

12.   Ibid., 138-47.

13.   Ibid., 138-40, 145.

14.   Ibid., 144, 89-95.

15.   Cf. 1 Cor. 4:15-16; 11:1; 1 Thess. 1:6.   The term "father" is found also in mystery religions; see R. Reitzenstein, *Die hellenistischen Mysterienreligionen nach ihren Grundgedanken und Wirkungen* (3d ed.; Leipzig: Teubner, 1927; reprinted, Darmstadt: Wissenschaftliche Buchgesellschaft, 1966), 20, 40, 98-99; M.J. Vermaseren, *Mithras, The Secret God*, trans. by T. and V. Megaw (London: Chatto and Windus, and Toronto: Clark, Irwin, 1963), 152-53.

16.   The imitation ethic is common in early Christian sources; see A. Heitmann, *Imitatio Dei: Die ethische Nachahmung Gottes nach der Väterlehre der zwei ersten Jahrhunderte*, Studia Anselmiana: Philosophica Theologica, 10 (Rome: Pontificium Institutum S. Anselmi, 1940); E. Larsson, *Christus als Vorbild: Eine Untersuchung zu den paulinischen Tauf- und Eikontexten*, trans. by B. Steiner, Acta Seminarii Neotestamentici Upsaliensis, 23 (Uppsala: Almqvist & Wiksells, Lund: Gleerup, and Copenhagen: Munksgaard, 1962).

17. Berger and Luckmann, *Social Construction* (see n. 6 above), 112-15.

18. E.g., 1 Cor. 14:24-25: when Christians prophesy in worship, Paul envisages that outsiders who enter will come to new self-knowledge through this communal witness and, falling on their faces, will worship God, proclaiming him to be present in the worshipping community.

19. W. Meeks, review of V.P. Furnish, *The Love Command in the New Testament* (1972), in *Interpretation* 27 (1973), 99.

20. In addition to references in the New Testament (Mk. 10:27 parr.; Mk. 14:36; Lk. 1:37) and in the Jewish scriptures (Job 42:2), cf. the first- and second-century writers cited in H. Chadwick, "Origen, Celsus, and the Resurrection of the Body," *Harvard Theological Review* 41 (1948), 84, and Robert M. Grant, *Miracle and Natural Law in Graeco-Roman and Early Christian Thought* (Amsterdam: North-Holland Publishing Co., 1952), ch. 9.

21. The Stoa: Cicero, *De natura deorum* 2.41.86 ("There is nothing, they say, which God is not able to accomplish" [Nihil est, inquiunt, quod deus efficere non possit]); similarly 3.39.92. Leiden Pap. J395 (3-4 c. C.E.), *PGM* 2, 119, lines 708ff.: a recipe designed to gain knowledge of the future instructs the operator not to despair if he receives a dire prediction but instead to ask the god to change it, for this god is capable of anything (*dunatai gar panta ho theos houtos*) (line 713).

22. A. Schweitzer, *The Quest of the Historical Jesus: A Critical Study of its Progress from Reimarus to Wrede*, trans. from the 1st German ed. by W. Montgomery (1910; reprinted, New York: Macmillan, 1955), 85.

23. R. Merton, *On Theoretical Sociology: Five Essays, Old and New* (New York: Free Press, and London: Collier-Macmillan, 1967), 9ff.

24. Cicero, *De divinatione* 2.16.17, amounts to a summary of what an educated person of his day might be expected to know about the causes of eclipses and other celestial phenomena. Cf. also Livy 44.37; Seneca, N.Q. 7.25.3.

25. Augustine, *De civitate dei* 3.15. As part of the self-education in astronomy that freed him from his belief in astrology (cf. *Confessiones* 4.3.4-6), Augustine read books by astronomers that explained the causes of eclipses;

see *Confessiones* 5.4.6 and cf. J.J. O'Meara, *The Young Augustine: The Growth of St. Augustine's Mind up to his Conversion* (London: Longmans, Green, 1954; reprinted, New York: Alba House, 1965), 100.

26.   Thomas Aquinas, *Summa Theologica* 1.105.7; ignorance of causes produces *admiratio,* which Aquinas takes as the root of the word *miraculum.* Similarly in his *Summa contra Gentiles* 3/2.101, Aquinas uses the terms *ignarus* and *astrologus.*

27.   K. Rahner, *Schriften zur Theologie,* Vol. 5, *Neuere Schriften* (Einsiedeln et al.: Benzinger, 1962), 524-26; Rahner argues for a "three-dimensional" scientific methodology that allows for the possibility of the operation of "higher," spiritual forces. Similarly J.B. Metz, "Wunder: systematisch," *Lexikon für Theologie und Kirche,* Vol. 10 (2d ed.; 1965), 1263-65; cf. his statement that "Wunder kann deshalb als solches nie in einem Welthorizont begegnen, der in seinem Entwurf diese von Freiheit getragene u. bestimmte Orientierung des Gesamtdaseins von vorherein (evtl. rein methodologisch, wie in den Naturwissenschaften) ausschliesst" (col. 1265). Also M. Schmaus, *Der Glaube der Kirche: Handbuch katholischer Dogmatik,* Vol. 1 (Munich: Max Hueber, 1969), 110-11.

28.   B. Spinoza, *The Chief Works of Benedict de Spinoza: A Theologico-Political Treatise and A Political Treatise,* trans. by R.H.M. Elwes (1883; reprinted, New York: Dover Publications, 1951), Vol. 1, ch. 6, "Of Miracles" (p. 84: "miracles were wrought according to the understanding of the masses, who are wholly ignorant of the workings of nature...the ancients took for a miracle whatever they could not explain by the method adopted by the unlearned in such cases"; pp. 92-93: narrators of events report, not "the plain facts seen or heard," but their own perception of them, which is often coloured by self-interest,as when the Hebrews at the time of Joshua reported that the sun and moon stood still, thus "convincing and proving by experience to the Gentiles, who worshipped the sun, that the sun was under the control of another deity who could compel it to change its daily course"); J. Toland, *Christianity Not Mysterious: Or, a Treatise Showing, That there is nothing in the Gospel Contrary to Reason, Nor Above it: And that no Christian Doctrine can be properly call'd A Mystery* (London, 1696; reprinted, with introduction and text-critical appendix by G. Gawlick, Stuttgart: Frommann, 1964), para. 71 (p. 152) (marvellous accounts "may be met with among the *Papists,* the *Jews,* the *Bramins* [sic], the *Mahometans,*

116   RELIGION AND THE SOCIOLOGY OF KNOWLEDGE

and in all places where the Credulity of the People makes
'em a Merchandize to the Priests"); para. 73 (p. 154)
("for it is very observable, that the more ignorant and
barbarous any People remain, you shall find 'em most
abound with Tales of this nature, and stand in far greater awe of Satan than Jehovah").
   In the same period, John Locke, in defending Christian
miracles, points to the evidential value of miracles for
the "bulk of mankind," which has little education nor the
leisure necessary to weigh abstract arguments; see *The
Reasonableness of Christianity* (1st ed.; 1695), ed. by
I.T. Ramsey, A Library of Modern Religious Thought (Stanford: Stanford University Press, 1958), 66-67, 75-76;
cf. *A Discourse of Miracles* (1st ed.; 1706), pp. 85-86
in Ramsey ed.

   29. See David Hume, *Enquiry Concerning Human Understanding, and an Enquiry Concerning the Principles of
Morals* (1777), ed. by L.A. Selby-Bigge (Oxford: Clarendon, 1894), 113-29.

   30. See J.B. Mozley, *Eight Lectures on Miracles*,
Bampton Lectures, 1865 (London: Rivingtons, 1865), 2;
W. Herrmann, *Offenbarung und Wunder*, Vorträge der theolo-
gischen Konferenz zu Giessen, 28 (2d ed.; Giessen: Töpel-
mann, 1908), 43-48.

   31. Van Harvey, *The Historian and the Believer: The
Morality of Historical Knowledge and Christian Belief*
(New York: Macmillan, 1966).

   32. Hume, *Enquiry* (see n. 29 above), 125.

   33. I. Kant, *Die Religion innerhalb der Grenzen der
blossen Vernunft (Kant's gesammelte Schriften*, 1st division, *Werke*, Vol. 6, ed. by Königlich Preussischen Akade-
mie der Wissenschaften [Berlin: Reimer, 1907]), 85-86
(E. T. by T. M. Greene and H. H. Hudson, *Religion within
the Limits of Reason Alone* [Chicago and London: Open
Court, 1934], 80-81): "Daher haben weise Regierungen
jederzeit zwar eingeräumt, ja wohl gar unter die öffentlichen Religionslehren die Meinung gesetzlich aufgenommen,
dass *vor Alters* Wunder geschehen wären, *neue* Wunder aber
nicht erlaubt. Denn die alten Wunder waren nach und nach
so bestimmt und durch die Obrigkeit beschränkt, dass keine
Verwirrung im gemeinen Wesen dadurch angerichtet werden
konnte, wegen neuer Wunderthäter aber mussten sie aller-
dings der Wirkungen halber besorgt sein, die sie auf den
öffentlichen Ruhestand und die eingeführte Ordnung haben
könnten."

THE STUDY OF EARLY CHRISTIANITY   117

34. Cf. above nn. 28, 29. This assumption underlies
much of the discussion in the modern period.

35. An exception is the scientist A. Lunn, "Miracles--
The Scientific Approach," *The Hibbert Journal* 48 (1950),
240-46, who regards the investigation of extraordinary
phenomena "for the presence of supernatural agencies" as
the most important task of scientists (242). R. Lembert,
Wunderglaube bei Römern und Griechen, Part 1, *Das Wunder
bei den römischen Historikern: Eine religionsgeschicht-
liche Studie*, Supplement to Jahres-Bericht über das Kön-
igliche Realgymnasium zu Augsburg im Schuljahr 1904/1905
(Augsburg: Druck des Literar. Instituts von Haas & Brag-
herr, 1905), 7, and G. Mensching, *Das Wunder im Glauben
und Aberglauben der Völker* (Leiden: Brill, 1957), see
the natural sciences as defining the limits of miracle
precisely whereas for ancients the line was not thus
demarcated.

36. For example, W. Paley, *View of the Evidences of
Christianity* (1794), who argues for the evidential value
of miracles but also asserts the priority of belief in
God (p. 7 in G. Fisk ed. [8th ed.; Cambridge: Hall, and
London: Simpkin, Marshall, and Co., Whittaker and Co.,
G. Bell and Sons, 1884]: of his "existence and power, not
to say of whose presence and agency, we have previous and
independent proof.... In a word, once believe that there is
a God, and miracles are not incredible"); F. Schleier-
macher, *Der christliche Glaube nach den Grundsätzen der
evangelischen Kirche im Zusammenhange dargestellt* (7th
ed., Vol. 1, ed. by M. Redeker; Berlin: de Gruyter, 1960),
99-100; D. F. Strauss, *The Life of Jesus Critically
Examined*, trans. by George Eliot from the 4th German ed.,
edited by P.C. Hodgson (Philadelphia: Fortress Press,
1972), 76, 419; J.S. Mill, *A System of Logic, Ratiocina-
tive and Inductive, Being a Connected View of the Principles of Evidence and the Methods of Scientific Investigation*, Vol. 2 (8th ed.; London: Longmans, Green, Reader,
and Dyer, 1872), 168; F.R. Tennant, *Miracle and its
Philosophical Presuppositions: Three Lectures Delivered
in the University of London 1924* (Cambridge: Cambridge
University Press, 1925), 61-69, 86-89, 94; A.E. Taylor,
"David Hume and the Miraculous" (1927), reprinted in his
Philosophical Studies (London: Macmillan, 1934), 359-63;
R. Bultmann, "Zur Frage des Wunders," in his *Glauben und
Verstehen*, Vol. 1 (Tübingen: J.C.B. Mohr [Siebeck], 1954),
distinguishing *Wunder* and *Mirakel* and defining the former
as *Offenbarung* and *Vergebung* (pp. 221, 226) and discernible only by faith, pp. 216, 219-21; N. Smart, *Philosophers and Religious Truth* (London: SCM, 1964), 2.53 (p.
46), 2.58 (p. 49); R.F. Holland, "The Miraculous,"

American Philosophical Quarterly 2 (1965), 44 (referring to extraordinary coincidences); R. Swinburne, *The Concept of Miracle* (London et al.: Macmillan, 1970), 46-47, 71. The Roman Catholic theologians cited in n. 27 above posit belief in God as prior to belief in miracle, rather than the reverse

37. H.S. Reimarus, "Unmöglichkeit einer Offenbarung, die alle Menschen auf eine gegründete Art glauben könnten," published posthumously by Lessing (Braunschweig, 1777); in K. Lachmann (ed.), *Gotthold Ephraim Lessings Sämtliche Schriften*, 3d ed., revised by F. Muncker, Vol. 12 (Leipzig: Göschen'sche Verlagsbuchhandlung, 1897), 335: "Ein jeder stelle sich unpartheyisch in die Stelle der Heyden, und urtheile denn, ob es wohl möglich sey, dass die durch gegründete Ueberführung zum Christemthume zu bringen sind. Sie sind erstlich von ihrer väterlichen Religion, so wie wir, von Jugend auf so eingenommen, dass sie sich um andere zu bekümmern so unnöthig als gefährlich halten. Wer ihnen dieses varargen wollte, der mag mir zuvor antworten, ob er den Talmud, die Misna und Gemara, den Alcoran, den Zendavesta des Zerduscht, den Sad-der der Destur, den Con-fu-zu und andere dergleichen Bücher gelesen? ob er Völker Religionen so genau zu kennen und so unpartheyisch zu untersuchen jemals Lust, Fähigkeit oder Zeit gehabt? ob er nicht glaube, die Religion, darin er erzogen worden, sey die einige wahre und seligmachende? ob er nicht daher unnöthig ze seyn glaube, sich um andere Religionen viel zu bekümmern? ja ob er es nicht fast für sündlich erachtet hätte, sich nach andern, als bessern, umzusehen, und aus Reizunq zu denselben ihre Bücher zu lesen und nach ihren Lehrern zu laufen?"

38. Ibid., 325.

39. Ibid., 325: "Und siehe, sie [*scil.* die Kinder] nehmen ihn [*scil.* den Glauben ihrer Eltern], wie alle übrige Religionen und Secten, nach den Ehe-Pacten, nach dem Willen und Bestimmung ihrer Aeltern, nach dem Exempel ihrer Vorfahren, getrost an; *und können nicht anders handeln.* Wer kann von solchen Kindern eine Fähigkeit fordern, dass sie die Wahrheit dessen, was sie lernen beurtheilen, und so sie im Irrthume wären, eine bessere Religion suchen und finden sollten? Wer kann ihnen verdenken, dass sie bey dem Vertrauen, bey dem Gehorsame, so sie ihren Aeltern schuldig sind, auch derselben ihre Religion für wahr und für die beste halten?...und sie sind ohne das von selbst geneigt, was ihnen ihre Aeltern und Lehrmeister sagen, was alle bekannte und angesehene Leute glauben, *ohne Untersuchung blindlings fur wahr zu halten* ... sie folgen den Aeltern so getrost auf dem unbekannten Wege zur Seligkeit, als auf einem unbetretenen Wege zu einem Luftschlosse" (emphases added).

40.   Ibid., 353.

41.   H.S. Reimarus, "Von dem Zwecke Jesu und seiner
Jünger," Part 2, published posthumously by Lessing (Braunschweig, 1778); in K. Lachmann (ed.), *Gotthold Ephraim
Lessings Sämtliche Schriften*, 3d ed., revised by F. Muncker, Vol. 13 (Göschen'sche Verlagsbuchhandlung, 1897),
para. 57 (pp. 315-16); E.T. in C.H. Talbert (ed.) and
R.S. Fraser (trans.), *Reimarus: Fragments*, Lives of
Jesus Series (Philadelphia: Fortress Press, 1970), 251-
52.

42.   "Zwecke Jesu," Part 2, para. 57, in Lachmann-
Muncker, Vol. 13, 316 (Talbert-Fraser, 252). Persons
who had a high regard for Jesus and had heard of his
miracles would find it credible that Jesus was resurrected.
"Dazu hatten die Apostel von ihrem Meister gelernet Wunder
zu thun, oder wenigstens wie man es machen müsste um den
Schein zu haben, und solches unter die Leute zu bringen,
und ich habe anderwärts gezeiget, dass es gar keine Kunst
sey, Wunder zu erzählen oder auch zu machen, wenn sich
viele mit Mund und Hand hierin einander behülflich sind,
und wenn sie mit einem Volke zu thun haben, des gewohnt
und geneigt ist, Wunder zu glauben." In interpreting the
miracle narratives in Acts as involving willful manipulation of beliefs, with an element of deception (cf. para.
60), Reimarus overlooks the function of social groups as
plausibility structures; otherwise, however, his observations adumbrate modern anthropological and sociological
research on the social matrices of extraordinary phenomena.

43.   "Zwecke Jesu," Part 2, para. 48, in Lachmann-
Muncker, Vol. 13, 303 (Talbert-Fraser, 232). When "enlightened" (*verständige*) Jews, such as the scribes and
authorities, demanded miracles of Jesus, so they could
investigate them, he scolded them instead, "so dass kein
Mensch von dieser Gattung an ihm glauben konnte" (Lachmann-Muncker, Vol., 13, 303-04; Talbert-Fraser, 232-33).

44.   "Unmöglichkeit einer Offenbarung" (see n. 37
above), in Lachmann-Muncker, Vol. 12, 320-21.

45.   Cf. ibid., Vol. 12, 353, and n. 37 above.

46.   "Unmöglichkeit einer Offenbarung" (see n. 37
above), in Lachmann-Muncker, Vol. 12, 335.

47.   Reimarus, like his contemporary Hume (see above,
pp. 115-6), pits the Romans, as persons more sophisticated
in assessing extraordinary phenomena, against other, non-

"classical" peoples like the Jews; "Zwecke Jesu," Para. 57, in Lachmann-Muncker, Vol. 13, 318 (Talbert-Fraser, 255). Reimarus thus fails to distinguish between various social and cultural strata among the Romans, though he elsewhere (see n. 43 above) distinguishes between educated and uneducated Jews.

48. V.A. Harvey, "D.F. Strauss' *Life of Jesus* Revisited," *Church History* 30 (1961), 191-211.

49. Strauss, *Life of Jesus* (see n. 36, above), para. 92, p. 420: Olshausen asks, "If the apostles were to enter our mad-houses, how would they name many of the inmates? We answer, they would to a certainty name many of them demoniacs, by reason of their participation in the ideas of their people and their age, not by reason of their apostolic illumination; and the official who acted as their conductor would very properly endeavour to set them right; whatever names therefore they might give to the inmates of our asylums, our conclusions as to the naturalness of the disorders of those inmates would not be at all affected."

50. Ibid., para. 92, pp. 420-21. Strauss's strictures would apply to Reimarus who, rather than attempting to understand the original matrix of miracle accounts, faults the reporters for not meeting his own criteria of credibility; cf. "Zwecke Jesu," Part 2, para. 48, in Lachmann-Muncker, Vol. 13, 303 (Talbert-Fraser, 232); para. 60, Vol. 13, 326 (267).

51. Strauss, *Life of Jesus* (see n. 36 above), para. 94, p. 438, contrasting Gibbon with Herodotus and faulting Paulus for not observing such distinctions.

52. Ibid., para. 15, p. 86.

53. Ibid., para. 14, p. 81.

54. Ibid., para. 13, pp. 74-75.

55. See R. Bultmann, *Die Geschichte der synoptischen Tradition*, FRLANT, 29 (3d ed.; Göttingen: Vandenhoeck & Ruprecht, 1957), 4-5; M. Dibelius, *Die Formgeschichte des Evangeliums* (5th ed., with an addition by G. Iber; ed. by G. Bornkamm; Tübingen: J.C.B. Mohr [Siebeck], 1966), 57.

56. O. Cullmann, "Les récentes études sur la tradition évangélique," *Revue d'Histoire et de Philosophie religieuses* 5 (1925), 573.

57. J. Geffcken, *Zwei griechische Apologeten*, Sammlung wissenschaftlicher Kommentare zu griechischen und römischen Schriftstellern (Leipzig and Berlin: Teubner, 1907), 245 ("einen gewaltigen Wirrwarr der Polemik"), 246 ("ein wahres Chaos der Polemik").

58. A. Harnack, *Medicinisches aus der ältesten Kirchengeschichte* (Leipzig: Hinrichs, 1892), 95 ("schlimmster Aberglaube" and "verständiger Kritik"); repeated verbatim in *Mission und Ausbreitung des Christentums in den ersten drei Jahrhunderten*, Vol. 1, *Die Mission in Wort und Tat* (4th ed.; Leipzig: Hinrichs, 1924), 135.

59. See e.g., L. Bieler, ΘΕΙΟΣ ΑΝΗΡ: *Das Bild des "Göttlichen Menschen" in Spätantike und Frühchristentum* (2 vols., 1935, 1936; reprinted in one vol., Darmstadt: Wissenschaftliche Buchgesellschaft, 1967), 84-87; G.P. von Wetter, *"Der Sohn Gottes": Eine Untersuchung über den Charakter und die Tendenz des Johannes-Evangeliums*, FRLANT, 26 (Göttingen: Vandenhoeck & Ruprecht, 1916), 73-82; R.M. Grant, *Gnosticism and Early Christianity* (2d ed.; New York: Harper & Row, 1966), 93 ("...in polemical writing, your magic is my miracle, and vice-versa"); A.B. Kolenkow, "A Problem of Power: How Miracle-Doers Counter Charges of Magic in the Hellenistic World," in G. MacRae (ed.), *Society of Biblical Literature 1976 Seminar Papers: One Hundred Twelfth Annual Meeting...* (Missoula, MT: Scholars Press, 1976), 105-10; J.Z. Smith "Good News is No News: Aretalogy and Gospel," in J. Neusner (ed.), *Christianity, Judaism and Other Greco-Roman Cults: Studies for Morton Smith at Sixty*, Part 1, *New Testament*, Studies in Judaism in Late Antiquity, 12 (Leiden: E.J. Brill, 1975), 21-38; R. Herzog, *Die Wunderheilungen von Epidauros: Ein Beitrag zur Geschichte der Medizin und der Religion (Philogus*, Supplementary Vol. 22/4 [Leipzig: Dietrichs, 1931]), 140 ("Aberglaube ist immer der Glaube der Anderen; für den römischen Staat waren das die Christen, für die Christen waren es die Altglaübigen"); G. Theissen, *Urchristliche Wundergeschichten: Ein Beitrag zur formgeschichtlichen Erforschung der synoptischen Evangelien*, Studien zum Neuen Testament, 8 (Gütersloh: Gütersloher Verlagshaus Gerd Mohn, 1974), 230 ("'Aberglaube' ist dann der in einer Gesellschaft abgelehnte Glaube, 'Glaube,' so könnte man ironisch formulieren, der offiziell anerkannte Aberglaube. Wo die Grenze zu ziehen ist, bestimmen die massgeblichen Kreise").

THE SOCIOLOGY OF KNOWLEDGE AND NEW

TESTAMENT INTERPRETATION

John Stanley

FROM PARADIGM TO PARADIGMS:
FROM BIBLICAL CRITICISM TO
BIBLICAL CRITICISMS

"Historical biblical criticism is bankrupt."[1] Thus
declared Walter Wink in 1973 and on a visit to Iliff
School of Theology in 1982.

"My former colleague Walter Wink claims 'historical
biblical criticism is bankrupt'. That isn't so," responded Raymond Brown on a visit in Iliff School of Theology
in 1981.[2]

This dialogue between Wink and Brown symbolizes the
creative ferment in contemporary biblical studies. If a
paradigm denotes a shared example of how to do things,
then a blurring of the paradigm has occurred in biblical
studies. This transition is analogous to the paradigm
shifts in the scientific world as described by Thomas
Kuhn in *The Structure of Scientific Revolutions*.[3] By a
paradigm shift in biblical studies, I mean that whereas
there used to be two basic ways of doing biblical studies
now there are many.

In 1962 Krister Stendahl outlined two basic ways of
doing biblical studies.[4] The first method was a descriptive theology which attempted to state what the biblical
text meant when it was composed. Descriptive theologians
use source criticism, form criticism, history of religions,

textual criticism, archaeology, and even disciplines such
as psychology and sociology to analyze what the text
meant in its original context. *The International Critical
Commentary* series was a high water mark of descriptive
criticism. In that series R.H. Charles spent 1,020 pages
detailing the background and message of The Revelation of
St. John.[5] However, in only two places do I recall Charles
relating the ancient message to his time in 1920. Charles
assumed that his task was to explain the background of the
ideas and sources used in writing Revelation. He function-
ed as a historian more than as an interpreter. The *Studies
in Biblical Theology* monograph series published by SCM
Press beginning in 1952 was a more recent collection which
used the historical descriptive approach. These essays
laid the foundation for what became known as the biblical
theology movement.[6] David Bartlett, in *The Christian
Century's* 1981-82 series "Emerging Trends in Biblical
Thought", testifies to his seminary training that followed the methods of descriptive theology. Bartlett reflects
in 1981:

> My graduate work in biblical studies ended just
> ten years ago. The courses I took and the re-
> search I did were dominated by the norms and
> concerns of the historical-critical approach to
> Scripture. We who were students in Bible thought
> of ourselves predominantly as nascent historians,
> seeking to apply all the canons of objective
> historical scholarship to the biblical texts.
> Our concern was to place the texts as accurately
> as we could in their original historical setting,
> to understand the history which lay behind those
> texts, and to draw conclusions about the sit-
> uations to which they originally spoke.[7]

Descriptive biblical study mimicked the glorification of rational inquiry and the reductionism which have been intrinsic features of the process of modernization.[8] Although descriptive theologians claimed to be guided by objective reason in seeking the literal meaning of texts they were children of the modern era. Wink criticizes traditional biblical criticism because

> it pretends to be unbiased when in fact the
> methodology carries with it a heavy rational-
> istic weight which by inner necessity tends
> toward the reduction of the irrational, sub-
> jective, or emotional data to insignificance
> or invisibility. It pretends to search for
> "assured results", "objective knowledge",
> when in fact the method presumes radical
> epistemological doubt.[9]

Stendahl mentioned Rudolf Bultmann, Karl Barth and Oscar Cullman as representative of interpreters who were not satisfied to be descriptive historians who merely stated what the text once meant. Instead, they wrapped the original message of the Bible into modern philosophi-cal systems in order to state what the Bible means today. They sought a theological core for the biblical litera-ture.[10] Bartlett highlights the contributions of these mid-twentieth century giants of biblical theology. He praises them for recognizing that

> the historical-critical school is not adequate
> even to tell us what the texts of the Bible
> "meant", because part of what they "meant"
> includes their claim to be significant for
> the ongoing life of faith. To restrict the
> study of their meaning to historical and
> linguistic questions is to miss an essential
> part of that meaning.[11]

These two approaches were the predominant ways of
doing biblical interpretation. Brevard Childs mused on
the monolithic method shared by descriptive and theological
exegetes. He asked:

> the basic hermeneutical assumptions are shared
> by both left and right within the full spectrum
> of biblical scholarship. Both left and right
> work within the parameters established for the
> discipline by the beginning of the nineteenth
> century. Is it possible to break out of this
> sterile impasse and to enter into a post-
> critical era?[12]

Cracks in the solidarity of these two walls began to
emerge. Childs' *Biblical Theology in Crisis*[13] in 1970
announced the demise of the biblical theology movement.
James Smart wondered about *The Strange Silence of the
Bible in the Church* (1970). Smart reminded readers that

> the steady progress of scholarship, constantly
> perfecting its methodology for dealing with the
> problems that the text of Scripture provides
> for it, has been paralleled by the steady
> recension in the attention that the church
> and Christians give to the Bible.[14]

Childs was calling for a new method. Smart was declaring
that the old methods had not moved from the professor in
the classroom to the pews and the Christian education
units in local parishes.

Kuhn explains how in a scientific revolution new
methods meet with resistance. Then a period of insecurity
ensues during which there is a blending of old and new
paradigms. Retooling can be justified only when a crisis
is perceived.[15] As Childs was declaring the futility of
the established paradigm, retooling was happening as new
paradigms were being tried out in biblical scholarship.

If one assumes that the rash of books that heralded new
methods which appeared in the mid-1970s required several
years of preparation, then retooling was taking place at
the very time when Childs was announcing the end of the
biblical theology movement. Exegetes were finding ways
to move beyond the historical method.

Four publishing events document the shift from paradigm to paradigms. A blurring of paradigms has occurred
which permits exegetes to use various methods and different degrees of appropriation of the texts. Even
though it is the most recent publishing event, I will
begin with Bartlett's "Biblical Scholarship Today: A
Diversity of New Approaches," because the article is
accessible and it summarizes the state of the discipline.
Bartlett reports on five models for biblical study. One
model draws upon sociology and anthropology to understand
the world which produced the biblical texts. This approach suggests that the communities which preceded and
produced biblical texts "may provide models for contemporary society".[16] A second model relies on psychology.
Robin Scroggs and Walter Wink represent this school. They
feel that the biblical symbols point to psychological
realities shared by modern readers. A third model involves
those exegetes who practice a "hermeneutics of the oppressed". Feminism, the black experience or the context
of the Third World furnishes the avowed partisan perspectives of these interpreters. Literary criticism comprises
the fourth method. Some literary critics want to study
the text as a literary form. Others hope that literary
criticism will lead to new ways of encountering the text.
The fifth approach is canonical criticism. Canonical
criticism interprets the text in its finished form rather
than majoring on the history behind the text.[17]

A comparison of surveys of New Testament issues illustrates the blurring of paradigms. Reginald Fuller's

The New Testament in Current Study[18] published in 1962,
listed questions that needed rethinking in light of the
monumental impact wrought by Bultmann. But Fuller's re-
considerations were encased within the methodology of
historical criticism and biblical theology. The old paradigm still prevailed. On the other hand, Patrick Henry's
New Directions in New Testament Study (1979)[19] lists
diverse methodologies as well as abiding historical problems. Even the popular, at times opinionated, style of
Henry when compared with the cool rationalism of Fuller
reflects a paradigm shift. The old school would not dare
to be so flamboyant.

A comparison of the 1962 *Interpreter's Dictionary of
the Bible* with the *Interpreter's Dictionary of the Bible:
Supplementary Volume,* published in 1976, confirms the
blurring of paradigms. Leander Keck and Gene Tucker's
1976 article "Exegesis" addresses the issues of methodologies and hermeneutics.[20] There was not an article on
exegesis in the 1962 edition! Elizabeth Achtemeier's
"History of Interpretation--Nineteenth and Twentieth
Century"[21] reviews the transition in the move from Biblical Criticism to biblical criticisms. Also, in his essay,
"Biblical Theology," James Barr elucidates the changing
debates among biblical scholars since 1962.[22]

Kuhn argues that textbooks usually are conservatizing
documents that

> record the stable outcomes of past revolutions...
> To fulfill their function they need not provide
> authentic information about the way in which
> those bases were first recognized and then em-
> braced by the profession...In short, they have
> to be rewritten in the aftermath of each sci-
> entific revolution, and once rewritten they
> disguise not only the role but the very existence
> of the revolutions that preceded them.[23]

Introductions to the Old, or New, Testaments have served
as the core textbooks that introduced the perennial historic problems of biblical studies. If one compares
standard introductions such as those of George Fohrer and
Werner Kummel[24] one finds a similar methodology undergirds
their books. They continue a tradition by reciting how
prior problems have been addressed by previous exegetes.
In essence, they summarize the research and viewpoints in
the field. But Brevard Childs' *Introduction to the Old
Testament as Scripture* breaks with the traditions. Childs
proclaims his departure from the established paradigm in
his Preface. He announces that

> this introduction attempts to offer a different
> model for the discipline from that currently
> represented. . . . It argues the case that the
> biblical literature has not been correctly
> understood or interpreted because its role
> as religious literature has not been correctly
> assessed. . . . I am acutely aware of the
> dangers inherent in any proposal which tries to
> challenge the critical methodologies which
> have been carefully developed over the last
> two hundred years.[25]

Note the polemical intention of this Preface. No wonder
that the response to *Introduction to the Old Testament as
Scripture* has been so vociferous![26]

This brief history of twentieth century exegesis reviews the shift from paradigm to paradigms in biblical
studies. There is not a solid center in biblical studies
today. I concur with Bartlett that

> the very variety of approaches to the task of
> biblical scholarship may imply that no single
> scholarly paradigm can be adequate to the
> varieties of biblical literature. . . . I doubt

very much that one ruling paradigm of
biblical studies will emerge in this century, and I suspect that the diversity of
approaches will help us to appreciate the
diversity of the texts and enrich our
understanding of Scripture itself.[27]

I suspect that biblical studies has taken its first
steps into the post-modern era. Many exegetes have sensed
the inadequacies of the historical inquiry alone. Among
those who still affirm the historical method, such as
Raymond Brown, many often alter that methodology to include dynamics from new methodologies. This blurring of
methodologies resembles what Kuhn calls the "blurring of
paradigms"[28]. But whereas in the hard sciences a paradigm
shift requires throwing out the previous methodology, in
biblical studies the current blurring of paradigms does
not necessitate repudiating the concern to determine what
a text meant and to what the text referred in its various
historical settings. Instead, the blurring of the paradigms allows exegetes to travel diverse routes in the
degree to which the meaning of the text is appropriated.
The blurring of the paradigm celebrates methodological
diversities.

IMPLICATIONS FROM THE SOCIOLOGY OF
KNOWLEDGE FOR BIBLICAL EXEGESIS

At least six tenets of the sociology of knowledge have
direct implications for biblical exegesis. The themes
which I will consider include reality as a social construction, knowledge as relational knowledge, the relationship
between symbolic universes and institutions, the search
for a group's ethos, humanity's longing to belong, and
the methods of the sociology of knowledge.

Reality as social construction means that persons and
groups build institutions. These institutions have a factual existence. They form a social reality which persons
enounter. They constitute, in the words of Berger and
Luckmann, "society as objective reality".[29] Whereas objective reality refers to life as it is institutionally
defined, society as "subjective reality" is reality "as
apprehended in individual consciousness".[30] Subjective
reality develops via the acquisition of an identity
through socialization. Identities and institutions do
not descend from on high, ontologically or idealistically.
Instead groups build social systems which then shape
identities. As Karl Marx put it, "consciousness is therefore from the very beginning a social product".[31] Marx
postulated that "life is not determined by consciousness,
but consciousness by life".[32] Karl Mannheim defined
knowledge as

> from the very beginning a co-operative process
> of group life, in which every one unfolds his
> knowledge within the framework of a common
> life, a common activity, and an overcoming of
> common difficulties.[33]

In *The Social Construction of Reality* Berger and Luckmann
state what Berger later affirmed in *The Sacred Canopy,*[34]
where Berger observed that

> every human society is an edifice of externalized
> and objectivated meanings, always intended a
> meaningful totality. Every society is engaged in
> the never completed enterprise of building a
> humanly meaningful world.[35]

Howard Kee's chapter "Constructing the Cosmos" in *Our
Origins in Sociological Perspective*[36] reflects his intellectual debt to this theme from the sociology of knowledge.

If reality is socially determined then knowledge is
relational. Mannheim maintains "all historical knowledge
is relational knowledge, and can only be formulated with
reference to the position of the observer."[37] Therefore
Mannheim instructs that "we must constantly ask ourselves
how it comes about that a given type of social situation
gives rise to a given interpretation".[38] Mannheim distinguishes between relationism and relativism. Relationism is aware that ideas, institutions and truth claims are
culturally conditioned. Relativism "denies the validity
of any standards and of the existence of order in the
world."[39] The awareness of cultural presuppositions marks
a step in the movement towards modernization.

The awareness that knowledge is relational has influenced contemporary biblical interpreters in three ways.
First, Kee suggests that the "current surge of interest in
the sociological setting of early Christianity is a manifestation of the spirit of this age."[40] Second, exegetes
have learned that their social situation shapes their
reading of texts just as much as do the sociological settings of the texts. Interpreters must examine the contexts in which modern exegesis occurs. As Abraham Milavec
asserts:

> Modern exegesis has made us painfully aware
> that the word of God must always be heard
> within a culturally fashioned world of par-
> ticular people in a particular epoch.[41]

Indeed, whereas Rudolf Bultmann argued that exegesis without philosophical and theological presuppositions is
impossible, persons like Milavec, Richard Rohrbaugh and
Walter Wink have shown that exegesis occurs in specific
cultural situations. Third, until recently most biblical
scholars were white European or North American males.
Recently Patrick Henry listed four new groups whose

cultural situations will lead to a diversification of
exegetical findings. These groups include interpreters
from the southern hemisphere who adhere to a liberation
theology, post-Vatican II Roman Catholics, Eastern
Orthodox thinkers and Pentecostal-charismatic scholars
such as James D.G. Dunn.[42] I would add feminists as a
fifth group. Their growing ranks include Phyllis Trible,[43]
Elisabeth Schuessler Fiorenza, Adela Yarbro Collins, Sally
McFague, and Mary Ann Tolbert. Although these feminists
represent different areas of exegetical specialization,
they are united by the feminist lens through which they
view texts. These interpreters bring a self-conscious
orientation to their exegetical tasks. These orientations
inject notes of dissonance in the former united front of
white male European-North American interpreters.

Through symbolic universes groups project a sense of
meaning onto their external world. Berger and Luckmann
list six things which symbolic universes do. They put
things in place. They deal with marginal situations.
They order phases of life. They set limits on social
interaction. They order history. They legitimate institutions.[44] Berger, Berger and Kellner show how persons
inevitably will construct institutions to order life and
to minimize choices. Once established, these institutions
become part of the objective reality which persons encounter as families, towns, voluntary associations and corpor-
ations. These institutions include world views, ideologies
and rituals.[45] A task of the sociology of knowledge is to
analyze and to detect the spheres of consciousness which
influence persons and groups.[46]

The notion of trajectories through early Christianity
builds upon this theme of symbolic universes. A trajectory
is a theme, an institutional form or a memory of a

venerated leader which appears in a connected fashion in
different communities. Different social worlds within
early Christianity developed different trajectories.
Biblical students such as Helmut Koester and James Robinson study how and why different groups developed different
theologies and institutional forms.[47]

Social groups are characterized by an ethos. Mannheim
traced the emergence of five ideal political types and
four utopian ideals in history. These types were ways of
relating to society based upon a group's interests and
ideologies. Even though he rejected the existence of a
"group mind", Mannheim's description of social types implies that groups can be characterized by specific
traits.[48] Berger, Berger, and Kellner spoke of an
identity acquired through self-definition.[49] Lewis
Wirth alleges that

the most important thing that we can know
about a person is what he takes for granted,
and the most elementary and important facts
about society are those that are seldom de-
bated and generally regarded as settled.[50]

Likewise, Kenneth Stikkers submits that

the most important implication of Scheler's
value sociology for the sociology of knowledge
is this: if, indeed, the essence of a group
is its ethos and this ethos is prior to and
determines all other social factors, then what
constitutes knowledge for a group, what a
group considers worth knowing, as well as
what it considers trivial, will likewise be
dictated by that group's ethos.[51]

I define "ethos" as a group's assumed, generally unarticulated way of perceiving how life is to be lived.

Some biblical interpreters are learning to delineate
the ethos of a society. Leander Keck comments on the
value of an ethos, as well as defining an ethos, when he
writes

> while an ethos can result from the working out
> of principles or convictions, it is never ex-
> plainable on this basis alone, for, among
> other reasons, an ethos always includes as-
> sumptions, values, and habits which are not
> produced by conscious reasoning but which
> may actually be the controlling factors in
> the formulation of the principles and con-
> victions themselves. In religion, as else-
> where, practices and habits more often
> receive interpretations than interpretations
> generate practices. . . ethos. . .has to do with
> what is customary, especially for a group.[52]

"Cognitive orientation" is Bruce Malina's synonym for
ethos. For Malina

> the term "cognitive orientation" refers to the
> unspecified, unverbalized explicit expression
> of a person's understanding of the "rules of
> the game" of social living as well as the
> rules for understanding and behaving in the
> total significant environment. Some synonyms
> for cognitive orientation include cultural
> paradigm, cultural theory, cultural world
> view, cultural perspective, basic assumptions
> about society, implicit assumptions about so-
> ciety, fundamental viewpoints and the like.
> The culture's cognitive orientation furnishes
> members of the cultural group with the basic
> premises and sets of assumptions neither
> reflectively recognized nor questioned.[53]

Jonathan Z. Smith seeks
    an empathetic reconstruction of the world of
    early Christians, i.e., what "it felt like"
    to live in a world determined by the symbols,
    rituals, and language of early Christians.[54]
Smith investigates "early Christianity as a social world,
as the creation of a world of meaning which provided a
plausibility structure for those who chose to inhabit it."[55]

Detecting and describing the diverse cognitive orientations of biblical communities can suggest why communities
formulated their theologies in distinct ways. For instance,
the social conservatism of the Pastoral Epistles can be
read as a way a church in Asia Minor reflected the hierarchical order and the spirit of the household order which
permeated society in Asia Minor. As time went on and Paul
increasingly became only a memory rather than a physical
presence in Asia Minor, his radical egalitarian ethic was
replaced in some churches by a social conservatism which
reflected the hierarchical ethos of the Roman Empire.
Dennis MacDonald's *The Legend and The Apostle*[56] spells
out the competing cognitive orientations of the church
struggles which occasioned the Pastoral Epistles.

A fifth theme of the sociology of knowledge is that
persons and groups long to belong. In their critique of
modernization Berger, Berger, and Kellner show how modernization has over-emphasized the rationalization of consciousness to the extent that religious symbols are often
regarded as outmoded. Rationalism and pluralism spawn
feelings of alienation, which Berger, Berger, and Kellner
characterize as a sense of homelessness. They contend
that even though "modern humanity has suffered from a
deepening condition of homelessness", this very experience
of homelessness engenders a yearning to belong to a group

with deep roots.[57] Responses to modernization include
nativism, a longing for reintegration, youth cultures,
and affiliation with authoritative institutions that make
choices for persons.[58] They define religion "as a cognitive and normative structure that makes it possible
for persons to feel 'at home' in the universe."[59] They
value symbols as significant themes that "span spheres
of reality...Religion, philosophy, art, and science are
the most important symbols systems of this kind."[60] As
a critique of modernization, *The Homeless Mind*[61] re-
sonates with Stikker's recollection of William James, who
    suggested that just as we look back upon former
    ages and laugh at what appear to us as silly
    beliefs and errors, so too future generations
    will look back in disbelief at our modern
    science's refusal to recognize the realm of
    spirit, of human subjectivity, as in any way
    significant.[62]
Stikkers introduces Scheler's *Problems of a Sociology of
Knowledge*[63] with the poignant awareness that "modern
humanity has become increasingly unable to address those
questions that burn most deeply in the human heart, questions of meaning."[64] Stikker's cure for this social frag-
mentation lies in discovering meaning as connectedness.[65]
Thus the sociology of knowledge affirms humanity's religious nature. Humans long to belong to institutions
which impart meaning to life. Humans live and die for
symbols.

     Some biblical interpreters have learned that exegesis
consists of more than a search for the historical essence,
the kernel of truth, in a text. It is customary nowadays
to speak of a text as being multivalent and having several
meanings or intentions. Later in this essay a recent mode
of parable interpretation which draws upon the legacy of

Amos Wilder and Paul Ricoeur will be analyzed. Wilder,
in the spirit of Stikkers, pleads for

doing more justice to the role of the symbolic
and the pre-rational in the way we deal with
experience. We should recognize that human
nature and human societies are more deeply
motivated by images and fabulation than by
ideas.[66]

Finally, the methods of the sociology of knowledge are
useful to biblical students. Interpreters have always reflected the spirit of their times as they tied biblical
hermeneutics to prevailing moods or philosophies. Thus
amid the contemporary quest for meaning and corporate
belonging some exegetes are finding that the sociology of
knowledge provides some tools, and even a framework, for
interpreting biblical texts. I have hinted how five
themes of this discipline can have implications for biblical interpretation. Now I will illustrate how to implement these themes methodologically in two ways.

    First, exegetes should reconstruct the social situa-
tions which gave rise to the composition of and the preservation of biblical texts. Here exegesis involves
historical reconstruction. But the reconstruction will
use sociological methods that discern roles, conflicts,
and the creation of symbolic universes and cognitive
orientations. However, mere sociology is not enough. For
instance, Gerd Theissen in *Sociology of Early Palestinian
Christianity*[67] lists four characteristics of the wandering
charismatics whom Jesus called to be apostles. They were
homeless (Mt. 8:20). They often left their families (Mk.
10:29). They were called to poverty (Mt. 6:25-32). They
lacked protection (Mt. 5:38-41).[68] If Theissen stopped
with listing these traits which he gleaned through a
sociological analysis of early Christianity, he would

only have employed sociological methods. Instead Theissen
indulges in the sociology of knowledge as he infers that
the social traits of the wandering charismatics became key
traits in their preaching. Which came first? Probably
the social traits.

A contrast to Theissen's sociology of knowledge approach are the social histories of Ramsay MacMullen such
as *Roman Social Relations*,[69] *Enemies of the Roman Order*,[70]
and *Paganism in the Roman Empire*.[71] MacMullen chronicles
how Romans related to each other. He documents how they
viewed and regarded each other. His research provides an
incredible resource for those who want to interpret the
New Testament via the sociology of knowledge. The trick
is to take MacMullen's portraits of Roman society and to
discern how Christian communities provided alternative
visions of how to order society; or to study what happened
when their competing symbolic universes collided; and to
infer how the conflict of consciousnesses produced social
change. [The sociology of knowledge involves a philosophy
as well as sociological methods. Hence, Howard Kee's
Our Origins in Sociological Perspective is long on sociological methods and short on the philosophical assumptions
intrinsic to the sociology of knowledge. The key is to
infer how social situations relate to ideologies, themes,
theologies, and institutional development.

Second, exegesis should not only describe what happened in the biblical world, but also it should enable us to
experience the social and ethical conflicts in our society
which are similar to those which occasioned the writing of
the biblical texts. Richard Rohrbaugh reckons that
> by asking what in our social perception of
> reality is similar to that of the biblical
> writers, we shall be able to enrich and deepen
> our understanding of the common ground we

> share with the text and this, in turn,
> offers the hope that preaching will be
> further justified by virtue of a larger
> reservoir of common concern between the
> biblical message and our own time.[72]

I assume there are some basic social conflicts which appear
throughout history despite changing cultural situations.
These dissensions include the quest for an ideal city
versus the tendency to settle for the injustice of actual
political systems; the rift between the affluent and the
poor; tensions between those who value honor over dignity;
the enmity between those who feel that self-development
means finding one's place in the social hierarchy and
those who assume that life is an invitation to overcome
hierarchical structures; and the yearning to belong to the
institutions of family and community in contrast to the
occasional, but inevitable threats to belonging which
come in the form of death, mobility and social disorder.
This list of social tensions is only a beginning.

In summary, the sociology of knowledge can inform
biblical exegesis in these six ways. An exegesis informed
by the sociology of knowledge begins with historical investigation. Then it analyzes what the text meant to
learn what social factors produced or influenced that
meaning. Finally, the exegesis looks for congruence between ancient and contemporary situations.

PARABLES VIA THE SOCIOLOGY OF KNOWLEDGE: FROM EXPLANATION TO ENCOUNTER

When I pastored for twelve years I seldom preached
from parables. Having been trained in the traditional
school of historical criticism I approached parables as

Joachim Jeremias and William Barclay did. Jeremias stated
his exegetical task as discovering

> what did Jesus intend to say at this or that
> particular moment? What must have been the
> effect of his word upon his hearers?[73]

Barclay reduced parable study to a search for the central
idea in each parable. These interpreters explained the
first century meaning of the parables.[74] They extracted
the kernel of moral truth from the husk of the parable.

But as a preaching pastor I felt frustrated by this
explanatory approach towards parables. It seemed to me
that once I grasped the central point of the parable and
then explained that point that there was nothing left to
do with parables. I was searching for the central idea
in the parable that would move minds.

Early in my first pastorate some parishoners told me
that I needed to learn how to inspire them through preaching as well as to instruct and inform them. I began to
search for ways to move the heart as well as to challenge
the mind. I observed how our local JC meetings featured
training in giving enthusiastic motivational talks. The
up-and-coming leaders of our community were motivating
each other with sales pitches tuned to the heartstrings
as well as to the mind waves. I listened to black preachers. Their use of biblical language and symbols fascinat-
ed me. Eventually I learned how to use symbols and images
to motivate persons. However, even in the last series of
Sunday school lessons which I taught as a pastor before
coming to graduate school, I approached parables with the
intentions of explaining the central idea of the parable.
I was functioning as a historian of ideas. Thus parish-
ioners would debate whether that central idea was truly
the essence of the parable. They questioned whether these
ideas were applicable to their lives.

Now when I share parables my goal is to allow the parables to encounter us with alternative visions of reality. I intend for parables to challenge the stories by which persons live and to suggest other stories as alternative lifestyles.

In 1980 H. Edward Everding introduced me to the writings of John Dominic Crossan. Crossan's *The Dark Interval*,[75] subtitled "Towards a Theology of Story," is an "indirect introduction to structural analysis."[76] Rather than evaluate the methodology of structural analysis, I want to demonstrate how what Crossan does via his method is paralleled in four ways by insights from the sociology of knowledge.

Crossan submits "the proposition that we live in story like fish in the sea."[77] Crossan defines a story as the structure of expectations in which a person lives.[78] I contend that what Crossan means by story is similar to what the sociology of knowledge means by a symbolic universe. A symbolic universe projects a sense of meaning onto the external world. A symbolic universe is the lens through which life is viewed. Recently, while teaching adult education classes in local congregations I have been stressing how we live by stories and symbolic universes. To get my point across I ask persons to sketch the stories which inform the political philosophies of Ronald Reagan and Thomas "Tip" O'Neill. People quickly outline the contrasting world views of these current leaders of the Democratic and Republican parties in the United States. Students sense that contrasting political philosophies are different stories of how society ought to be structured. Thus they are prepared to understand parables as stories embodying life styles and social theories. Parables are stories which offer alternative symbolic universes.

Crossan speaks of the expectations of the hearer and speaker of parables.[79] He calls the parable of The Good Samaritan "an attack on the structure of expectation."[80] Parables of reversal, such as the stories of Ruth and Jonah, reverse normal expectations.[81] The sociology of knowledge refers to these expectations as the ethos, or cognitive orientation, which characterizes a group's assumed, generally unarticulated way of perceiving how life is to be lived.

Crossan and the sociology of knowledge affirm that knowledge is relational. Karl Mannheim maintains "all historical knowledge is relational knowledge and can only be formulated with reference to the position of the observer."[82] What one knows is related to the culture in which one lives. Crossan contends in his chapter, "A Theology of Limit," that parables enable us to explore beyond the edges of customary relationships. Parables invite us to step beyond our normal cultural confines. Crossan suggests

> that the experience of transcendental experience
> is found only at the edge of language and the
> limit of story and that the only way to find
> that excitement is to test those edges and
> those limits. And that, as we shall see is
> what parable is all about.[83]

Parables and the sociology of knowledge provide en- counters with alternative world views. Parables and an exegesis informed by the sociology of knowledge aim at encounter as well as explanation. Crossan portrays the parables of Jesus as

> stories which shatter the deep structures of
> our accepted world and thereby render clear and
> evident to us the relativity of story itself.
> They remove our defenses and make us vulnerable

to God. It is only in such experiences that
God can touch us.[84]
Parables, for Crossan, "are meant to change, not reassure
us."[85] Parables address the imagination as well as the
will. I submit that Berger, Berger, and Luckmann's *The
Homeless Mind* critiques the assumption that modern persons
are primarily rational beings. Instead, Berger, Berger,
and Luckmann demonstrate humanity's need for a spiritual
foundation for life. Humanity needs symbols and institutional meanings. Likewise, Kenneth Stikkers pleads for a
rediscovery of "the realm of spirit, of subjectivity."[86]
The issues of life's meaning and a cultural ethos involve
a spiritual and poetic dimension that Crossan and the
sociology of knowledge affirm. Parables encounter hearers
and readers with unaccustomed ways of envisioning reality.
The sociology of knowledge can elucidate different cultural
stories. Once these different cultural paradigms are
explained, persons are free to choose which symbolic universe they prefer and perhaps even to state why they prefer
that particular story.

     Sometimes the sociology of knowledge is discredited as
an exercise in uncovering cultural determinism. Here
parable studies provide an answer to that accusation. For
if parables are alternative ways of envisioning symbolic
universes, then the very fact that parables exist demonstrates that persons and societies are not completely
culturally determined. Parables illustrate our capacity
for picturing different ways of relating, for imaging
different value systems, and for constructing different
concepts of God. Parables encounter us with new possibilities. The sociology of knowledge reminds us that once we
confess that knowledge is relational, we are more open to
grasp the possibilities inherent in other specifically
culturally conditioned truth claims. Encounter with new

possibility, rather than mere explanation, is the goal
of parable studies and an exegesis informed by the sociology of knowledge.

This comparison of methodologies intends to show how
an exegesis informed by the sociology of knowledge can be
a multi-disciplinary venture which supplements the former
normative paradigm of the historical critical method.

NOTES

1. Walter Wink, *The Bible in Human Transformation* (Philadelphia: Fortress Press, 1973), 1.

2. Raymond Brown, Doctoral Colloquium, Iliff School of Theology, Denver, 1981.

3. Thomas Kuhn, *The Structure of Scientific Revolutions*, Second Edition,(Chicago: The University of Chicago Press, 1970), 175-187.

4. Krister Stendahl, "Biblical Theology, Contemporary," *Interpreter's Dictionary of the Bible I*, Edited by George Buttrick (Nashville: Abingdon Press, 1962), 148-432.

5. R.H. Charles, *The Revelation of St. John* (New York: Charles Scribner's Sons, 1920).

6. James Barr analyzes this movement between 1945-1960 as "the biblical companion and parallel to the neo-orthodox movement in general theology." See "Biblical Theology," *Interpreter's Dictionary of the Bible: Supplementary Volume* (Nashville: Abingdon Press, 1976), p. 105. The biblical theology movement was undermined by its rationalistic methodology, its failure to address new linguistic awarenesses, by the social upheavals of the 1960's which undermined its assumed consensus, and by its failure to address the problem of evil.

7. David Bartlett, "Biblical Scholarship Today: A Diversity of New Approaches," *The Christian Century*, 98 (1981), 109.

8. Peter Berger, Brigette Berger and Hansfried Kellner, *The Homeless Mind* (New York: Vintage Books, 1974).

9. Wink, *The Bible in Human Transformation,* 6-7.

10. A summary of Stendahl's "Biblical Theology, Contemporary."

11. Bartlett, "Biblical Scholarship Today," 109.

12. Brevard Childs, *Introduction to the Old Testament as Scripture* (Philadelphia: Fortress Press, 1979), 16.

13. Brevard Childs, *Biblical Theology in Crisis* (Philadelphia: The Westminster Press, 1970).

14. James D. Smart, *The Strange Silence of the Bible in the Church* (Philadelphia: The Westminster Press, 1970), 18.

15. Kuhn, *The Structure of Scientific Revolutions*, 64-84.

16. Bartlett, "Biblical Scholarship Today," 1091.

17. Ibid., 1091-1094. For bibliographies on this approach see John Elliott's *A Home For the Homeless* (Philadelphia: Fortress Press, 1981). Also, the articles by Bruce Malina, Burke Long, John Gager and Wayne Meeks in *Interpretation* 36 (1982) have good bibliographies in this issue devoted to the theme "Social Studies and Biblical Interpretation."

18. Reginald Fuller, *The New Testament in Current Study* (New York: Charles Scribner's Sons, 1962).

19. Patrick Henry, *New Directions in New Testament Study* (Philadelphia: The Westminster Press, 1979).

20. Leander Keck and Gene Tucker, "Exegesis," *Interpreter's Dictionary of the Bible: Supplementary Volume*, 296-303.

21. Elizabeth Achtemeier, "History of Interpretation—Nineteenth and Twentieth Century," *Interpreter's Dictionary of the Bible: Supplementary Volume*, 455-456. The fact that she is one of seven women writers in this volume signifies a tiny shift of the paradigm since the 1962 publication of *Interpreter's Dictionary of the Bible*.

22. James Barr, "Biblical Theology," *Interpreter's Dictionary of the Bible: Supplementary Volume*, 104-111.

23. Kuhn, *The Structure of Scientific Revolutions*, 137.

24. George Fohrer, *Introduction to the Old Testament* Translated by David Green. (Nashville: Abingdon Press, 1978) and Paul Feine, Johannes Behm and Werner Kummel, *Introduction to the New Testament*, Translated by A.J. Mattill, Jr. (Nashville: ABingdon Press, 1966).

25. Childs, *Introduction to the Old Testament as Scripture*, 16.

26. *Old Testament Abstracts* 3 (1980) lists nine reviews that debate the merits of Childs' approach.

27. Bartlett, "Biblical Scholarship Today," 1094.

28. Kuhn, *The Structure of Scientific Revolutions*, 84.

29. Peter Berger and Thomas Luckmann, *The Social Construction of Reality* (Garden City: Anchor Books, 1967), 47-128.

30. Ibid., 147, 129-183.

31. Karl Marx, "Existence and Consciousness," *Selected Writings in Sociology and Social Psychology*, Translated by T.B. Battomare(New York: McGraw-Hill, 1956), 71.

32. Ibid., 75.

33. Karl Mannheim, *Ideology and Utopia*, Translated by Louis Wirth and Edward Shils (New York: Harcourt, Brace, Jovanovich, Inc., 1936), 29; also, 31.

34. Peter Berger, *The Sacred Canopy* (Garden City: Anchor Books, 1969).

35. Ibid., 27; also, 3, 89. See *The Social Construction of Reality*, 1, 14-15, 49, 50, 51, 52, 61.

36. Howard Clark Kee, *Our Origins in Sociological Perspective* (Philadelphia: The Westminster Press, 1980), 30. Bruce Malina notes that this awareness "teaches us that the world we live in, the world that we think, or assume, has ontological foundations, is really socially constructed and is created, communicated and sustained through language and symbol," "Limited Good and the Social World of Early Christianity," *Biblical Theology Bulletin* 8 (1978), 175.

37. Mannheim, *Ideology and Utopia*, 79.

38. Ibid., 80; also, 176, 282.

39. Ibid., 283. Berger and Luckmann compare relationism and relativism in *The Social Construction of Reality*, 10.

40. Kee, *Our Origins in Sociological Perspective*, 8.

41. Aaron Milavec, "Modern Exegesis, Doctrinal Innovations, and the Dynamics of Discipleship," *Anglican
Theological Review* 60 (1978), 57. Richard Rohrbaugh provides a hermeneutic based upon the sociology of knowledge
in *The Biblical Interpreter* (Philadelphia: Fortress Press,
1979). He treats this point on pp. 8-9. Walter Wink, in
The Bible in Human Transformation, argues for an awareness
of the partisan nature of knowledge on pp. 8, 25.

42. Patrick Henry, *New Directions in New Testament
Study* (Philadelphia: The Westminster Press, 1979), 21-23.
James D.G. Dunn is a practicing Pentecostal. His *Unity
and Diversity in the New Testament* (Philadelphia: The
Westminster Press, 1977) has been well received.

43. Phyllis Trible's "Feminist Hermeneutics and
Biblical Studies," *The Christian Century* 99 (1982) 116-118
does not represent her best work. The impact of her *God
and the Rhetoric of Sexuality* (Philadelphia: Fortress
Press, 1978) culminated in an invitation to give the
Beecher Lectures on preaching at Yale University.

44. Berger, Luckmann, *The Social Construction of
Reality*, 97-104.

45. A summary of *The Social Construction of Reality*,
60ff. Also, see *The Homeless Mind*, 96-102.

46. Berger, Berger, Kellner, *The Homeless Mind*, 12-14.

47. Helmut Koester and James Robinson, *Trajectories
Through Early Christianity* (Philadelphia: Fortress Press,
1971).

48. Mannheim discusses the five ideal political types
on pp. 117-146 and the four utopian ideals on pp. 211-247
of *Ideology and Utopia*. He rejects a "group mind" on p.
269.

49. Berger, Berger, Kellner, *The Homeless Mind*, 76.

50. Lewis Wirth, "Preface," *Ideology and Utopia*,
xxiii.

150   RELIGION AND THE SOCIOLOGY OF KNOWLEDGE

51. Kenneth Stikkers, "Introduction," Max Scheler's *Problems of a Sociology of Knowledge*, Translated by Manfred Frings (Boston: Routledge & Kegan Paul, 1980), 26.

52. Leander Keck, "On the Ethos of Early Christianity," *Journal of the American Academy of Religion* 42 (1974), 440.

53. Malina, "Limited Good and the Social World," 35.

54. Jonathan S. Smith, "The Social Description of Early Christianity," *Religious Studies Review* 1 (1975), 21.

55. Ibid.

56. Dennis MacDonald, *The Legend and the Apostle* (Philadelphia: The Westminster Press, 1983).

57. Berger, Berger, Kellner, *The Homeless Mind*, 82.

58. Ibid., 158 ff.

59. Ibid., 79. In *The Sacred Canopy* Berger shows how religion addresses life's marginal situations on pp. 22-24, 44.

60. Berger and Luckmann, *The Social Construction of Reality*, 40.

61. Berger, Berger, Kellner, *The Homeless Mind*, 5.

62. Stikkers, "Introduction," 5.

63. Scheler, Max, *Problems of a Sociology of Knowledge* Translated by Manfred Fringes (Boston: Routledge & Kegan Paul, 1980).

64. Stikkers, "Introduction," 6.

65. Daniel Day Williams speaks of this quest for meaning from a process theology perspective in *The Spirit and Forms of Love* (Philadelphia: The Westminster Press, 1968).

66. Amos Wilder, *Theopoetic* (Philadelphia: Fortress Press, 1976), 2; also 9, 25, 27, 39, 74, 78-79.

67. Gerd Theissen, *Sociology of Early Palestinian Christianity*, Translated by John Bowden (Philadelphia: Fortress Press, 1978).

68. Ibid., 8-16.

69. Ramsay MacMullen, *Roman Social Relations, 50 B.C. to A.D. 284* (New Haven: Yale University Press, 1974).

70. Ramsay MacMullen, *Enemies of the Roman Order* (Cambridge: Harvard University Press, 1966).

71. Ramsay MacMullen, *Paganism in the Roman Empire* (New Haven: Yale University Press, 1981).

72. Rohrbaugh, *The Biblical Interpreter*, 26.

73. Joachim Jeremias, *The Parables of Jesus*, Translated by S.L. Hooke (New York: Charles Scribner's Sons, 1963), 22.

74. William Barclay, *And Jesus Said. A Handbook on the Parables of Jesus* (Philadelphia: The Westminster Press, 1970).

75. John Dominic Crossan, *The Dark Interval* (Niles, Illinois: Argus Publications, 1975).

76. Ibid., 10, 48.

77. Ibid., 47.

78. Ibid., 86.

79. Ibid., 107.

80. Ibid., 108.

81. Ibid., 67-77.

82. Mannheim, *Ideology and Utopia*, 79.

83. Crossan, *The Dark Interval*, 45-46.

84. Ibid., 122. Here Crossan seems related to Paul Ricoeur who achieves a unified hermeneutic combining insights from philosophy, phenomenology and biblical studies in a manner similar to Paul Tillich's search for a cultural synthesis. Ricoeur posits self-reflection as the goal of his hermeneutic. Regarding the parables of Jesus Ricoeur writes, "To listen to the parables of Jesus, it seems to me, is to let one's imagination be opened to the new possibilities disclosed by the extravagance of these short dramas. If we look at the parables as at a word addressed first to our imagination, rather than to our

will, we will not be tempted to reduce them to mere di-
dactic devices, to moralizing allegories. We will let
their poetic power display itself within us," "Listening
to the Parables: Once More Astonished," *Christianity and
Crisis* 34 (1975), 307. Also, see his *Essays on Biblical
Interpretation*, Edited by Lewis Mudge (Philadelphia:
Fortress Press, 1980).

85. Ibid., 156.

86. Stikkers, "Introduction," 5. Lewis Mudge warns
us not to "dismiss realms of meaning beyond the literal
either as confusion to be cleared away by the logicians
or as emotional embellishment to be kept in check,"
"Introduction," Paul Ricoeur's *Essays on Biblical Interpretation*, 4.

PART III

SOCIOLOGY OF KNOWLEDGE AND THE
RELIGIOUS INSTITUTION

CHARISMATIC AUTHORITY AND ITS ROUTINIZATION

Max Weber

THE PRINCIPAL CHARACTERISTICS
OF CHARISMATIC AUTHORITY AND
ITS RELATION TO FORMS OF
COMMUNAL ORGANIZATION

The term "charisma" will be applied to a certain quality of an individual personality of virtue by which he is set apart from ordinary men and treated as endowed with supernatural, superhuman, or at least specifically exceptional powers or qualities. These are such as are not accessible to the ordinary person, but are regarded as of divine origin or as exemplary, and on the basis of them the individual concerned is treated as a leader. In primitive circumstances this peculiar kind of deference is paid to prophets, to people with a reputation for therapeutic or legal wisdom, to leaders in the hunt, and heroes in war. It is very often thought of as resting on magical powers. How the quality in question would be ultimately judged from any ethical, aesthetic, or other such point of view is naturally entirely indifferent for purposes of definition. What is alone important is how the individual is actually regarded by those subject to charismatic authority, by his "followers" or "disciples."

It is recognition on the part of those subject to authority which is decisive for the validity of charisma. This is freely given and guaranteed by what is held to be a "sign" of proof (*Bewährung*), originally always a miracle, consists in devotion to the corresponding revelation, hero worship, or absolute trust in the leader. But

where charisma is genuine, it is not this which is the
basis of the claim to legitimacy. This basis lies rather
in the conception that it is the *duty* of those who have
been called to a charismatic mission to recognize its
quality and to act accordingly. Psychologically this
"recognition" is a matter of complete personal devotion
to the possessor of the quality, arising out of enthusiasm, or of despair and hope. No prophet has ever regarded
his quality as dependent on the attitudes of the masses
toward him. No elective king or military leader has ever
treated those who have resisted him or tried to ignore him
otherwise than as delinquent in duty. Failure to take part
in a military expedition under such a leader, even though
recruitment is nominally voluntary, has universally been
met with disdain.

If proof of his charismatic qualification fails him
for long, the leader endowed with charisma tends to think
his god or his magical or heroic powers have deserted him.
If he is for long unsuccessful, above all if his leadership fails to benefit his followers, it is likely that
his charismatic authority will disappear. This is the
genuine charismatic meaning of the "gift of grace."
(*Gottesgnadentum*)

The corporate group which is subject to charismatic
authority is based on an emotional form of communal
relationship. The administrative staff of a charismatic
leader does not consist of "officials"; at least its
members are not technically trained. It is not chosen
on the basis of social privilege nor from the point of
view of domestic or personal dependency. It is rather
chosen in terms of charismatic qualities of its members.
The prophet has his disciples; the war lord his henchmen;
the leader, generally, his followers. There is no such

thing as "appointment" or "dismissal," no career, no
promotion. There is only a "call" at the instance of the
leader on the basis of the charismatic qualification of
those he summons. There is no hierarchy; the leader
merely intervenes in general or in individual cases when
he considers the members of his staff inadequate to a
task with which they have been entrusted. There is no
such thing as a definite sphere of authority and of
competence, and no appropriation of official powers on
the basis of social privileges. There may, however, be
territorial or functional limits to charismatic powers
and to the individual's "mission." There is no such
thing as a salary or a benefice. Disciples or followers
tend to live primarily in a communistic relationship with
their leader on means which have been provided by voluntary gift. There are no established administrative
organs. In their place are agents who have been provided
with charismatic authority by their chief or who possess
charisma of their own. There is no system of formal
rules, of abstract legal principles, and hence no process
of judicial decision oriented to them. But equally there
is no legal wisdom oriented to judicial precedent.
Formally concrete judgments are newly created from case
to case and are originally regarded as divine judgments
and revelations. From a substantive point of view, every
charismatic authority would have to subscribe to the
proposition, "It is written . . ., but I say unto
you . . ." The genuine prophet, like the genuine military
leader and every true leader in this sense, preaches,
creates, or demands *new* obligations. In the pure type of
charisma, these are imposed on the authority of revolution
by oracles, or by the leader's own will, and are recognized by the members of the religious, military or party
group because they come from such a source. Recognition

is a duty. When such an authority comes into conflict
with the competing authority of another who also claims
charismatic sanction, the only recourse is to some kind
of contest, by magical means or even an actual physical
battle of the leaders. In principle, only one side can
be in the right in such a conflict; the other must be
guilty of a wrong which has to be expiated.

Charismatic authority is thus specifically outside
the realm of everyday routine and the profane sphere. In
this respect, it is sharply opposed to traditional authority, whether in its patriarchal, patrimonial, or any
other form. Both rational and traditional authority are
specifically forms of everyday routine control of action;
while the charismatic type is the direct antithesis of
this. Bureaucratic authority is specifically rational in
the sense of being bound to intellectually analyzable
rules; while charismatic authority is specifically
irrational in the sense of being foreign to all rules.
Traditional authority is bound to the precedents handed
down from the past and to this extent is also oriented
to rules. Within the sphere of its claims, charismatic
authority repudiates the past, and is in this sense a
specifically revolutionary force. It recognizes no
appropriation of positions of power by virtue of the
possession of property, either on the part of a chief or
of socially privileged groups. The only basis of legitimacy for it is personal charisma, so long as it is proved;
that is, as long as it receives recognition and is able to
satisfy the followers or disciples. But this lasts only
so long as the belief in its charismatic inspiration
remains.

THE ROUTINIZATION OF CHARISMA
AND ITS CONSEQUENCES

In its pure form charismatic authority has a character specifically foreign to everyday routine structures.
The social relationships directly involved are strictly
personal, based on the validity and practice of charismatic personal qualities. If this is not to remain a purely
transitory phenomenon, but to take on the character of a
permanent relationship forming a stable community of
disciples or a band of followers or a party organization
or any sort of political or hierocratic organization, it
is necessary for the character of charismatic authority
to become radically changed. Indeed, in its pure form
charismatic authority may be said to exist only in the
process of originating. It cannot remain stable, but
becomes either traditionalized or rationalized, or a
combination of both.

The following are the principal motives underlying
this transformation: (a) The ideal and also the material
interests of the followers in the continuation and continual reactivation of the community, (b) the still stronger
ideal and also stronger material interests of the members
of the administrative staff, the disciples or other
followers of the charismatic leader in continuing their
relationship. Not only this, but they have an interest
in continuing it in such a way that both from an ideal
and material point of view, their own status is put on
a stable everyday basis. This means, above all, making it
possible to participate in normal family relationships or
at least to enjoy a secure social position in place of the
kind of discipleship which is cut off from ordinary worldly connexions, notably in the family and in economic
relationships.

These interests generally become conspicuously
evident with the disappearance of the personal charismatic
leader and with the problem of succession, which inevitably arises. The way in which this problem is met--
if it is met at all and the charismatic group continues
to exist--is of crucial importance for the character of
the subsequent social relationships.

Concomitant with the routinization of charisma with
a view to insuring adequate succession, go the interests
in its routinization on the part of the administrative
staff. It is only in the initial stages and so long as
the charismatic leader acts in a way which is completely
outside everyday social organization, that it is possible
for his followers to live communistically in a community
of faith and enthusiasm, on gifts, "booty," or sporadic
acquisition. Only the members of the small group of
enthusiastic disciples and followers are prepared to
devote their lives purely idealistically to their call.
The great majority of disciples and followers will in the
long run "make their living" out of their "calling" in a
material sense as well. Indeed, this must be the case if
the movement is not to disintegrate.

Hence, the routinization of charisma also takes the
form of the appropriation of powers of control and economic advantages by the followers or disciples, and the
regulation of the recruitment of these groups. This process of traditionalization or of legalization, according to
whether rational legislation is involved or not, may take
any one of a number of typical forms.

1. The original basis of recruitment is personal
charisma. With routinization, the followers or disciples
may set up norms for recruitment in particular involving
training or tests of eligibility. Charisma can only be
"awakened" and "tested"; it cannot be "learned" or

"taught." All types of magical asceticism, as practiced
by magicians and heroes, and all novitiates, belong in
this category. These are means of closing the group
which constitutes the administrative staff.

2. It is easy for charismatic norms to be transformed into those defining a traditional social status on
a hereditary charismatic basis. If the leader is chosen
on a hereditary basis, it is very easy for hereditary
charisma to govern the selection of the administrative
staff and even, perhaps, those followers without any
position of authority.

3. The administrative staff may seek and achieve the
creation and appropriation of individual positions and the
corresponding economic advantages for its members. In
that case, according to whether the tendency is to traditionalization or legalization there will develop (a) benefices, (b) offices, or (c) fiefs.

For charisma to be transformed into a permanent
routine structure, it is necessary that its anti-economic
character should be altered. It must be adapted to some
form of fiscal organization to provide for the needs of
the group and hence to the economic conditions necessary
for raising taxes and contributions. When a charismatic
movement develops in the direction of praebendal provision,
the "laity" become differentiated from the "clergy"; that
is, the participating members of the charismatic administrative staff which has now become routinized. These
are the priests of the developing "church." Correspondingly, in a developing political body the vassals, the
holders of benefices, or officials are differentiated from
the "tax payers." The former, instead of being "followers
of the leader" become state officials or appointed party
officals. This process is very conspicuous in Buddhism
and in the Hindu sects. The same is true in all states

resulting from conquest which have become rationalized
to form permanent structures; also of parties and other
movements which have originally had a purely charismatic
character. With the process of routinization the charismatic group tends to develop into one of the forms of
everyday authority, particularly the patrimonial form in
its decentralized variant or the bureaucratic. Its
original peculiarities are apt to be retained in the
charismatic standards of honor attendant on the social
status acquired by heredity or the holding of office.
This applies to all who participate in the process of
appropriation, the chief himself and members of his staff.
It is thus a matter of the type of prestige enjoyed by
ruling groups. A hereditary monarch by "divine right"
is not a simple patrimonial chief, patriach, or sheik;
a vassal is not a mere household retainer or official.
Further details must be deferred to the analysis of social
stratification.

As a rule the process of routinization is not free
of conflict. In the early stages personal claims on the
charisma of the chief are not easily forgotten and the
conflict between the charisma of office or of hereditary
status with personal charisma is a typical process in
many historical situations.

THE TRANSFORMATION OF CHARISMA
IN ANTI-AUTHORITARIAN DIRECTION

A charismatic principle which originally was primarily directed to the legitimization of authority may be
subject to interpretation or development in an anti-
authoritarian direction. This is true because the validity of charismatic authority rests entirely on recognition
by those subject to it, conditioned as this is by "proof"

of its genuineness. This is true in spite of the fact
that this recognition of a charismatically qualified, and
hence legitimate, person is treated as a duty. When the
organization of the corporate group undergoes a process
of progressive rationalization, it is readily possible
that, instead of recognition being treated as a consequence of legitimacy, it is treated as the basis of
legitimacy. Legitimacy, that is, becomes "democratic."
Thus, for instance, designation of a successor by an
administrative staff may be treated as "election" in ad-
vance; while designation by the predecessor is "nomina-
tion"; whereas the recognition by the group becomes the
true "election." The leader whose legitimacy rested on
his personal charisma then becomes leader by the grace of
those who follow him since the latter are formally free
to elect and elevate to power as they please and even to
depose. For the loss of charisma and its proof involves
the loss of genuine legitimacy. The chief now becomes
the freely elected leader.

        Correspondingly, the recognition of the charismatic
decrees and judicial decisions on the part of the community shifts to the doctrine that the group has a right to
enact, recognize, or repeal laws, according to their own
free will, both in general and for an individual case.
Under genuine charismatic authority, on the other hand, it
is, to be sure, true that conflicts over the correct law
may actually be decided by a vote of the group. But this
takes place under the pressure of the feeling that there
can only be *one* correct decision and it is a matter of
duty to arrive at this. The most important transitional
type is the legitimization of authority by plebiscite.
The commonest examples are to be found in the party leaders of the modern state. But it is always present in

cases where the chief   feels himself to be acting
on behalf of the masses and where his recognition is
based on this.

Once the elective principle has been applied to
the chief by a process or reinterpretation of charisma,
it may be extended to the administrative staff. Elective
officials whose legitimacy is derived from the confidence
of those subject to their authority and to recall if
confidence ceases to exist, are typical of certain types
of democracies, for instance, the United States. They
are not "bureaucratic" types. Because they have an
independent source of legitimacy, they are not strongly
integrated in a hierarchical order. To a large extent
their "promotion" is not influenced by the superiors
and, correspondingly, their functions are not controlled.
There are analogies in other cases where several charismatic structures, which are qualitatively heterogeneous,
exist side by side, as in the relations of the Dalai Lama
and the Taschi Lama. An administrative structure organized in this way is, from a technical point of view,
a greatly inferior "instrument of precision" as compared
with the bureaucratic type consisting of appointed
officials.

The introduction of elected officials always involves
a radical alteration in the position of the charismatic
leader. He becomes the "servant" of those under his
authority. There is no place for such a type in a technically rational bureaucratic organization. He is not
appointed by his superiors and the possibility of promotion is not dependent on their judgment. On the contrary,
his position is derived from the favour of the persons
whose action he controls. Hence he is likely to be little
interested to win the favour of superiors. The tendency
is rather for electoral positions to become autocephalous

spheres of authority. It is in general not possible to attain a high level of technical administrative efficiency with an elected staff of officials. This is illustrated by a comparison of the elected officials in the individual states in the United States with the appointed officials of the Federal Government. It is similarly shown by reform mayors with their own appointed staffs. It is necessary to distinguish the type of democracy where positions of authority are legitimized by plebiscite from that which attempts to dispense with leadership altogether. The latter type is characterized by the attempt to reduce to a minimum the control of some men over others.

It is characteristic of the democracy which makes room for leadership that there should in general be a highly emotional type of devotion to and trust in the leader. This accounts for a tendency to favour the type of individual who is most spectacular, who promises the most, or who employs the most effective propaganda measures in the competition for leadership. This is a natural basis for the utopian component which is found in all revolutions. It also indicates the limitations on the level of rationality which, in the modern world, this type of administration can attain. Even in America it has not *always* come up to expectations.

RELIGION IN MODERN SOCIETY: A
SYSTEMS-THEORETICAL APPROACH

Peter Beyer

The sociology of knowledge, including the questions
it asks of religion, is one reflection of a profound series
of changes in Western society that is often subsumed under
the heading of modernization. The development of modern
society is a condition for the possibility of the sociology
of knowledge. It is therefore not surprising that the
questions it asks of religion are an aspect of the changed
position of religion in society as a result of modernization. The examination of religion's response to the
challenge presented it by the sociology of knowledge is
then but one way of approaching the question of religion
and modernization. What is religion's position in modern
society? What have been some of religion's responses to
its changing and changed situation? What are the possibilities for further response?

It is the purpose of this essay to examine the relation of religion and modernization by offering certain
answers to these questions just posed. Given the limitations of space, this requires a certain amount of restriction of the great many ways this task can be tackled. In
what follows, I will take the following approach: I shall
present an analysis of what, sociologically speaking,
modernization is, specifically what it is from the point
of view of its effect upon religion as a social phenomenon.
This presentation will essentially be a reading of the
analysis of modernization offered by Niklas Luhmann.[1]

In the course of this analysis, I will illustrate the
points that are made predominantly with examples drawn
from the responses to the development of modern society
by the Christian tradition. These responses can be seen
not only as illustrations of the structural and ideological transformations, but also as a critique of modernity
insofar as much of religious thought and many religious
attitudes have seen themselves as opposed to the major
consequences of modernity for religion and for human
existence more generally. Having benefitted less than
other social domains (e.g., the economic or the scientific) from the hitherto dominant features of modernity,
religion has preserved alternatives that other domains
have abandoned. Thus the examples will lead to a consideration of the possible role that religion can play in
today's society as an agent of constructive change and
not simply of reaction. This last section of the paper
will of necessity be highly tentative, being justified
mainly as a way of showing how religion can continue to
have social relevance under the conditions of modernity.

WHAT IS MODERNIZATION?

The discussion as to the nature of modernization has
a long history dating back at least to the French Revolution. Although this event was only one particularly prominent symptom of basic transformations in the structures
of Western society that began in the Middle Ages and are
still continuing today, it seemed to give European thinkers a benchmark that allowed the analysis of the before
and the after. Certain responses, such as that of Edmund
Burke,[2] simply considered the new as a negation of the
old, contrasting the revolutionary order with what was
called "legitimate society." Others made more positive

distinctions: de Bonald distinguished the agricultural
and the industrial family;[3] Marx distinguished feudalism
and capitalism;[4] Maine discriminated status and contract.[5]
These polar contrasts, including later ones such as Tönnies'
separation of *Gemeinschaft* and *Gesellschaft*[6] and Durkheim's
analysis of mechanical and organic forms of solidarity,[7]
express the notion that Western society was undergoing a
basic transformation. It will be evident from the examples
given that the thus established distinction between traditional and modern societies begs the question of what it
is that fundamentally distinguishes the one from the other.
Marx gives primacy to economic changes; Durkheim and
Tönnies look at contrasting forms of sociality; Weber often
focuses on changes in individual consciousness.[8] All these
approaches as well as others have maintained relevance in
the current discussion of the issue. The approach that I
have adopted here has been chosen in part because it makes
room for the insights of the other approaches within its
own analytic framework, but mainly because it can shed
particular light on the changing and changed place of religion in society as a correlate of modernization. It
uses as its fundamental distinction a contrast between two
types of primary social differentiation: stratified and
functional.

Another important concept for the discussion is that
of secularization. Although it is used by scholars in many
different ways, its dominant application is to focus attention on the idea that religion in modern society has lost
social relevance. The implication is that more and more
things in social and personal life have become secular,
that is, non-religious, as a result of modernization;
whereas before, in traditional society, religious considerations played a greater role. The idea includes the
notion that religion has been privatized, that religious

beliefs and practices have become matters strictly for
individual choice. Unfortunately, the use of secularization as a research variable has tended unnecessarily to
harden the distinction between secular and religious into
one of polar opposites. A re-analysis may provide a
better idea of what precisely the concept, secularization,
is trying to express. It is to such a re-analysis that I
now turn.

MODERNIZATION AND THE
DIFFERENTIATION OF SOCIETY

The notion that modernization is connected with changes
in the way society is differentiated internally is not new.
The best known supporters of this thesis are undoubtedly
Durkheim[9] and Parsons.[10] For Durkheim, the new modern
society differentiates various functional roles whose
organic interplay constitutes the integrative solidarity
of the society. This functional differentiation is seen
to be at the heart of what characterizes modern society
and distinguishes it from older forms which relied on en-
forced likeness of all members of the society to a particular mold in order to assure its (mechanical) solidarity. Parsons develops this idea significantly further:
he posits not only an increase in the number and autonomy
of functional roles in modern society, but further the
development of entire functional systems as characterizing
what modern society essentially is. The thesis that a
society as such is a system of actions and that modernization brings about the functional differentiation of this
system into subsystems provides the basis of an explanation
of the secularization phenomenon. Religion, becoming
identified with *only one* of his four fundamental subsystems, each with equal importance for the society, can no

longer claim to be the foundation of all social existence.
Actions can have their meaning and value relatively inde-
pendently of the religious reference, above all if they
refer primarily to one of the three functional spheres
other than that to which religion is assigned.[11]

Although the Parsonian theory provides essentials for
understanding what modernization has meant for religion,
several of the pieces of the puzzle are still missing. Of
these, important ones can be found in theoretical endeav-
ours in this direction by Parsons' student, Niklas Luhmann,
in particular a better understanding of what precisely it
was about *traditional* society that made religion so much
more central in its structures;[12] and a more complete understanding of the different kinds of response to modernization by the Protestant and Catholic branches of Christianity.

Luhmann makes several basic revisions to the Parsonian
model, two of which are of special relevance here. To begin, unlike Parsons, Durkheim, and many others, Luhmann
departs from a polar model of the traditional/modern shift.
Parsons and Durkheim, as key examples, have only one type
of differentiation and therefore see the change from traditional to modern as an increase along the quantitative
axis of this unique type: modern societies display a higher degree of functional differentiation than do traditional
societies. Luhmann breaks this continuity by positing not
only a change in the degree of functional differentiation,
but also a change in the type of primary, inner-societal
differentiation. There are accordingly three types of
social differentiation: segmentary, stratified, and functional. The first and last ways of grouping social
action are already present in previous models, corresponding roughly to Durkheim's mechanical and organic solidari-
ties respectively. The middle term is the addition and
provides the basis for a more thorough understanding of

traditional societies. Modernization, or better, the
emergence of modern society, is thus seen as the transformation of a society or societies exhibiting a primacy[13]
of stratified differentiation (division into distinct
social strata) into a society that relies in the first
instance on functional differentiation for its internal
differentiation. Luhmann's theory therefore lets us see
modernization as a more radical change. Not only does
functional differentiation become increasingly dominant
as the primary structure of reference for the orientation
of social action, but this development is paralleled by
the loss of a primacy of stratified differentiation.
Accordingly, in order to understand more fully the challenge that modernization presents to religion and religious organizations, it is also necessary to appreciate the
way that religion was structurally and ideologically im-
plicated in the basic patterns of traditional Western
European society. This aspect of the question is particularly important for comprehending the 19th and 20th
century attitudes of the Roman Catholic Church and the
significance of the radical shift announced by Vatican II.

The second basic revision of the Parsonian model by
Luhmann that is of relevance for the present discussion
concerns the societal functions. By discarding the Parsonian restriction to four such basic functions, the
Luhmannian model opens the door for a more flexible approach to the question of religion's position with respect
to the other functional spheres of modern society. This
flexibility becomes particularly important when considering
the relation of religion, which is here assigned its own
functional subsystem, to such areas as education, the
family, and morality. In the Parsonian system, religion,
education, and the family are all primarily located in the
same subsystem, the one for latent pattern maintenance.

Luhmann sees each of these as separate functional subsystems and can therefore regard the development of modern society as including the differentiation of these spheres as well.[14] Historically, it has been primarily in relation to these spheres that Western religion has sought to stem the tide of what seemed to it to be a progressive erosion of its social importance. To be sure, this primacy has not and does not today exclude the assertion of the social relevance of religion in other functional spheres, notably the economic and political ones. However, in these latter cases, the contributions have most often been, as it were, from the outside: religious professionals most often do not seek to control government and business, whereas such control is precisely what has been sought and in many quarters still is sought in relation to education, the family (including sex roles), and individual morality.

STRATIFIED VS. FUNCTIONAL DIFFERENTIATION

Traditional Society

These introductory remarks by way of a comparison of Parsonian and Luhmannian theory need to be fleshed out considerably. In what follows, I shall present an analysis of the main structural differences between traditional and modern societies, including the place of religion in each. This objective analysis will include a short temporal one that outlines some of the main historical steps taken by Western society between its Middle Ages and the present in its passage from traditional to modern structures. In addition, I shall examine the place and importance of the notion of privatization in the model of modernization thus described.

Distinguishing traditional from modern societies on
the basis of different types of dominant internal differentiation does not mean that one seeks to characterize
these societies simply on the basis of this distinction.
The great variety of traditional societies, from Aztec to
Greek city-state to Ancient Chinese to medieval European,
would be sufficient to confute such an attempt. However,
to understand what fundamentally happened in the transformation of Western society between the 15th and 20th
centuries, the distinction can be instrumental. We begin
with a description of some of the implications dominance
of stratification has for a traditional society and for
religion in such a society.

In contrast to simple, segmentarily differentiated
societies,[15] traditional societies are larger (in terms of
population) and wealthier. These two factors correlate
with two fundamental possibilities: increased differences
in the styles of life individuals of the society can lead,
and sufficient surplus resources above a basic subsistence
level to allow relatively large groups of individuals
(more precisely: families) to concentrate on activities
other than the provision of basic needs. Correspondingly,
these two interrelated factors bring about a certain communication problem: the greater variety of life-styles and
life-situations combined with the increase in the absolute
number of members of the society makes it impossible to
base that society on interaction between all members of
the society on the basis of some restricted and uniform
view of reality.[16]

Stratification addresses itself to the possibilities
as well as the resulting problems. It divides the society
into fixed social strata within each of which numbers are
sufficiently small and life-styles sufficiently uniform to
permit equality of communicative potential,[17] or potential

influence, to all members of a particular stratum. This
equality within strata combines with inequality between
strata: the upper and much smaller strata tend to monopo-
lize communication that can be relevant for the society
as a whole by having control over most of the wealth,
political power, and other media of social influence.
This concentration of social influence in the hands of the
few makes possible a self-definition of the society by
these upper strata, and this on their own terms. Owing
to their control over the media of social communication,
the ruling classes can impose their own vision of society
on the lower classes. Functional differentiation is the
division of social actions on the basis of which fundamental social problem each addresses, or more simply, on
the basis of what one does. It is certainly present in
these societies, but it serves to support the dominant
stratification rather than competing with it. Thus the
more influential roles within any functional sphere, for
example, king, general, abbott, bishop, and above all
landowner, are assigned to members of the upper strata.
Functional differentiation reinforces the communication
barriers that are at the very heart of stratification.

For the further description of the characteristics of
traditional societies, I shall restrict myself to the
single example of medieval Western European society. To
begin, it should be noted that membership by individuals
in a particular stratum is inherited and therefore ascribed. That is, one belongs to one's stratum by virtue
of one's membership in a family. Strata are composed of
families and not of individuals as such. The centrality
of the kinship group should be kept in mind for what
follows.

Further description can follow two interrelated lines:
the modes of integration of such a society and its self-

conception. A word has already been said about the latter
in terms of how the upper strata can conceive the society
in terms of themselves. In order to impose their vision
on the society as a whole, both structural and ideological
achievements are required. On the level of structure,
the upper strata must have the means by which they can
assure collective action on their part, collective action
that will maintain the over-all societal structures, especially the very uneven distribution of power and wealth.
In a very real sense, the integration of stratified societies is achieved at the level of the upper strata.
Collective upper class action comes about through the
structured interaction among members of the upper class
families. This, in turn, is co-ordinated through the
moral code.[18]

Luhmann's model here does not see morals as simply a
system of general values and norms that determine an outlook on the world. Rather morals are seen as the code of
rules that govern the granting and withholding of respect
in social systems.[19] As such, they are rules of behavior
which determine the degree to which a particular person
is accepted as a socially valuable person. They co-ordi-
nate the behaviour and outlooks of people in a society
and they do so in close connection with concrete behaviour.
Accordingly, morals gravitate towards interaction situations. An example of this tendency is the reflection of
group pressure expressed in the statement: "But I have to
live with these people!" The close relation of morals and
interaction makes it understandable that, in the case of
traditional societies, upper-stratum solidarity or coordination of experience and action should be achieved
through morally directed interaction. This makes possible
the collective action that integrates the basic social
structures. The moral code defines who is a member of the

upper class group and also controls behaviour so as to
integrate upper class action.

In the light of these structural characteristics of
traditional societies, one can now ask as to the ideological dimension that expresses these structures, justifies
them, and thereby reinforces them. It is at this point
that religion enters the picture most clearly. The central
role of morals in the structural integration of these
societies already points to why this is the case. At
least in Western society (but not exclusively there), the
most important way of responding to the increased social
complexity[20] brought about by stratified societies, on the
level of the coordination of behaviour, was the increased
moralization of religion. The increased variety of social
situations, both within and between strata, with their
corresponding pressures for different sorts of behaviour,
requires an appropriate development in the morals that
guide behaviour. Increased generalization of the moral
code is a partial response, but the most global and perhaps most successful solution to this type of problem has
been to tie the moral code more closely to the sanctioning
power of religion.[21]

The Judeo-Christian tradition gives a good example of
how this development can come about and how it works. The
high god becomes more and more interested in moral questions
beyond the plane of ritual observance. He comes to be seen
as himself a moral being whose behaviour is guided by a
moral code that has its direct counterpart in the human
moral codes. Eventually the high god becomes identified
with the morally good. His demands on human beings now
exceed ritual observance to include standards of behaviour
for human beings *during* their lifetimes. A happy life and
a happy afterlife depend on conformity to the divinely
sanctioned moral code and not just on the correct

performance of rituals. Moralized religion can now justify
a moral code that in principle applies to all members of
society and to all interaction situations. The granting
or withholding of respect is now supported by religious
beliefs and, indirectly, through religious rituals. It
can thereby integrate all social communication.

Inasmuch as morally guided upper stratum interaction
represents the structural aspect of traditional societal
integration, moralized religion can be seen as its ideological aspect. Such religion provides not only a unified
and general moral code but also legitimation for the over-
all stratified structures themselves. The necessarily
differing standards of behaviour of the different social
strata, differences that correspond to the variations in
the kinds of lives that members of the different strata
lead, can be unified through an overarching religious
vision. Thus, for example, the moral peasant accepts his
inferior status as God-willed and treats the upper class
member with the deference due an inherently more noble
person. The lower class person who breaks such moral
rules is considered presumptuous. The nobleman who be-
haves without the proper decorum is also morally censured.
To sit in the presence of one's lord is as reprehensible
as to take a drink with one's serfs at their home. In
each case, the divinely willed order is being threatened.

A further aspect of the role of moralized religion in
traditional societies is its relation to functional communication, particularly economic and political action.
Although these types of action have their specific values
and their specific roles, these are fundamentally tied to
religious values and, in medieval Europe, largely subordinated to them. Morals and the religious belief code
that legitimates them are the underpinning of all social
action, including political and economic. This assertion

is an aspect of the dominance of stratified differentiation, since it effectively subordinates functional criteria to the considerations of stratum membership and stratum
maintenance.

Modern Society

Since, on this model, structure and ideology are interdependent, it is to be expected that the degree to
which the structures change is also the degree to which the
ideological correlates will be under pressure to change
accordingly. To the extent that the communicative barriers
between strata are broken down, the unifying function, that
is, the integrative function of religion, will be able to
lose its critical importance. Its centrality depends on
the continued existence of the structures with which it
correlates. The central position in a society of moralized
religion is part and parcel of the societal structures that
give it such a central position. As stratification is
replaced in its structural dominance by functional differentiation, not only does the old necessity for a unifying moral-religious code become less acute, but the
exigencies of the new structures may dictate that religion
both lose its paramount position *and* that it become somewhat more dissociated from the moral codes of the newly
emerging societal structures.[22]

A shift from a primacy of stratified to a primacy of
functional differentiation means fundamentally that social
action or social communication shifts in its primary orientations from action or communication that is before
anything else the action of a stratum, to action or communication that is directed by the values and priorities
of a particular functional sphere, that is, a particular

problem area. The nobleman in medieval society will act
economically, politically, religiously, etc., but will do
so only to the extent that such action affirms the hierarchical order of the society or at least does not question
it. Thus, for example, even though religious belief asserts that all persons are equal as sinners before God and
that it is difficult for a wealthy person to attain salvation, such religious "equality" does not result in action
so as to eliminate the rich (i.e., the upper strata) but
rather in the formation of a monastic tradition that em-
bodies the religious value without questioning the primary
structures. By contrast, a very important feature of
Protestantism was the transfer of this religious orientation to a position where it was expected of everyone,
regardless of their level of economic, political, and
other social influence. That this Protestant pattern correlated with significant increases in the economic performance of the society in which it held sway reinforces
the idea that economic and religious action are being increasingly differentiated rather than the idea that economics simply benefitted from a new religiosity to which
its value system was still subordinated.[23]

     This shift in orientation involves more than the pre-
cedence of function over stratum. Functional differentiation, historically in the West, has also meant the creation
of functional subsystems, each relatively independent of
the others and yet all mutually interdependent. These
functional subsystems for political decision-making, for
science, for the economy, for religion, etc., are based
on already existing functional spheres which in traditional societies already have specific roles, specific values,
and often specific organizational structures representing
them. Thus one finds political rulers controlling elaborate state apparatuses and ruling according to some

conception of the common good, priests organized into
churches working towards the salvation of the society's
members, and merchants amassing wealth through the use of
money. For functional differentiation to become primary,
however, more is required. One dominant contributing feature has been the greatly increased development of abstract,
symbolic, and generalized media of influence, each specific
to one functional subsystem, with its own specific value-
orientation. Examples of such media that control communication in most functional subsystems are money (economic
system), scientific truth (science system), art (art system), and belief (religious system).[24] The value-orientations that correlate with such media and with the functional subsystems are based on specific formulations of the
constraints of reality under which human action operates,
and on a particular binary schema which orients the responses to the problems presented by these real constraints.
This abstract formulation can be illustrated by taking some
of the just mentioned systems as examples. The economic
system formulates reality constraints through the idea of
scarcity: there is a limited amount of goods and services.
Therefore, if someone possesses or has the use of an item,
someone else may have to do without. Accordingly, the
binary schema that is at the basis of the functioning of
the medium of economic communication, money, is having/not
having or owning/not owning. The science system formulates the constraints inherent in reality through a principle of limitations: the acceptance or rejection of a
given statement about reality by that fact alone limits
the possible statements that can be accepted or rejected
subsequently. The principle is thus founded on a system
of logic. Accordingly, the appropriate binary schema is
true/false. For religion, a concept of the ultimate
nature of reality, and in Western religion a concept of

God, formulates the reality constraints. The corresponding
binary schema appears in different forms in different religious traditions: examples are salvation/suffering and
in the Christian tradition, grace/sin.

Under functional differentiation, it is around such
structures of these and other subsystems that the most
important social communication is organized. In the present context, the most important consequence of these
structures is that, under this regime, society loses its
previous or traditional unity, a unity structured by
hierarchy and supported by a dominant moral-religious code.
In the place of this unity, functional differentiation
sets up a situation in which several value systems stand
side by side with more or less equal claims to importance
and often contradictory demands. The requirements of a
sound economy may compete with political efforts to assure the common good of all citizens. And both or either
of these may contradict fundamental religious beliefs.
For example, the demands for efficiency of economic enter-
prises may at some point contradict the political good
of guaranteeing a basic material welfare to all citizens.
In addition, both economic concern for future production
of wealth and political decisions taken to support such
economic expansion may run counter to religio-moral ideals
concerning the desirability of first helping the poor and
powerless rather than waiting for the benefits to trickle
down. Accordingly, a government may decide to allow high
unemployment if it believes this to be in the long-run
public good and more politically expedient than another
course. And sections of the Roman Catholic Church in
Latin America will oppose on religious and moral grounds
governments that seem to place certain economic and
political considerations above all others. In all these
cases, each value-oriented position, representing different

functional subsystems, can claim the importance of its
concerns but cannot effectively claim priority of its
orientation. To counter the arguments of the other subsystems, one must assume the value-orientation of these
systems in addition to maintaining one's own orientation.
To counter the political and economic arguments of a
Latin American government requires that one use alternative
political and economic arguments and not restrict oneself
to religious and moral ones, even if one is a priest.
What starts as religiously motivated action can quickly
take on economic, political, and other functional overtones;
from here it is but a small step to its *perception* as
economic or political action. Similarly, one can expect
the governments to support their positions with religious
or quasi-religious arguments, perhaps the idea that the
policies will help to maintain Christian values.

    Without traditional claims to priority, religio-moral
concerns in modern society become just one consideration
beside several others. The relative autonomy which other
functional spheres establish in the process of the differentiation of subsystems can therefore be interpreted as
a loss of religious orientation in addition to a gain for
other functional orientations, hence secularization.
Before proceeding to examples of religion's responses to
the consequences of modernization, we must examine the role
of privatization in this transformation.

PRIVATIZATION

    Under the conditions of stratified differentiation,
all the actions of a particular person are attributed to
one sub-system of society, to the person's stratum.
Under modernization and functional differentiation, the
conditions change radically in this regard. Persons can

no longer be identified nearly as much with one subsystem;
politicians are consumers, are members of families, and
may go to church; businessmen believe and vote; scientists
go to art galleries; etc. Put into different terms, functional differentiation becomes dominant in a society only
to the extent that there develop complementary roles for
each functional subsystem, roles which, unlike professional roles, in principle are accessible to everyone. Examples are consumer (producer), patient (doctor), voter
(politician), believer (priest), student (teacher).
Whereas a person can usually only occupy one of the professional roles at a time, one can and does occupy all or
most of the complementary roles.

The importance of complementary roles can be made
clearer by looking at two of the most notable features of
modern society: the value placed on the individual as the
centre of choice and the emphasis on a certain equality
among these individuals. Translated into the terms of
the model presented here, the modern ideals of freedom
and equality are expressions of the consequences of the
dominance of functional differentiation. All people must
have access to all the main functions and this without
regard for other social roles:[25] from the standpoint of
the political system, all persons must at least politically (i.e. legally) be considered equal as potential
voters and office holders without prior regard for their
economic, sexual (i.e., familial in a broad sense), or
other social roles. Similar statements can be made for
the other functional subsystems. For religion in modern
society, this feature already goes a long way to explaining the tendency towards privatization. In terms of one's
complementary role, as believer, a person's decisions will
tend to be considered according to the dominant structural
pattern and be a matter of private decision. Access to

other functional spheres cannot be affected, positively
or negatively, by the person's beliefs. Religion does not
by this fact alone lose social relevance, any more than
do economic concerns. But it does lose its automatic
relevance for the other spheres, especially the political
and economic, and even with increasing frequency for the
educational and the familial. Denominational schools are
weakening in importance and interfaith marriages are less
and less problematic.

Nevertheless, if this were the only factor contributing to the tendency to restrict religious matters to the
private domain, then one would expect religion to be no
more privatized than politics or economics. Such is not
the case, for reasons that have to do both with the specific historical development of modern society in the West
and with responses to modernization within the religious
system.

The concrete reactions of the various branches of the
Christian tradition in the West to the modernization of
their society have been varied, depending on denominational, cultural, political, and other factors. Generally,
Protestantism has been considered to have affirmed the development of modernity. Important aspects of this more
or less positive reaction can be subsumed under the heading of interiorization of the religious. The distinction
between internal faith and external acting out of that
faith was of course not new with the Protestant Reformation.[26] However, the devaluing of ecclesiastical structures, especially the idea of priestly mediation, and the
consequent de-ritualization[27] of Protestant Christianity
point to an increasing localization of the religious in
the domain of "inner" or personal experience. This development can be seen as reflecting an effort to restructure the religious domain along lines consistent with the

gradual dominance of functional differentiation. Specifically, the development of faith as a generalized medium of
communication for religion distinct from others, especially
scientific (rational) truth, political power, and love,
required the development of a domain unique to religion.[28]
Faith as communications medium could serve as the basis
for the differentiation of a religious system from other
functional subsystems also based on their own respective
media. This aim could potentially be achieved if faith
were to be seen as a non-rational (based for instance on
revelation or feeling) and experiential mode of human
determination. Under this conception of the actually
religious domain, the exterior aspects of religion would
have to be devalued to a position of secondary or even suspect importance, resulting in a relative de-ritualization
and the relocation of the *public* manifestation of religious
faith in domains *other than* the religious, for example, in
the economic sphere.

        The elimination or at least reduction of the impor-
tance of professional mediation of religious goods and of
public participation in rituals that have religious (i.e.,
salvific) efficacy beyond the symbolic reflection of internal commitment, contributed to the tendency to see religion as predominantly a private decision with no more
overall social relevance than, say, one's choice of entertainment. In addition, it is no longer simply the Protestant traditions that are following in this direction. The
increasing emphasis in the Roman Church, especially since
Vatican II, on individual conscience and lay participation,
both factors decreasing the mediation power of the priest,
can be interpreted as concessions to the structural exigencies of the modern world.

        The specific historical development of modern Western
society must also be seen as contributing, at least temporarily, to the privatization tendency. Above, I outlined

the position of moralized religion in the structures of
traditional, stratified societies. It would not be entirely unexpected if, in the gradual drift towards modernization, one witnessed a progressive marginalization of
religio-moral structures as an aspect of the dismantling
of the old structures. The history of these developments
is well beyond the scope of the present article. Here I
shall restrict myself to certain key points which touch
on the present subject. To begin, the division of Christianity into denominations in the wake of the Protestant
Reformation destroyed the old religious unity of Western
European society. Political and economic considerations
by themselves began to dictate the bracketting of religious
determinations as, for example, in the Edict of Nantes of
the late 16th century. More fundamental, however, was the
gradual undermining of the dominant stratification. With
increasing wealth, more people came to be in a material
position (i.e., with sufficient leisure) from which they
could claim communicative competence in upper stratum
interaction. The religio-moral code that reinforced the
stratified structures made possible the *ascription of the
moral capacity that defined communicative competence*. A
person was "noble" or "common" by birth. The increased
number of people claiming such communicative competence
on the basis of *achieved* moral capacity weakened and then
ruptured the old unity. The destruction of the self-evi-
dence of the question of moral capacity and ascribed social
status was an important feature of the progressive removal
of religion and morals from their privileged positions.
The subsequent retreat of this unity of morals and status
to a secondary and less influential level of the upper
strata in the 17th and 18th centuries contributed not only
to an increased marginalization of the religio-moral code,
but also to the loss by the family of its structurally
privileged position.[29]

This retreat created a sphere which most people, but
especially those in the upper strata, still considered to
be the foundation of *any* (traditional!) social order, but
which nevertheless no longer had the practical clout it
used to have. The fact that this secondary sphere was so
closely tied to morals, religion, and the family structures
reinforced the already touched-upon tendencies towards the
creation of a privatized domain centered on just these
societal structures. The word, private, must be given a
slightly more extended meaning here: this domain can be
considered as private as opposed to public in the sense
that it was and still is seen as that which forms individual persons for (at least logically) subsequent public
life. Conceived as that which makes social order of any
kind possible, this religio-moral-familial domain can be
styled as the privileged domain of socialization. And it
is here that the educational sphere enters the picture.
As a societal sphere that under traditional society was
primarily an affair of the family and religion, the functional subsystem for education that began to differentiate itself under the dominant pattern, beginning
especially in the 18th century, did so by finding alternative systemic allies in the political and scientific
systems, specifically the state and the universities.[30]
Because of this domain's close identification with socialization, it is not surprising that such a development
would be greatly resisted by those interested in defending
traditional structures, especially representatives of the
religious system.

THE RESPONSES OF THE
ROMAN CHURCH

What has been described theoretically until now can
be filled out somewhat by looking a little more closely at
certain aspects of the response of the Roman Catholic
Church to these developments, especially in the 19th and
20th centuries. That the Roman Church, in its organization
and in its dogma, was the largest part of what made religion
such a dominant influence in the traditional society that
was Christendom, can hardly be questioned. The development
of modern Western society therefore threatened the privileged positions of religion in general and of the Roman Church
in particular.

The first most apparent symptom of this developing
syndrome was undoubtedly the Protestant Reformation. One
of its greatest effects was to destroy the hegemony of the
Roman Church in much of what still had to be considered as
one society. Roman Catholicism's response to modernization
was, in its earlier phases especially during the 16th and
17th centuries, virtually identical with its fight against
Protestantism. One thinks particularly of the appearance
on the scene of important new religious orders such as the
Jesuits, whose role in the struggle is universally acknowledged; and of the increased emphasis on public education
to combat the spread of Protestantism.[31]

In the present context, the most interesting phases
of this reaction occurred during the 19th and 20th centuries. The almost two centuries since the French Revolution have seen attempts by the Roman Church, especially its
hierarchy, successively to restore the traditional order,
to compete with the modern structures once this proved impossible, and finally, to contribute positively to the
modern structures. For the moment, I will concern myself

with the first two aspects. Although I shall have in mind
both the European and the New World branches of the church,
I shall at certain points draw my examples from the Roman
Catholic Church of Quebec, first because it is this area
with which I am most familiar, but also because local conditions resulted in the relative success of the Catholic
reaction here and, as a result, some of the features of
the general reaction can be seen in sharper profile.

The attempt to preserve or restore at least the major
political feature of traditional society, the absolutist
and legitimist monarchies and their close alliance with the
Roman hierarchy, can be regarded as having ended anywhere
between 1830, the year of the fall of Charles X and the
restoration monarchy, and 1870, the year of the loss by the
pope of the papal states. It was above all during these
years that there developed a strategy within the Roman
hierarchy that, with appropriate ideological correlates,
sought to make of the church an alternative structure to
the increasingly prevailing liberal bourgeois one. This
strategy took both a negative and a positive form. Negatively, especially popes Gregory XVI and Pius IX condemned
attempts to reconcile Catholic religion and modern tendencies. Examples are Gregory's condemnation of the liberal
Catholicism of Lamennais during the 1830s and Pius'
Syllabus of Errors of 1864.[32] Among other doctrines, these
actions and others condemned the separation of Church and
State, that is, the differentiation of religious and political systems; freedom of conscience, that is, the segmentation of the religious system which, as was shown
above, encouraged the secularization of society and the
privatization of religion; and rationalism, that is, the
attempt to separate the value criteria of religious belief
from those of other societal spheres, a separation fundamental to the dominance of functional differentiation.

On the positive side of this reaction, one can look especially at the declaration of the dogma of the Immaculate
Conception in 1854 and the definition of papal infallibility
at the Vatical council of 1870. Both these were steps in
the direction of carving out and defending a specifically
ecclesiastical source of knowledge that was unavailable to
other forms of human endeavour. The pope and the Roman
Church, through the use of a medium of social communication
peculiar to them, attempted through its use to demonstrate
both the legitimacy and the superiority of their alternative. Ironically, in thus developing the faith medium
away especially from scientific or rational truth, these
actions of the Roman hierarchy were contributing to the
differentiation of religion from other societal domains
rather than to their reintegration.

Among the other important characteristics of this
19th century reaction is an emphasis on the control of
education by the church and the advocacy of a religiosity
that lays great stress on the external manifestation of the
faith. This defensive religiosity displayed publicly its
disagreement with the world around it. The promotion of
numerous devotions, especially to saints such as Mary and
Joseph; the encouragement of frequent use of the sacraments,
both the eucharist and penance; the advocacy of grand public
processions on the occasion of major religious feasts, all
were aspects of a religious style that ran counter to the
inward tendency of Protestantism.

THE CASE OF QUEBEC

This ultramontane reaction to modernization took on
particularly clear form in 19th century Quebec. Here,
especially under the guiding hand of the Archbishop of
Montreal, Ignace Bourget, the entire strategy was given a

nationalist and isolationist flavour. Under his regime,
successive laws were passed by governments, assuring the
Roman Catholic hierarchy of Quebec complete control over
the education of Catholics from the primary to the university levels.[33] Bourget and his allies saw such control as
the key to the survival of the French Canadian nation and   ·
the maintenance of a true social order in their domain.
They imported teaching orders such as the *Frères des écoles
chrétiennes* to reinforce the clerical nature of education.
In addition, Bourget not only encouraged the kind of public
religious expression just described, but also worked to
build up numerous religious organizations, such as religious
confraternities and temperance societies, in order to make
religious communication more of a presence, if not dominant,
in the everyday lives of his subjects. The temperance
societies point to another aspect of the whole movement:
the use of moral issues and moral arguments to structure
and justify the action of the church in domains other than
the strictly religious. The supposed indissolubility of
religion and morals was used to justify the control of
schools and of libraries. In the 1870s a movement arose
which virtually demanded of Catholic voters to cast their
ballots only for those candidates who supported the dominant role that the church wanted to play in societal life;[34]
Bourget waged vicious and often successful battles against
any French Canadian organization, whether it was a political
party, a literary club, or a newspaper, that dared to
advocate the liberal ideas condemned in the Syllabus of
Errors.[35]

    In addition to these features, Quebec ultramontane
social action and ideology made much of the family as the
indispensable foundation of society along with religion.
Moreover, the family structure that was idealized was an
extended family situated in a rural subsistence economy.

Ultramontane thought never tired of praising the family
and agriculture as characteristics that, along with Catholic
religion and French language, made French Canadians a
unique and blessed nation with a divine mission in North
America to preserve the true social order.[36] The emphasis
on the family, a rural economy, and religiously controlled
education helped to create a Quebec in which the problems
that came with industrialization and urbanization were made
worse because of the underdevelopment of a specifically
political consciousness, and in which compulsory education
and the vote for women were not introduced until the 1940s.

In sum, the specific version of Catholic reaction that
was so powerful in Quebec until well into the 20th century
made of this province just that kind of alternative society
towards which the European version of the same movement
tended. The contrast between traditional and modern society
in Quebec was, as it were, superimposed on the already
existing distinction and conflict between French and English
speaking cultures. Its combination of emphasis on religion,
family, morals, religiously controlled education, and a
rural subsistence economy tried to make of Quebec a revised
(in the light of the fact of the modernizing world around
it) version of a traditional society in which religion
would once again play a fundamental and unifying role. One
should note, however, that this version was almost a traditional society turned on its head: the ideological elite
(if not the power elite) was the rural peasant and not the
upper stratum noble, who did not exist here. The unified
conception of society, so characteristic of traditional
societies, was here conceived from the point of view of
the peasant, who was the one who came closest to having
moral capacity and social status identified. At least,
true moral existence was conceived to be more difficult
outside the peasant's situation, especially in the

increasingly industrialized and growing urban centres.
Moreover, the success of this reactionary nationalism made
Quebec a nation that, until recently, had control over its
own destiny only in what above I have tried to style as
the private sphere: the other major societal subsystems,
especially economic, political, and scientific power, were,
as it were, "exported" from Quebec. Through church control
over education, universities and scientific pursuits were
neglected until well into the 20th century: the research
was done elsewhere in Canada or in the United States.
Because of the distrust and even disapproval of an independent and powerful state, the Quebec government remained
weak in terms of its influence on the society: transformative political decisions often came from Ottawa even in
areas clearly under provincial jurisdiction. And because
of the distrust of industrialization and its consequences,
the economic power, already in the hands of the English-
speaking population, remained there and made of Quebeckers
a nation of farmers and proletarians.

RELIGION AS GUARANTOR OF
MODERN PLURALISM

The foregoing analysis of the Roman Catholic reaction
gives a fairly negative image of the role that religious
institutions have had in modern society, negative in the
sense of being at best defensive and at worst blindly reactionary. I wish to balance this presentation a bit by
exploring the possibility of a positive contribution by
religion and religious institutions to modern society, a
positive contribution that is discernible in already present tendencies. By positive contribution, I mean a role
that provides directions for solutions to some of the
major problems of modernity rather than trying to preserve
or recapture past glory.

For this conjectural portion of the analysis, one can
use a distinction between pluralism and what I shall call
integrism. The latter term refers to a view of society in
which all the values that support the societal structures
are seen to flow from one key domain that, as it were, takes
primacy over all the others. Traditional societal models
fall in this category: society is *basically* a political
unity, a religious community, a moral whole, or better, a
religio-moral-political community. Under this category
also fall views of society that see it as basically economic. These include many bourgeois visions, especially
the economic laissez-faire liberalism of the 19th century,
but also doctrinaire Marxist visions such as the official
positions of countries such as the USSR and China. The
integrist vision sees society as a unified whole which
must be positively integrated to keep from becoming chaotic.

Inasmuch as the integrist position is to a large degree a reflection of traditional societal structures, the
pluralist position is a reflection of modern structures.
The pluralism comes from the impossibility of establishing
a consistent hierarchy of values for most social situations.
According to this idea, rather than being based on a high
degree of shared value orientations, modern society is
possible only if the integration is achieved negatively:
by the relative non-interference of different value systems
rather than their reconciliation and unification. Since,
according to the model used here, modern society is fundamentally characterized by a dominance of functional differentiation, these different value systems would be those
that flow from the various functional perspectives.
Pluralism is therefore not synonymous with utilitarian
individualism, an idea that identifies modernization with
privatization of decision-making under the assumption that
society is basically economic. Rather it is the belief

that social and personal reality looks different *depending on which systemic point of reference one takes.* From the point of reference of a world-wide economic system based on a market, the plight of the third world countries may appear as a problem of lack of capital, lack of managerial expertise, interference by governments, etc. However, actions taken from the point of reference of this value orientation can appear as intolerable oppression from the point of reference of a political system that is segmentarily differentiated into sovereign states, from the point of reference of personal systems (individual persons) who are adversely affected both materially and psychologically by such action, and from the point of reference of artistic or cultural systems that see their orientations being wholly ignored.

The disadvantages of either of these positions are not difficult to find. The integrist position, in consistently favouring one system of values over others, tends to assume the necessity of limiting diversity in all spheres. On the scale of our developing global society, this can and does lead to the destruction of social and personal possibilities that have grown out of particular situations, and thereby to the marginalization of lands and peoples who do not have the power to impose their own sense of integrist priorities. The pluralist position, on the other hand, in not being able to establish priorities, has a problem of underdeterminacy, leading perhaps to just those fluid situations in which an integrist solution, with its attendant problems, becomes attractive and possible to implement.

It is in this context that one can envisage a societal role for religion and religious organizations, a role that derives both from religion's societal function and from its former unifying position in traditional societies. From

the point of view of function, religion addresses the conditions for the possibility of the constraints under which
human existence seems to have to operate. It is more
general than the other functional spheres: religion does
not posit scarcity and go from there but rather asks why
there is scarcity in the first place. Religion does not
simply posit the existence of a common good but rather
asks why there is good and bad in the first place. From
this more general functional position, religion, through
religious organizations, can play, if not an integrating
role, then at least a balancing and critical role in modern
society. Having played a unifying role in traditional
societies, it can in modern society hope to enhance the
advantages of pluralist structures by countering temp-
tations towards integrism, whether this integrism be done
from a political, economic, or even religious point of
departure.

       This idea may seem rather utopian. An illustration
can serve to clarify the point. Since the late 19th century, various Christian perspectives have been concerned
by the problems of industrialization, especially the plight
of the workers. The social gospel of Protestantism and
social Catholicism both responded to major problems in
Western industrialized countries, problems raised largely
by the increasing dominance of an economic system that
operated as much as possible on the basis of its own value
criteria. The attempt by laissez-faire capitalism to conceive and structure society on the foundation of its predominantly economic conceptions of the social was countered
by, among others, movements that had their source in the
religious system. Today these balancing efforts continue.
For example, Pope John Paul II's recent encyclical, *Laborem
exercens*,[37] carries further the tradition of social Catholicism by applying the religious balancing argument not only

to Western countries with their private enterprise economies,
but also to the socialist states of the second world where
a different economically dominated conception of society
has resulted in similar if not identical problems. Moreover, one can regard recent pronouncements by American
Catholic bishops on the question of nuclear arms as an
analagous attempt to counter an imbalance that is located
more in the political system.

It should be noted that this way of looking at the
social role of religion in today's global society assumes
the continuation and further evolution of the structures
of modernity as described above. As such, my analysis
assumes that the global religious system will continue to
be segmentarily differentiated into religious traditions,
and that religion will remain to a certain degree privatized, at least on the level of belief and ritual. This
statement means no more than that, failing the re-estab-
lishment of some kind of traditional society or societies,
religion will not be able to occupy the unifying and integrating place that it once did: differentiation into functional subsystems will limit the possible roles that
religion can have *on the level of society as a whole*.
Although still relevant for the society as a whole, it
will be called upon at this level only in certain situations, perhaps situations of the sort described above.

These suggestions as to the possible societal role
for religion in modern society are of course rather tentative. They have been presented here because they seem to
flow out of the foregoing analysis of the place of religion
in modern society and because one can discern manifestations
of such a role in current events. Secularization can therefore be seen to indicate a changed role for religion but by
no means an insignificant one. Privatization need not take
on the extreme atomistic flavour that it would if driven to

its logical conclusions. On the basis of the analysis
presented above, the term is a designation of one of the
features of religion in modern society, but not the only
or even necessarily the most important one. Secularization
does mean that religion is now but one functional subsystem
among others. But this fact alone does not erase the societal relevance of religion anymore than the same structural
fact makes our society less political.

NOTES

1. Although Luhmann has written a great deal that bears on this subject, major statements are found in Niklas Luhmann, *Funktion der Religion* (Frankfurt: Suhrkamp, 1977), esp. pp. 225-271; and *Gesellschaftsstruktur und Semantik: Studien zur Wissenssoziologie der modernen Gesellschaft*, 2 vols. (Frankfurt: Suhrkamp, 1980-81).

2. *Reflections of the Revolution in France* . . . (London, 1790).

3. Louis de Bonald, *Oeuvres II* (Paris, 1880).

4. See, for example *Manifesto of the Communist Party* (London, 1848).

5. Henry J.S. Maine, *Ancient Law* (London, Dent, 1972), first published 1861.

6. Ferdinand Tönnies, *Community and Society*, Charles, P. Loomis, trans. (East Lansing, MI: Michigan State Univ. Press, 1957).

7. Emile Durkheim, *The Division of Labor in Society*, George Simpson, trans. (New York: Free Press, 1933).

8. Max Weber, *The Protestant Ethic and the Spirit of Capitalism*, Talcott Parsons, trans. (New York: Scribner, 1958).

9. See *The Division of Labor*.

10. See Talcott Parsons, *Societies: Evolutionary and Comparative Perspectives* (Englewood Cliffs, N.J.: Prentice-Hall, 1966): and *The System of Modern Societies* (Englewood Cliffs, N.J.: Prentice-Hall, 1971).

11. See Parsons, "On the Concept of Value-Commitments", *Sociological Inquiry* XXXVIII (1968), 135-160.

12. See *Funktion der Religion*, pp. 72-181; and *Gesellschaftsstruktur und Semantik*, Vol. I, 72-161.

13. Primacy here means not that the other types are not found in a particular society, but rather that the other two are used only to the extent that they reinforce or at least do not contradict the primary type. Thus, for

example, Luhmann sees that modern society, although showing
a dominance of functional differentiation, still uses stratified differentiation in its economic system, specifically
the distinction between labour and management. (see Luhmann,
Funktion der Religion, p. 229). This stratification is however, at least ideally, restricted to the economic sphere
and should not penetrate to others.

14. See Parsons, *The System of Modern Societies*, pp.
94-101; Luhmann, *Funktion der Religion*, p. 234; and Niklas
Luhmann and Karl-Eberhard Schorr, *Reflexionsprobleme im
Erziehungssystem* (Stuttgart: Klett-Cotta, 1979).

15. Such societies, as exemplified in Native North
American tribal societies, are on this model seen as divided
primarily on the basis of clan, village, or living communities, even though they exhibit a certain amount of stratification and functional role differentiation. For Luhmann's
description, see "Differentiation of Society", *Canadian
Journal of Sociology*, II (1977), 29-53.

16. As is the case in segmentarily differentiated
societies; see Luhmann, "Einführende Bemerkungen zu einer
Theorie symbolisch generalisierter Kommunikationsmedien",
in *Soziologische Aufklärung 2: Aufsätze zur Theorie der
Gesellschaft* (Opladen: Westdeutscher Verlag, 1975), pp.
170-192 (176).

17. Equality of communicative potential does not mean
equality in terms of actual social influence. Rather it
means that there are no structural barriers preventing
families of the same stratum from rivalling fellow families
of this stratum for the maximum of influence available.
Thus, for example, various noble houses in a given territory
may be rivals for determining the royal lineage, resulting
in the phenomenon of dynasties.

18. See Luhmann, *Gesellschftsstruktur und Semantik*,
Vol. I, 131 ff.

19. See Luhmann, "Soziologie der Moral", in Niklas
Luhmann and Stephan H. Pfürtner, *Theorietechnik und Moral*
(Frankfurt: Suhrkamp, 1978), pp. 8-116, esp. 43-63.

20. This increase has fundamentally to do with the
introduction of writing, which made possible communication
outside of interaction situations and thus control over
much wider areas and greater populations. Cf. Harold A.
Innis, *Empire and Communication*, revised by Mary Q. Innis,
foreword by Marshall McLuhan (Toronto: Univ. of Toronto

Press, 1972); and Eric A. Havelock, *Preface to Plato* (Cambridge: Harvard Univ. Press, 1963).

21.   See Luhmann, "Soziologie der Moral", p. 80.

22.   Benjamin Nelson, "Scholastic Rationales of 'Conscience', Early Modern Crises of Credibility and the Scientific-Technocultural Revolutions of the 17th and 20th Centuries", *Journal for the Scientific Study of Religion* VII (1968), 157-177, sees in such a dissociation one of the conditions for the possibility of the development of modern society.

23.   This position is of course in contrast with Weber's classic thesis; cf. Weber, *The Protestant Ethic*.

24.   See Luhmann, "Einführende Bemerkungen . . ."; and *Funktion der Religion*, pp. 121 ff.

25.   Parsons and Luhmann both analyze this feature of modern society under the concept, inclusion. See Parsons, *The System of Modern Societies*, pp. 88-94; Luhmann, *Funktion der Religion*, pp. 232-242.

26.   Thus, from among many examples, see Thomas Aquinas, *Summa Theologiae*, IIa-IIae, 81-90.

27.   Ritual being here considered as the primary social expression of religion. Cf. Jean Cazeneuve, *Sociologie du rite (Tabou, magie, sacré)* (Paris: Presses Universitaires de France, 1971), esp. pp. 9-38; Mary Douglas, *Natural Symbols: Explorations in Cosmology* (New York: Random House, 1973), pp. 19-43, 69-80.

28.   For the problems attendant upon such an attempt see Luhmann, *Funktion der Religion*, pp. 121-125.

29.   For an analysis of these developments with consideration of the attempts, especially by moralists such as Nicole and Pascal, to forestall this questioning of the old moral unity with adjustments in the religious sphere, see Luhmann, *Gesellschaftsstruktur und Semantik*, Vol. I, 109-119. Cf. also, Guy Chaussinand-Nogaret, *La noblesse au XVIIIe siècle   De la Féodalité aux Lumières* (Paris: Hachette, 1976); Lawrence Stone, *The Crisis of the Aristocracy, 1558-1641* (Oxford: Oxford Univ. Press, 1966).

30.   See Luhmann and Schorr, *Reflexionsprobleme im Erziehungssystem*, pp. 46ff.

31. See Margaret Gillet, *A History of Education, Thought and Practice* (Toronto: McGraw Hill, 1966); and Francois de Dainville, *Les Jésuites et l'éducation de la société française. La naissance de l'humanisme moderne* (Paris: Beauchesne, 1940).

32. See Roger Aubert, "La liberté religieuse de 'Mirari Vos' au 'Syllabus'", *Concilium* (Sept., 1965), 81-93.

33. See Louis-Phillipe Audet, *Histoire de l'enseignement au Québec*, 2 Vols. (Montreal: Holt, Reinhart and Winston, 1971).

34. A. Lavallee, "20 avril 1871: Un programme électoral catholique", in *Histoire du Canada: Une expérience tricentenaire* (Cahiers UQ-5) (Montreal: Presses de l'Université du Québec, 1978), pp. 109-128.

35. Cf. Nadia F. Eid, *Le clergé et le pouvoir politique au Québec. Une analyse de l'idéologie ultramontaine au milieu du XIXe siècle* (Montreal: Hurtubise-HMH, 1978).

36. For an excellent example, see Louis François Laflèche, *Quelques considérations sur les rapports de la société civile avec la religion et la famille* (Montreal: Senécal, 1866).

37. For an English translation of the text and an analysis in keeping with the present analysis, see Gregory Baum, *The Priority of Labor: A Commentary on Laborem Exercens, Encyclical Letter of Pope John Paul II* (New York: Paulist Press, 1982).

FUNDAMENTALISM: BASTION OF TRADITIONALISM
IN A MODERN WORLD

Nancy T. Ammerman

In the world we call "modern," pluralism and tolerance are assumed. We recognize that others live by different rules, that there may be as many versions of truth
as there are observers of that truth, that what is "right"
for me may not be "right" for you. We are surrounded by
others whose heritage and culture endow them with different assumptions about life and different languages in
which to express those assumptions. We live with uncer-
tainty and doubt precisely because we have no clear,
commonly-accepted, pre-ordained rules for living.

Such is the heritage of the intellectual, social and
economic revolutions of the late nineteenth century.
After the Civil War, American cities began to boom.
Science, technology and business were taking over where
tradition, prayer and faith had left off. At the same
time, streams of European immigrants were arriving, bringing Catholic and Jewish traditions that began to introduce
a more dramatic pluralism into American religion. Among
intellectuals, an objective view of the universe was
rapidly giving way to a subjective one, and even the
trusted dogmas of Protestantism were quivering under the
onslaught of historical critical scholarship.[1] From every
direction, the world was changing, losing its taken-for-
granted homogeneous, rural, Protestant character.

And at this moment of historical change, Fundamentalism began to emerge. To many religious people, Christianity itself seemed under attack, and concerned believers

began to gather in Bible conferences and to publish newspapers, to hold revivals and to write pamphlets defending
what they saw as the historic foundations of the faith--
      doctrines such as the virgin birth, man's
      depravity, the substitutionary atonement of
      Christ, the bodily resurrection, and the sure
      destiny of all men in Heaven or Hell.[2]
To these traditional Protestant doctrines were added the
popular new ideas of dispensational pre-millenialism and
the techniques of aggressive revivalism. By the end of
World War I, these concerned believers had begun to call
themselves Fundamentalists. They were a recognizable
movement, with an organizational structure and leadership
sufficient to mount attacks on most of the major denominations during the decade that followed.[3] Though they failed
to gain control of the denominations, they were able to
capture enough territory from each of their opponents to
create a new place for themselves on a re-drawn map of
American religion. During the years since 1930, Fundamentalists have built a vast and thriving "independent"
institutional network.[4] Today that network includes thou-
sands of churches in every part of the country and the
independent mission boards, publishing houses and other
agencies that identify themselves and each other as Fundamentalist, as the Bible-believers who carry on and defend
the timeless truths of Christianity.

        One such group of Bible-believers is Southside Gospel
Church.[5] Located in a comfortable suburb of a Northeast-
ern city, this congregation averages about five hundred in
Sunday morning attendance--about two hundred member adults,
another one hundred more or less regular visitors, and
nearly two hundred children, many of whom are bused in from
distant public housing projects. Except for the "bus kids,"
the people who come to Southside are not deprived or down-

trodden. They are white, middle-class, home-owning families. They are both younger and better educated than the
rest of the community. Southside's members are distinguished from the surrounding community not by demo-
graphics, but by the Fundamentalist ideas that become
for them an all-encompassing alternative to the modern
world in which their neighbors live.[6]

CONSTRUCTING A WORLDVIEW;
ORDER V. CHAOS

The alternative world Southside members construct is
by definition a world in opposition, an orderly well-
mapped territory in the midst of an uncharted chaotic
modern wilderness. Theirs is a world where there *are*
rules, where only one truth applies. To be a Christian
is to live by God's rules and to seek to understand God's
reasons for making life the way it is. The believer's
task is to find and live by God's perfect will.

> Everything is measured against a certain
> standard, a Christian standard, and the Holy
> Spirit leads you. . . . That's what I need
> right now. I need a regimen.

> You either believe God all the way or not
> at all. Then it begins to add up. If you can
> believe him on one thing, you gotta believe
> him on everything.

> I love the absolutes. . . . I'm glad I
> serve a living God that is absolute. He has
> all the answers. I don't have responsibility.
> He gives us all the answers.

When Southside members say that God has the answers,
they mean that there is a plan and a purpose to life, an
exact plan they can understand and explain. They not only

claim that there *is* a reason; they claim they *know* the
reason.

The Lord moved us here for--there's a
reason we live thirty minutes from the
church. Why didn't God move us right next
door to Southside Gospel Church? There's
a reason we live in Westfield. Now certainly
the Forester family is not going to evangelize
Westfield. But at the same time, if we're
following the Lord, if we're in the Lord's
will, God can use our testimony in our
community to possibly lead somebody to the
Lord.

This house is directly put here by the
Lord. We were in Centerville for six years,
and four of those years I was travelling back
and forth to Southside. . . . For two years
straight I prayed and several people with
me about moving to Valley View. . . . I
remember saying to Pastor one day, "When
the Lord decides we're gonna move, our
feet are never gonna touch the ground."
And it was like that. Our house sold in
four days. . . . By the time we saw our
direction and we came to the builder, this
was the only lot left, and somebody else was
already showing interest in it. But because
we could spend just about two or three hundred
dollars more than this other family--so that's
how we got here. It was all the Lord's timing.
God's plan, of course, includes far more than where people
live. It begins with who will be saved and when, and it
continues with which church those saved people should
support, who they should marry, which job they should

hold, and what they should do each day. For each decision, there is a right way and a wrong way, God's way and
the way of the world.

In addition to individual Christian lives, God is
also concerned with the history and future of the world.
Southside members are sure that nothing happens except as
a part of God's grand scheme of reward and punishment.
Above all, they are sure that their moment of reward--the
Rapture--is not far away.

> We believe in the Second Coming. We believe
> that a lot of things that are going on in Iran
> and Israel really show that the Lord will be
> coming really soon, and I am looking forward
> to that day.

> The time is really close. It's building to
> a crescendo, with the missiles and the Arabs and
> the oil, and the rebel groups having atomic
> weapons, and the wars in Africa, and the move-
> ment of communism today.

> Just the way the nations are aligning now
> are exactly the way Ezekiel spoke in chapter 38.
> The nations are gonna come against Israel.
> And he mentions Ethiopia, Libya, Egypt, Togar-
> mah, which you know is considered to be Turkey,
> and the lands of Gomer and eastern Europe--
> Poland, Hungary, you know, all of the countries
> that have been taken over by Russia. In par-
> ticular it mentions . . . Gog and Magog,
> Meshech and Tubal. All that means Russia.

> This is all pointing to the end times.
> You know, it's hard to talk about our children
> in college. You know, I don't think they'll
> ever make it to college. I don't think we'll
> be around. 'Cause you look at the world and
> you say, "How much worse can it get?"

I have been reading *The Sword of the Lord*.
He said in the end times men would be lovers
of themselves; there would be signs in the
sky, different changes in the weather, earth-
quakes. Just see the way men are living. I
see people dancing on TV, and they remind me
of Sodom and Gommorrah. . . . I just know that
the Lord is not going to let this go on much
longer without some kind of Judgment.

The world believers construct is one in which God can
be in control of everything. He has an orderly and absolute plan and knows exactly what will happen. Life has
rules and reasons, and the believer's task is to live
according to the rules and understand the reasons. To
the extent that the individual person's will is surrendered to the Divine will, "all things work together for
good." To the extent that the world seeks to live without God, only chaos can result. The "sacred cosmos" of
the Fundamentalist is constructed in defense against the
terrible chaos they perceive in the modern world. Peter
Berger's description of religious world-building is
expecially apt:

> The sacred cosmos, which transcends and
> includes man in its ordering of reality,
> thus provides man's ultimate shield against
> the terror of anomy. To be in a "right" rela-
> tionship with the sacred cosmos is to be pro-
> tected against the nightmare threats of chaos.
> To fall out of such a "right" relationship is
> to be abandoned on the edge of the abyss of
> meaninglessness.[7]

The social constructions of Fundamentalism enable believers
to protect themselves from a world that denies that absolute order is possible. Where explanation is not possible,

God does not exist. The social world of Fundamentalism
is built on the assumption that explanation *is* possible.

LIVING IN THE WORLD:
DISCIPLINE V. PERMISSIVENESS

     In most of the everyday world, Fundamentalist rules
and explanations are treated as ludicrous. As believers
face unbelieving friends and relatives, secular work
environments, and mass media that assume pluralist norms,
one of their most persistent tasks is to define and defend
their own boundaries. They know that most basically they
are separated from the rest of the world by their salvation, and they expect salvation to make a difference.
People who are lost are headed for eternity in hell's
torments, while those who are saved can look forward to
heaven's eternal bliss. Therefore, saved people should
have an inner peace and confidence that changes their
lives. Yet eternal destiny is not an easily measured
quantity. Neither, for that matter, are peace and joy.
In everyday life, a person's invisible status before God
must be measured with a visible social yardstick.
          I'm not totally sure whether Herb's saved
     or not. One conversation when he speaks, you
     know he's saved, for sure you know. But then,
     he'll say the next day that he knows he's not.
     . . . He loves to come to service, and he loves
     to talk about the things he's learned, which
     you don't get from someone who's not saved.
     But there's a lot of things in his life that
     haven't been cleared out yet.
Believers have very definite ideas about what things need
to be "cleared out" once a person is saved.

At the heart of the matter, a saved person's life is characterized by discipline, by the ability to say "No" to worldly pleasures. Drinking, smoking, illicit sex, rock music, dancing, and going to movies are among the practices that separate the people of the world from God's people. God's people know that they must not engage in frivolous pleasures and that being a Christian means accepting God's rules, even if no one else agrees.

This same theme of discipline and obedience pervades the distinctions believers make between their families and the families of people who are not saved.

You can see a stark contrast between our home life and our habits and our ideals and the way we run our household, compared to some others.

The way believers run their households is to expect obedience from children, priestly guidance from fathers, and submission from wives. The divine imperatives seem so clear that Southside members expect anyone who is really saved to establish a family according to God's rules.

These behavioral yardsticks work together with the strict doctrine on which Fundamentalists insist to exclude not only most of the secular humanists and everyday agnostics in the world, but also the members of most other Christian churches. Anyone who does not espouse the beliefs Fundamentalists hold dear and live by the disciplined rules they embrace is an outsider, part of the permissive world in which God is not honored. Believers recognize themselves as a small minority in a hostile unsaved world.

My own family gives me a hard time about [drinking]. You know, they have different names for me. It's really important, and they can't understand why.

> When you're with someone who's not saved,
> you can almost sense a total difference.
>   When people write in your yearbook, they
> always say, "You're so different."
>   People just don't invite you . . . [but]
> as long as you feel you are right, the
> majority isn't right.

DEFENDING THE FAITH:
AUTHORITY V. ANARCHY

People on the outside do notice that Fundamentalists
are different. Sometimes they respond with ridicule when
believers insist on living by "God's rules," but sometimes, they ask "Why?". Non-believers look at the many
available versions of truth in the world and wonder how
believers can know which one is God's perfect truth. What
believers answer them is that God's truth is found in the
Bible. All anyone needs to know about life or the universe, about history or the future, can be found in the
words of the King James Bible.

> Of course, when you accept the Lord, you
> accept the Bible, and you accept God's Word.
> And if God says it, then there's really no
> argument. Our line is drawn. If it is against
> what we believe and what the Bible says, we will
> not do it.

At Southside, the words "scriptural" and "biblical"
are synonymous with "good." Sermons are good if they are
filled with references to many verses of scripture. Plans
and conduct are God's will if there is a Bible verse to
support them. The ultimate authority to which believers
turn in everyday practice is not the God of scripture,
but to the scripture itself. And the scripture to which

they turn is not the Bible as a whole, but its small
individual parts. Though members often read the Bible
from cover to cover, they find answers to their questions
by "searching the scripture" for words and phrases that
seem to apply. For instance, one man shared with an
adult Sunday School class how the Bible had helped him
make a decision. He had been worried about whether to
buy a new tent from Sears, since the last one he bought
there had leaked. He was just about to leave for the
store when he sat down to search the scriptures one more
time. He turned to Deuteronomy 14 and began to read. In
the fifth verse, among the list of animals that Jews would
be permitted to eat, he found the name "roebuck." Since
roebuck was on the list of things God approved, the man
concluded that he should indeed buy his tent from Sears.

     Biblical authority is the basis for how believers
choose to live, but that does not completely answer the
question of how they discern God's will out of the rather
massive (and sometimes contradictory) volume of scripture.
It seems at times that messages almost leap off the page,
but more often individual searching of the scripture is
guided by some other authority of more human dimensions.
And in a Fundamentalist church, that human authority is
most likely to be the pastor. At Southside, the pastor
teaches the largest adult Sunday School class, preaches
twice on Sunday, and leads the Wednesday night service.
A member goes to church to "hear the pastor," and when
they talk about who helps them understand the Bible, they
point to the pastor.

          Those first few years, you know, I quit
     wearing my slacks, threw them away. You know,
     that's it! Part of it was because people at
     Southside don't dress that way, and I had--my

thought, my uppermost thought all the time
was, "What will Pastor think?"

   At first, I had a hard time reconciling how
I was supposed to act, how I was supposed to
talk, how I was supposed to just conduct myself as a Christian. But the influence of our
pastor in Ohio helped me considerably in that
area.

What the pastor preaches helps to shape what the congregation sees as important. He explains what the Bible means
and tells the people how the Bible says they should live.
Though they are to seek God's will in prayer and Bible
study, they understand what they find because the pastor
has guided them.

   The world Southside members construct is a world
where authority and tradition are honored. Since there
is only one eternal truth, neither change nor competing
ideas are welcome. Inside this Fundamentalist territory,
there is order. There are clear rules to be obeyed and
recognized authorities to interpret and enforce those
rules. The outside world, on the other hand, is doomed
and can only get worse until Christ returns. Just as
surely as God created the earth in exactly its present
form, so God will soon rescue true believers from the
trials they now endure. God is in charge of every detail
of human history and of individual lives.

SUPPORTING EACH OTHER:
THE COMMUNITY OF THE SAVED

   A Fundamentalist understanding of the world does indeed mark the members of Southside as different. They
recognize it when they describe their relationships in the
outside world. Among unsaved people, they feel different,

as if they do not know what to expect, what to say or do.
Yet there is a place where they can feel at home, where
things work as they should. The ideas and behavior
Southside members expect of themselves and others are not
merely a matter of scriptural authority and eternal destiny; they are also a matter of participation in a this-
worldly social structure that creates and sustains this
Fundamentalist view of the world.

The foundation of the social structure in which believers live is the church. Southside provides work,
activities, and relationships that become the focus of
the believer's life. Almost no one who is a member of
Southside attends less than once a week. Over half attend
two or more times a week, give ten percent or more of their
incomes to the church, and hold at least one church job.
For the most devoted of its members, Southside Gospel
Church is the dominating institution in their lives, a
presence not unlike the parish church in a medieval
village. Though they may not hear church bells calling
them to morning prayers or evening vespers, their days
and weeks and lives are no less regulated by the church's
cycle of events. It dedicates their newborns, sanctifies
their marriages, and buries their dead. They awaken each
day to a time of prayer and Bible reading, and they spend
many waking hours telling their neighbors and co-workers
about being saved. The church provides activities for
every day of the week and work for any spare moment
between.

In addition, the church provides believers with
friendships with like-minded people. Members not only
see each other at church, they also share meals together,
go on outings together, and do all the things that friends
always do. But Christian friends can be depended on to

understand and give advice that others could not give.
Believers know about God's will, and they know how to
pray and search the scriptures.

> All through those first couple of years, when
> I first came to Southside, but was still hav-
> ing a hard time, all I needed to do was call
> Elaine, and she would just hear my voice, and
> she would say, "I'll be right there." She
> would get in the car and come over, and she
> would open the Bible, and whatever it was
> that I was struggling with or discouraged
> with, she would not back down. She would not
> let me say, "I give up." . . . She always came
> back to the Word.

These two women are still good friends who help to sustain each other. They share prayer concerns with each
other, and they work together in their spare time to
witness to friends and strangers.

Since the friendship between Christians is so special,
it is not surprising that very few of the most committed
members have close relationships with people outside.

> We couldn't have the form of fellowship; we
> knew it was different. Their thinking was
> different, and we knew that if we were ser-
> ious, we would have to change that. And we
> said, "It is going to be sad to lose all of
> our friends." But to tell you the truth, as
> time went on the new friends that we got were
> really wonderful. There were so many, and
> they thought the way we did, what they wanted
> to do. We still kept in contact with the
> old friends, but the fellowship ended.

RELIGION AND THE SOCIOLOGY OF KNOWLEDGE

I really don't see much of my other friends.
These are the girls who when I have gone back
to being burdened for them and gone back and
tried to witness to them, you know, . . . I
just don't share the same things even in what
we like to talk about or what we like to do,
so there isn't very much contact. . . . I don't
want to go to waste an afternoon talking about
worldly things.

Though sometimes separation occurs in a heated battle or
in a prolonged struggle, most often it is a gradual mutual
decision that there is no longer enough common ground to
maintain a relationship.

The story is more poignant when the outsiders being
left behind are family members.

My brother used to be like number one in my
life. He was very close with me. . . . We're
almost on different ends of the spectrum now,
whereas we were very close being brought up.
He just doesn't understand now why certain
things have to be left out, whereas I don't
understand why he has to include certain things.

When one person in a family converts to Fundamentalism,
strains are likely to follow. The situation is particularly acute for spouses. The bond of marriage cannot
easily be broken by a believer, yet differences in life-
style and priorities make marriages between believers
and non-believers difficult. Even if a saved wife learns
to accept her unsaved husband's eternal fate, she still
must chafe at the temporal decisions he makes about their
money, their friends, and their time. Though she may
abandon other worldly relationships, she cannot abandon
her husband.

A much easier separation is the one that comes
between Southside's most committed members and the secular
organizations to which they used to belong. They simply
become convinced that most community activities and leisure pursuits are not worthy of their time.

> As far as the community, the only thing I did
> was to do volunteer work in the hospital. Al-
> though it was very interesting, and I enjoyed
> it, I knew that--I kept praying that "If you
> don't want me here, Lord, just let it happen
> that I don't come here anymore." And then,
> before I knew it, I was so busy I couldn't get
> there anymore.

> I tried the Women's League, because I was asked
> to be in it, and it's something perhaps you
> don't turn down easily--it's quite a respected
> group in town--but I tried it, and as a Chris-
> tian, I really didn't fit in, not personally,
> but there were so many things that I couldn't
> be wholeheartedly for.

Believers leave behind competing activities and relationships because they no longer share common interests and
thereby establish for themselves a social universe in
which one set of ideas is assumed to be true.

The church, however, is not the only institution in
the world believers establish. The social structures of
Fundamentalism extend far beyond the local church. Southside may not belong to a denomination, but it participates
in a network of institutions that connects it with other
believers throughout the world. There are a few other
area churches that are recognized as "sound." There are
publishing houses to supply church literature and mission
boards to deploy approved, locally-funded missionaries.
Most important, Bible colleges train the next generation

of Fundamentalist leaders (and leaders' wives). They
are trusted with the purity and vitality of the faith and
are supported by the informal network of ties among pastors, churches, and institutions that comprise Fundamentalism.

Those same colleges also provide more direct resources for churches and opportunities for lay members to
take "Christian vacations" away from the wiles of the
world. Similar Christian resort facilities are located
at Schroon Lake in New York and the Bill Rice Ranch in
Tennessee, among other places. When believers just want
to relax with a good book, they have plenty of Christian
material from which to choose--newspapers, magazines,
books and tapes--perhaps purchased from their local
Christian book store. When they want to listen to radio
or watch television, their local Christian stations supply
an endless variety of preaching, hymn singing and Christian
talk. Now, with the Christian Yellow Pages to help, even
trips to the dry cleaners or dentist can be accomplished
within the confines of the world Southside members call
Christian.

Though all of these alternative structures make the
believer's life more possible and pleasant, the most important Christian institution outside the church is none
of these; it is the home. Believers are encouraged to
marry other believers and to structure their marriages by
biblical rules. The ideal Christian home has a father
whose authority is patterned after the pastor's. Prayer
and Bible reading are a constant part of the family's
routine.

Because Christ is a way of life for us, it
does enter into our daily life. So he [Ray]
does come home sharing who he is talking with,
and I would come home doing the same thing.

> Then, of course, you would have to go look up
> a verse, and you would have to go to the Bible.
> We were doing a lot about evolution at one
> time. That seemed to be our area of sharing,
> because the children were challenged with it
> in school.

In Christian homes, rules and discipline and order take
shape just as they do at church. In both places believers
are supported rather than challenged.

At the same time that adult believers are being supported in their life-style and ideas, Christian homes also
provide an ideal environment for raising believing children. Churches and homes work together in shaping the
development of the young.

> When you have a little one, you think, "How do
> I want to raise her?" So she was raised in
> the church. The church became her second home.
> She loved Sunday School. We worshipped to-
> gether always. We had Bible stories together.
> I remember when we first started, we used a
> little folder of verses. Then we had family
> devotions, time to pray together. For our
> children, church was always a place they wanted
> to be. . . . Children have a way of knowing
> something you really believe in and are not
> just saying.

The people of the church become a kind of extended family,
with relationships that carry over into weekday activities.
Church kids become best friends with each other and help
each other to learn the ways of the faith. Together they
learn that they must obey those in authority and that they
can find answers to anything in the Bible.

Church kids, in fact, begin to memorize verses from
the Bible before they can read, and they will know the

names and order of all sixty-six books about as soon as
they know their own home address. Both at church and at
home, they will hear Bible stories instead of fairy tales
and will learn more about Mary and Joseph than about Dick
and Jane. By the time they are six or seven, they are as
likely to have a favorite Bible verse as to have a favorite color, to be able to tell a Bible story as to be able
to recite a nursery rhyme, to be able to sing a hymn as
any other song. The people and places of the Bible simply
become a part of the everyday world of Southside's children.

        Yet for many parents, church and home are no longer
enough; Christian schools are needed, as well. Many
parents fear the lack of discipline in public schools and
regret the poor quality of public education. But more
important, Southside parents recognize that public schools
are repositories of knowledge that is contrary to Fundamentalist ways of thinking. The very logic of scientific
explanation that is taught in public schools presumes a
natural, human cause and the possibility for humanly-
initiated change. Evolution is but the tip of the iceberg
of differences between Fundamentalist ways of thinking and
the prevailing wisdom of the public classroom.

        Southside Christian Academy provides an alternative.
Students are taught basic skills and extensive Bible
knowledge in an atmosphere of strict discipline. Almost
all of the church's parents send their children there and
see it as a way of screening out "worldly" influences,
while maximizing Christian ones.

        I think she is going to have less options thrown
    at her in a Christian school than if she was in
    a public school, where there might be a few more
    things she might have to choose about. I would
    rather control her environment as much as possible

> while she is young, until she is old enough
> to be let go.
>   I didn't want them to think that salvation and
> the love of the Lord and living a Christian
> life was just my opinion. I wanted Sunday
> School and home and school. I wanted them to
> see as many Christians living a Christian life
> as they could. I wanted as much influence in
> their life as possible.

What parents also say is that they just like the "good Christian atmosphere" at the Academy. What they mean is that the ideas and behavior and people there are consistent with the Fundamentalist worldview that children experience at home and at church. Children are being educated within the bounds of the world they call Christian.

It remains to be seen whether academies will be effective in reducing Fundamentalism's rate of attrition among youth and young adults.[8] At Southside, about fifteen percent of church families have teens who have dropped out, and three times that percentage have adult children who have strayed. Even with an academy, the church's efforts are sometimes not enough to counter the definitions of reality and standards for behavior that exist outside of Fundamentalism. As Fundamentalist ideas and life-styles become more and more divergent from those in the larger culture, it is becoming more necessary for parents to limit their children's opportunities to choose, to isolate them from the people and activities of the world. Some children can maintain a conviction that everything outside Fundamentalism is inherently evil, but others begin to encounter people, ideas and activities they simply cannot bring themselves to condemn. In neighborhoods and in school, children are very likely to find the outside world not nearly so offensive as they had

been warned. If parents, in cooperation with the church
and the Academy, are able to isolate their children from
such positive experiences with the world, those children
are less likely to stray. But the opportunities for
failure are legion.

THE RESULTS: LIVING ˙AS
GOD'S CHOSEN REMNANT

Choosing and maintaining a life in opposition to the
world is a difficult business for both children and
adults. Living by "biblical" rules about drinking,
dancing, movies and marriage requires both inner discipline and support from a community where others live by
the same rules. Finding explanations for life's events
requires not only prayer and Bible study, but conversa-
tions with others who construct explanations by the same
principles of order and divine control. Even when the
outside world does not attack them, Fundamentalists know
that their ideas are alien to "godless" secular minds.
They are resigned to being a minority in a world that
rejects their message. Listen to them describe the
feeling.

It's almost like we're on the spectator end
of a demonstration, like when you've gone to
the aquarium and you're watching through the
window everything that's going on inside, and
you're protected from what's in there. It's
like the Lord's put up a hedge around us.

I live in this little world--my little Christian
world, my little work world, and everything else
seems sorta pointless.

It just seems like I'm in a separate world.

> It's just like a feeling in the back of my
> mind that I don't fit in with some of the
> other people . . . because I feel like a lot
> of things people do I just don't like. . . .
> I don't think it's right, and a lot of the
> times I'll get left in the corner.

The members of Southside have no desire to be part of
a world where there are no rules, where everyone lives by
whatever selfish, wanton standard they please. Believers
may sometimes use political activity to try to make the
social climate less alien, and they often seek to convert
individual outsiders and thereby to change their more
immediate social world. But for most believers, the orderly world inside is so much more attractive then the
chaos outside that they choose to retreat into the protective shelter of the fellowship. They leave behind
non-believing friends, family members and organizations
to devote all of their time to the Bible, the church, and
to Christian friends. Inside the fellowship, those who
are saved form a tightly-knit family, a brotherhood that
is distinct in belief, language and life-style from the
unsaved world outside.

The ideology of Fundamentalism is based on an assumption that truth is truth, with no allowances for human
subjectivity. All that needs to be known about life and
the world can be found in the Bible. Having taken such
a stance of ideological purity, organizational purity is
necessary, as well. Since there is no room for compro-
mise, the borders of God's kingdom must always be care-
fully guarded. So long as churches like Southside are
able to erect social structures within which believers
can live out their faith, certainty can remain alive. In
the world outside, there is pluralism, tolerance and un-
certainty--the very forces of modernity against which

Fundamentalism has always reacted. To resist those
forces, the ideas and institutions of the Fundamentalist
world attempt to provide an all-encompassing sacred canopy
for those who believe. As the outside world has become
more demanding, Fundamentalist social inventions have
largely kept pace, allowing large numbers of people to
find in the ideas, activities, and relationships of a
church like Southside an alternative social world.

But no matter how valiant the effort to fortify the
walls of the holy city, the secular world remains ever-
present outside the gate. The very firmness of belief
that makes Fundamentalism so attractive to many also pre-
vents its boundaries from bending to accommodate the
changing needs of its members and their worlds. Change
and doubt by definition bring individual and collective
walls of faith tumbling down. Fundamentalism's strength
is at the same time its weakness.

NOTES

1. Among the many sociologists of religion who have examined the modernizing trends of the last century and their effects on religion are Martin E. Marty, in *The Modern Schism* (New York: Harper & Row, 1969); Peter L. Berger, in *The Sacred Canopy* (New York: Anchor Books, 1969); and Thomas Luckmann, in *The Invisible Religion* (New York: MacMillan, 1967). George Marsden, in *Fundamentalism and American Culture* (New York: Oxford University Press, 1980), provides an excellent discussion of Fundamentalism's relationship to the intellectual and social changes of the nineteenth century.

2. George W. Dollar, *A History of Fundamentalism in America* (Greenville: Bob Jones University Press, 1973), p. 27.

3. A variety of histories of Fundamentalism are available. Sidney Ahlstrom, in *A Religious History of the American People* (Garden City: Image Books, 1975), provides a brief overview of the movement and details its relationship to the rest of American religion. Ernest R. Sandeen, in *The Roots of Fundamentalism* (Chicago: University of Chicago Press, 1970), and Marsden, *op. cit.*, provide the most thorough investigation of the ideas and structures that formed Fundamentalism. Stewart G. Cole, in *The History of Fundamentalism* (New York: Smith, 1931), and Norman F. Furniss, in *The Fundamentalist Controversy, 1918-1931* (New Haven: Yale University Press, 1954), offer special insights into the denominational battles of the 1920s, and Dollar, *op. cit.*, supplies an insider's point of view.

4. Joel A. Carpenter, "Fundamentalist Institutions and the Rise of Evangelical Protestantism, 1929-1942," *Church History* 49 (1980), pp. 62-75.

5. As is customary, the names of people and places have been changed to protect the anonymity of those who were studied.

6. For a more complete description of this church and how it was studied, see Nancy T. Ammerman, "The Fundamentalist Worldview: Ideology and Social Structure in an Independent Fundamental Church," an Unpublished Ph.D. Dissertation, Yale University, 1983.

7. Peter L. Berger, *op. cit.*, pp. 26-27.

8. C. Kirk Hadaway, in "Denomination Switching and Membership Growth," *Sociological Analysis* 39 (1978), pp. 321-337, and W. C. Roof and C. K. Hadaway, in "Shifts in Religious Preference in the Mid-Seventies," *Journal for the Scientific Study of Religion* 16 (1977), pp. 409-412, present data from the General Social Survey that indicate that about forty percent of the people who grow up in "sectarian" churches switch to some other denomination (or out of religion entirely) by the time they are adults. Since the General Social Survey has no category that accurately identifies Fundamentalists, however, these data must be taken as only suggestive.

EARLY MODERN VERSUS MODERN RELIGION
IN SUBURBAN PROTESTANTISM

Howard S. Fuller

A DEFINITION OF RELIGION

According to Robert Bellah there are five stages of
religious evolution which may be called primitive, archaic,
historic, early modern, and modern. These are ideal types,
and only the last two are particularly relevant to this
discussion. Early modern religion began with the Protestant Reformation.

> Early modern *religious symbolism* concentrates
> on the direct relation between the individual
> and transcendent reality . . . since the re-
> formers re-emphasized the radical separation
> between divine and human, still by proclaiming
> the world as the theatre of God's glory and
> the place wherein to fulfill his command, the
> Reformation reinforced positive autonomous
> action in the world instead of a relatively
> passive acceptance of it.

> *Religious action* was now conceived to be
> identical with the whole of life. . . . The
> service of God became a total demand in every
> walk of life. The stress was on faith, an
> integral quality of the person rather than on
> particular acts clearly marked "religious."[1]

Salvation was not to be found in withdrawal from the
world, but in the midst of worldly activity. The "picture"
of God as defined by the new legitimizers such as Calvin,

230   RELIGION AND THE SOCIOLOGY OF KNOWLEDGE

Luther, and Wesley was of a transcendent being who was
intimately concerned with individuals and who demanded an
activist attitude toward life.

Life is not regarded as a time of enjoyment
and contemplation but as a sphere of labor.
Business is the very essence of existence and
industry, the method of all attainment. . . .
The values of religion are regarded less as a
divine gift than as an end of a striving; the
method of religion is held to be the method
of constant activity; the conception of God is
the conception of dynamic will; the content of
the faith is a task rather than a promise.[2]

The individual today is socialized into a world which
is quite different from the Reformation period or even the
world of 100 years ago. One is now confronted with a
startling array of religious symbol systems, none of which
have claims for ascendancy in the modern world. Bellah
wrote:

It is difficult to speak of a *modern religious
symbol system*. It is indeed an open question
whether there can be a religious symbol system
analogous to any of the preceding ones in the
modern situation, which is characterized by a
deepening analysis of the very nature of symbolization itself. . . . In the world view
which has emerged from the tremendous intellectual advances of the last two centuries there
is simply no room for a hierarchic dualistic
religious symbol system of the classical historic type. This is not to be interpreted as
a return to primitive monism: it is not that
a single world has replaced a double one but
that an infinitely multiplex one has replaced
the simple duplex structure. It is not that

life has again become a "one possibility thing"
but that it has become an infinite possibility
thing.[3]

If this is the case, then a definition of religion
must be sought which is broad enough to describe the
meaning systems which people develop in this infinitely
multiplex world. A definition which identifies the existing "religious" organizations as religion is not broad
enough. Luckmann argues that recent sociological definitions of religion were deficient because only religious
organizational behavior was studied. "On occasion this
assumption is explicitly formulated as a methodological
principle: religion may be many things but it is amenable
to scientific analysis only to the extent that it becomes
organized and institutionalized."[4]

The changing symbolization in modern society suggests
that the individual must create his or her own meaning
systems in order to function in an increasingly differentiated and complex social situation. Individuals do
create meaning systems as they are socialized. Symbolic
interactionists and sociologists of knowledge such as
Peter Berger and Thomas Luckmann drew upon the pioneer work
of such theorists as George Herbert Mead as they described
how an individual's meaning system emerges out of the process by which he or she is socialized.[5]

The individual obtains a notion of the world originally from other human beings who are the legitimators of
the roles one plays as child, sibling, son, daughter,
parent, employee, student, and so forth. Each of these
roles consists of the shared expectations of significant
others. These shared expectations aid in acting appro-
priately.

As a person grows he or she develops a perspective of
reality which attempts to make meaningful the roles one

plays, bring order out of conflicting role expectations,
and to deal with life situations of death, loneliness, and
of anxiety. One constructs a "symbolic universe" or overarching value system which helps one to live with some
sense of purpose and of meaning.[6]

Human beings of course do not construct "symbolic
universes" from scratch. They are born into them. They
internalize an historically given universe of meaning
rather than construct it *de novo*. Human beings encounter
other selves who are socialized and internalize a configuration of meaning underlying an historical social
order. This configuration of meaning, as Luckmann argues,
is a world view. It is religion, and the process by which
it occurs is religious and universal. The world view
which becomes a subjective reality for the individual is
a "social fact" and an historical reality. Thus it has
a transcendent quality which arises above an individual's
unique self and exerts influence upon conduct. It is an
elementary social form of religion.[7]

The world view has several characteristics. It is
non-specific. Being universal, it has no special or distinct institutional basis, but has a domain of meaning
which may be specifically called "religious."[8]   As
Luckmann wrote:

> This domain consists of symbols which represent
> an essential "structural" trait of the world
> view as a whole--to wit, its inner hierarchy
> of significance. It is the fact that this
> domain stands for the religious function of
> the world view as a whole that justifies calling
> it religious. The typifications, interpretive
> schemes, and models of conduct contained in a
> world view are not discrete and isolated units
> of meaning. They are arranged in a hierarchy

of significance. Formally speaking, this
hierarchical arrangement of meaning is an
essential "structural trait" of the world
view.[9]

On the lowest level of the world view are typifications of concrete objects and events in the world of
everyday life (trees, eating, green, round, etc.). On
the next level, significant elements of pragmatic *and*
moral evaluation are added ("there should be no marriage
between first-degree cousins."). To this level are super-
ordinated more general interpretive schemes and models of
conduct which chart a morally significant course of conduct against a background of problemmatic alternatives
("early to bed and early to rise, keeps a man healthy,
wealthy, and wise"). These interpretive schemes in concrete instances depend on an element of reflection--as
slight as that may be--and are, typically, accompanied by
a subjective realization of the "moral" significance involved. These models and schemes are closely linked to
evaluations and prescriptions formulated in terms of encompassing biographical categories (such as "he lived and
died a man"). These are related, in turn, to a super-
ordinated level of interpretation referring to social and
historical wholes (such as, a just social order, the human
community). They claim jurisdiction over individual
conduct.

As one moves from the lower to the higher levels of
meaning in a world view, Luckmann argued, one enters a
domain of reality that is set apart from everyday life and
may be called a sacred cosmos, which originates in each
individual as he or she is socialized and which provides
a meaning system. Luckmann argued that this sacred cosmos
is part of the world view. It is socially objectivated
and is capable of articulation. It does not require a

distinct and specialized institutional basis, but rather
permeates all institutional areas such as kinship, division of labor, and the exercise of power.[10]

A DEFINITION OF RELIGION
APPROPRIATE FOR THE STUDY
OF WEST COAST SUBURBANITES

The preceding discussion suggests that there are as
many religions or symbolic representations of the Sacred
available for internalization by individuals as there are
meaningful worlds. Some religions, like Americanism or
the civil religion, have characteristics similar to the
meaning systems of primitive society which Durkheim described. They function to integrate an entire national
social system. Others function to buttress church organizations. These symbolize a Protestant or Catholic God
who stands over against the individual. But for many
today the older hierarchic religious symbol system has
collapsed. Theological belief statements developed by the
churches do not have saliency. For many, the word "God"
is empty of meaning. Robert Wuthnow, in *The Consciousness
Reformation*, says of the religious consciousness survey
(1973) that "In the Bay Area one in three no longer believes in God, and another eleven percent believe in
'something more or beyond' but feel uncomfortable about
using the word 'God' to describe it."[11] A definition of
religion which is broad enough to encompass the present
day experience of individuals who may exist in many worlds
is necessary.

Clifford Geertz defined religion as

. . . a system of symbols which acts to establish powerful pervasive and long-lasting moods
and motivations in men by formulating concep-

tions of a general order of existence and
clothing the conceptions with such an aura
of factuality that the moods and motivations
seem uniquely realistic.[12]

Bellah suggested that "religion is a set of symbolic forms
and acts that relate man to the ultimate conditions of his
condition."[13] These definitions eliminate the distinction
between the sacred and profane which Durkheim and Glock
and Stark used, but are broad enough to define the religion of those whose symbols of ultimate meaning include
images of a reality which is wholly Other. Such a broad
definition still demands some specification of the particular symbols which constitute the ultimate meaning systems
which distinguish religion from other perspectives. Luckmann's description of the development of a hierarchy of
significance within an individual's world view suggests
that values which are defined by sociologists as "statements of what ought to be" are appropriate symbols to
describe the broad perspectives and statements of ultimate
meaning which are religious.[14]

Values are preferences for some state of being. They
are "complex but definitely patterned (rank ordered)
principles . . . which give order and direction to the
everflowing stream of human acts and thoughts as these
relate to the solution of 'common human problems.'"[15]
They are a "generalized and organized conception . . . of
nature, of man's place in it, of man's relation to man
and of the desirable and non-desirable as they relate to
man--environment and interhuman relations."[16] An example
of such a value for Americans is "freedom." Freedom is
a symbol which American individuals use to define to
themselves their preference for a certain state of human
existence. It is a symbol which is taught to the individual by significant others as one is socialized, and which

functions in helping one to make choices between alternative forms of behavior. One particular value statement
is the norm which is a prescription that states what human
beings should or should not think, say or do. The norm is
usually more specific than a value though the distinction
is often fuzzy. "Loving" is usually considered a norm
but it may, in some cases, be considered a value.

Some values are more pervasive than others, that is,
they are statements of what "ought to be" which all participants in a national social system espouse. Some
values like "oneness with God" or "salvation" are symbols
for those who are socialized into religious organizations.
Again certain roles or social statuses would be defined by
such values as "a sense of accomplishment" or "equality."
An occupant of a professional work status might rank the
former high while a black might value the latter.

Value statements function as religious symbols which
help individuals and groups bring some order out of the
chaos of images--the oughts and musts--which come from
significant legitimizers. For the purposes of this
study then, religion is defined as:

A system of value symbols by which individuals
interpret to themselves what is most important
to them as they attempt to find meaning in a
highly pluralistic world. These value symbols
may or may not be institutionalized conceptions
held by family, church, state, or economic
organizations. They may or may not define
ideal relationships to the wholly Other.

SOME ASSUMPTIONS

If the generalizations of Bellah, Luckmann, et al.,
are correct, then the religion of West Coast suburbanites,

described by values, is likely to be a modern religion
which affirms self-actualization and social relevance, and
gives less assent to an early modern religion which em-
phasizes values representing supernaturalism and ascetic
Protestantism.

Furthermore, if early modern religion is salient at
all, given the relation Bellah makes between that form
and Protestantism, it would be assumed that Protestants
would assent to these values more than non-Protestants,
and that active Protestant church attenders would be more
likely than less active church attenders to hold early
modern religious values.

It is with this thought in mind that, as we move to
an empirical test of these hypotheses, Protestants will be
defined as members of the following "mainline" churches:
United Presbyterian Church in the USA, American Baptist,
American Lutheran, Episcopal, United Methodist, and the
United Church of Christ. Those who attended worship two
or three times a month are defined as "active" members,
those once a month or less as "inactive" members.

A MEASURE OF RELIGION

The Rokeach Value Survey was used as a measure of
religion in a research study of the religious faith and
practice of residents of two suburbs east of San Francisco. In a matter of ten to twenty minutes, the survey
yields reasonably reliable measures of a respondent's
value ranking.

Rokeach presented two sets of values in the Value
Survey. He argued that the distinction between preferable
modes of conduct and preferable end-states of existence
is a distinction between values representing means and
ends. A means value was defined as a single belief that

always takes the following form: "I believe that such-
and-such a mode of conduct (for example, honesty,
courage) is personally and socially preferable in all
situations with respect to all objects." An end value
took a comparable form: "I believe that such-and-such
an end-state of existence is socially and personally worth
striving for."[17]

The value survey has been easy to use in large sampling efforts. Its linguistic symbols are taken from a
cross section of the population and not merely the representatives of religious groups. It assists the individual
to replicate the experience of creating one's own value
structure, as Luckmann and other symbolic interactionists
have described this process.

Certain values are chosen from the Rokeach Value
Survey to represent an aspect of early modern or modern
religion. For example, the value *salvation* stands for the
aspect of supernaturalism in early modern religion; the
values *a sense of accomplishment, social recognition,
ambitious, self-controlled, obedient,* and *a comfortable
life* represent ascetic or secular Protestantism. Similarly, the values *family security, mature love, freedom,
helpful, forgiving, independent* and *loving* stand for the
self-actualization aspect of modern religion; *world at
peace, world of beauty,* and *equality* represent the social
relevance aspect of this religion. The selection of
values to represent these types is a logical deduction
from the descriptions and themes of these religions
offered by Luckmann and Bellah.

In order to compare the ranking of these various
values in clusters, the rank of each individual's values
representing, for example, social relevance is summed and
divided by the number of values in the cluster. The sum
of the means for all those individuals in the group rank-

ing the values is the common mean. The common means for
the various clusters of values is then compared. The
common mean for each group was obtained, and then a chi
square test used to determine if there was a significant
difference between these groups.

THE SAMPLE: THE VALLEY
COMMUNITY (LIVERMORE AND
PLEASANTON, CALIFORNIA)

Since World War II (and particularly since 1960)
white middle-class people have been settling in great
numbers in once-rural towns about forty-five minutes driv-
ing time east of San Francisco. In 1960 there were 16,058
persons living in Livermore; in 1970, 36,520. Ten years
ago there were 4,203 residents of Pleasanton; today,
18,418.[18]
The Valley is a community of people living in single
family residences with a sprinkling of apartment houses
and trailer courts. About two percent of the population
is non-white. At the time of the study, two-thirds to
three-quarters of the people were buying their homes which
range in value from $20,000 to $40,000. Many new developments were being carved from former ranchland and vine-
yards. Seventy-one percent of the people who worked were
employed in the Valley, but thirty-six percent traveled to
nearby cities and towns.[19] VW buses, campers, and tent
trailers were parked in many driveways.
The major industry in the Valley is the Lawrence
Radiation Laboratory which employs 5,800 people and has a
payroll of $121 million a year.[20] These funds come from
the Atomic Energy Commission through the University of
California. Sandia Corporation and Livermore Electronics,
Incorporated, are also large employers. There are three

wineries, some sand and gravel plants, a few dairies, a
toy factory, distribution centers for VW parts, research
operations for Kaiser Aluminum and Chemical, General
Electric, book publishing operations by Harper & Row, and
scholastic publications. The Bank of America has a
records center in the Valley, and Santa Rita Prison Farm
is nearby. There are two daily newspapers, *The Herald*
and *The Times*, and a weekly, *The Independent*.

There is a high percentage of engineers, metallur-
gists, and geologists, chemists, physicists, and medical
scientists working at the research labs. A sizeable
number of government and construction workers also live
in the Valley.

In April, 1969, a cluster sample of individuals,
living in Livermore and Pleasanton, California, was drawn
in such a way that every individual fourteen years and
older in these two communities had an equal chance of
being included. The total sample drawn was 400. The
responses of 283, or 71%, were completed and useable.

THE FINDINGS

The data support the conclusion set forth in our
first assumption; namely, that the religion of West Coast
suburbanites, described by value ranking, is a modern
religion. The values representing modern religion consistently and significantly are ranked higher than those
representing early modern religion in the total population
and in each group, by sex, age, education, income, marital
status, and family role.

As to our other assumption, is it possible that
Protestant churches are plausibility groups for early
modern religion? If this religion is held by any group,
it would be assumed that it would be manifest in those

who join and become active in Protestant churches. Here
we find that the values representing modern religion consistently and significantly are ranked *higher* than those
representing early modern religion in every group and
status within the Protestant sample. Therefore, the
assumption that the early modern religion is "carried" by
the mainline Protestant population is not correct.

This is clearly indicated in Table 1. Active Protestants differed significantly from less active Protestant
attenders in their ranking of the values describing modern
religion. There was no significant difference between
both groups in their ranking of values describing early
modern religion. Both groups ranked those values lower
than values describing modern religion.

TABLE 1

PERCENTAGE OF ACTIVE AND INACTIVE PROTESTANT
CHURCH ATTENDERS WHO SCORE ABOVE OR BELOW
THE COMMON MEAN OF VALUE CLUSTERS
DESCRIBING MODERN RELIGION

	Active Protestant Church Attenders		Inactive Protestant Church Attenders	
Common Mean 8.57				
Modern Religious Values Ranked High	(35)	74.5%	(32)	53.3%
Modern Religious Values Ranked Low	(12)	25.5%	(28)	46.7%
Totals	(47)	100.0%	(60)	100.0%

chi square - 4.20

p. = less than .05

It is puzzling that active mainline Protestants rank
modern religious values higher than the less active members. Are mainline churches, contrary to what some theorists have assumed, actually groups which West Coast suburbanites seek out to express modern religious values? Is
this a source of the churches' attraction in a time of the
decline of supernaturalism?

Mainline Protestant churches are "plausibility groups"
for a certain segment of the Valley population. Those who
are most active in their attendance rank salvation higher
than those who are less active, but the most active also
rank the values associated with modern religion and self-
actualization higher than the less active. Those who have
time and energy for leisure time voluntary organizational
activity and who have been brought up to regard the church
as a place where values associated with self-actualization
are espoused will be more likely to become active in mainline Protestant churches.

This proved true among the Protestants sampled here.
Those who had high social status were more likely to join
and become active in mainline Protestant churches than
those who had less social status. Active Protestants
differed significantly from the inactives in that they
achieved a higher level of formal education and had more
family income. To a near significant degree they also
expressed more satisfaction with the social status as
measured by education and income which they had achieved.
They were not socially deprived. But members of secular
organizations also differed from those who were not
members of such organizations in this same aspect.

Finally, because active Protestants ranked the self-
actualization aspect of modern religion high and because
Protestant churches "presented" themselves to their suburban communities as organizations which served the entire

family, it seemed plausible that those Protestants who had
been socialized into church activity by their parents would
be more likely to join and become active in mainline Protestant churches than those who had not been socialized
into such activity. This was found to be the case. Not
only did active Protestant church attenders differ significantly from the less active in that one or both parents
of the active respondents had been a member or attended a
church, but they also differed from members of secular
organizations in this regard.

The religions of mainline Protestants in the Valley
were found to be quite similar to religions of other
groups. Only when the Protestant group was separated
according to degree of church attendance did significant
differences appear. Active Protestants ranked salvation
and the values describing modern religion, particularly
self-actualization, significantly higher than the less
active. Active Protestants did have the same status
characteristics as those who were members of secular
voluntary organizations. But they differed from that
group in that they had been socialized into the church
ethos because one or more of their parents had belonged.

The data of this study indicate that, contrary to our
assumptions, Protestant churches are regularly attended by
those Protestants who espoused values describing modern
religion. They also have high social status and were
socialized into church activity by their parents.

These findings are contrary to those of some social
theorists who argue that people join and become active in
mainline Protestant churches because they are expressing
social status dissatisfaction or deprivation.[21]

However, active mainline Protestant church attenders
do rank the value *salvation* significantly higher than less
active participants. One of the weaknesses of the study,

however, may be that differences in definitions of *salva-tion* were not tested.

CONCLUSIONS

If values do measure religion and if Rokeach's Value
Survey obtains value rankings which accurately reflect the
phenomenon of religion in individual lives then it seems
evident that there is emerging in western society--if
residents of West Coast suburbs are typical--an attempt by
individuals to put together systems of meaning which focus
on personal and private social relations. The position of
the individual vis-a-vis the institutions of the state,
church, and economic order is changing. There is no
longer a Roman Catholic, Protestant, or Jewish sub-
community which is meaningful. Supernaturalism is dis-
appearing. Ascetic Protestantism is fading. A heavy
religious emphasis is put on defining the self and the
family as sacred. The old culture is fading away; a new
culture is emerging.

There is evidence of a shift from achievement orientation to personal satisfaction. Among some groups there is
a shift from the incentive structure of external salvation, satisfaction in work in vast bureaucracies, and
even political power to systems of meaning involving in-
trapersonal relationships. The placement of values such
as *freedom, wisdom* (as opposed to salvation), *inner harmony, mature love, happiness* and *self-respect* in high
position for all segments of the West Coast suburban
population points to a contemporary religious consciousness which is intensely preoccupied with authentic personal experience. This contemporary turn "within" is
intensely preoccupied with the self. This quest for personal experience, personal choice and personal authentic-

ity is not identical with the "individualism" which perhaps was salient in the 19th century. The present-day
quest for innerness is intensely concerned with the self,
but it is also concerned with intimate others in the
family or in a "family" substitute.

There is evidence in the Valley study that values
describing early modern religion are still sought by males
and older people. The social relevance values defining an
individual's ideal of community, probably redefined especially by the young not in chauvinistic nationalistic terms
but in the ideals of the original American Dream embodied
in the Declaration of Independence, still has meaning.
Perhaps some of the young are identified with and assume
responsibility for the sufferings of others anywhere in
the world, especially the Third World. What may be
emerging is a new religion of humanity whose basic tenets
are the sanctity and dignity of the individuals and the
full flowering of personality. It is in this context
that the importance of the new religions from the East
may be assessed.

This study with its emphasis on values as a measure
of religion emerged serendipitiously after the data of the
field study on the Valley were superficially analyzed.
But the new focus seems essential if the new cultural
movements are to be more clearly understood and related
to traditional findings. The Value Survey as a measure
of religion is a radical methodological approach especially when viewed in the context of traditional studies of
organized churches. But it--or something like it--seems
to be a necessary instrument for future field studies of
the emerging and ever changing religions of modern
America.

For future studies it would be helpful to redesign
some of the value labels so that comparisons can be made

and theories concerning the origins of the emerging new religions (only now being put forth) might be tested. There needs to be further elaboration of the proposition describing the preoccupation of certain segments of the population with maintaining the nuclear family.

But if religion is defined as the attempt by all individuals and groups to describe what ought to be in terms which are not completely identified with existing institutions, then some kind of methodology like the Value Survey is needed. It puts a minimum of preliminary definition in existing institutional terms and thus is admirably suited for studies of religion in a time of radical cultural change.

NOTES

1. Robert N. Bellah, *Beyond Belief: Essays on Religion in a Post-Traditional World* (New York: Harper & Row, 1970), p. 37.

2. H. Richard Niebuhr, *Social Sources of Denominationalism* (New York: Meridian Books, 1957), p. 83.

3. Bellah, *Beyond Belief*, p. 40.

4. Thomas Luckmann, *The Invisible Religion* (New York: MacMillan Co., 1967), Chapter III.

5. Peter L. Berger and Thomas Luckmann, *The Social Construction of Reality: A Treatise on the Sociology of Knowledge* (Garden City, NY: Doubleday, 1966), pp. 47-57.

6. Ibid., Chapter III.

7. Ibid., p. 61.

8. Ibid., p. 37.

9. Ibid., p. 56.

10. Ibid., pp. 57-58.

11. Robert Withnow, *The Consciousness Reformation* (Berkeley: University of California Press, 1976), pp. 86-87.

12. Clifford Geertz, "Religion as a Cultural System," in *The Religious Situation* (Boston: Beacon Press, 1968), p. 643.

13. Bellah, *Beyond Belief*, p. 21.

14. Florence Kluckhohn and Fred Strodtbeck, *Variations in Value Orientations* (Evanston: Row, Peterson, 1961); Talcott Parsons and Edward Shils, eds., *Toward a General Theory of Action* (New York: Harper Torchbooks, 1961); Neil J. Smelser, *A Theory of Collective Behavior* (New York: The Free Press of Glencoe, 1963): Talcott Parsons, "Value Belief Patterns," in *Theories of Society*, Vol. II, ed. by Talcott Parsons, et al., (New York: The Free Press of Glencoe, 1962); and, Robin M. Williams,

"Values," in *International Encyclopedia of the Social Sciences* (New York: MacMillan, 1968).

15. Kluckhohn and Strudtbeck, *Variations in Value Orientations*, p. 4.

16. Clyde Kluckhohn, "Values and Value-Orientations in the Theory of Action: An Exploration in Definitions and Classification," in *Toward a General Theory of Action*, p. 411.

17. Milton Rokeach, *Beliefs, Attitudes, and Values* San Francisco: Jossey-Bass, 1968), p. 160.

18. 1960-1970 Census Comparisons, *San Francisco Chronicle*, September 7, 1970.

19. "Housing and Population Characteristics--Cities of Livermore and Pleasanton," 1960-1967.

20. *San Francisco Chronicle*, March 2, 1970.

21. Charles Y. Glock, Benjamin B. Ringer, and Earl R. Babbie, *To Comfort and to Challenge* (Berkeley: University of California Press, 1967), p. 101.

A COMPARATIVE ANALYSIS OF THE IMPACT OF SECULARIZATION ON THE NEW RELIGIOUS RIGHT AND THE LIBERAL CHURCH

Kenneth E. Merrick-Webb

INTRODUCTION

With the high media visibility in recent years of
such religiously fundamental groups as the Christian
Voice, the Moral Majority, and the Religious Roundtable[1]
one gains the impression that the religious fundamentalists are the polar opposite of religious liberals with
regard to secularization. Secularization, secular humanism, and secularity are all categorized together and
labeled as unbiblical or ungodly. This position on the
part of religious fundamentalists is the opposite of the
liberal church's position of embracing secularization.
The uninformed person is quite likely to see the religious
fundamentalists as anti-secular and the religious liberals
as secular. This perspective is inappropriate, since
fundamentalists functionally utilize the benefits derived
from the secular world-view as frequently and as extensively as the most secular liberals. Thus as one moves
from the realm of rhetoric to the realm of functionalism,
the basis for such a perspective collapses. To demonstrate
this issue, the question of the impact of secularization
upon these two elements of American Christianity will be
investigated.

The placement on a continuum of the elements that
make up the mainstream of American Christianity can be
argued with good cause. Yet, wherever one with good

reason might finally decide to place the liberal church,
the evangelical Protestant church would certainly be to
the right of the liberal church. Moreover, the fundamentalist would be the furthest right of the mainstream
evangelical groupings. Thus, generally one can call the
liberal church the religious left, and the fundamentalist
church the religious right, when the two are being
compared.

It is the hypothesis of this paper that secularization has thoroughly permeated both the religious left and
right, though perhaps in different ways, to such a degree
that the anti-secular rhetoric of the right is little
more than nativistic propaganda that is an appeal to a
popular though no longer viable world-view. With this
hypothesis in mind let us examine these elements in
American mainstream Christianity with an eye toward
secularization.

DEFINITIONS

In Martin E. Marty's work on the three pathways to
the secular, he identifies two evidences of the rise of
secularism. He wrote, "Formal secularization . . . was
. . . when the colleges and universities passed out of
church control and Darwinism prevailed in the sciences."[2]
This historical note most directly applies to the religious left, who readily adopted the scientific world-view.
The attraction of this view for many was:

    The dissolution of the ontocratic society (which)
    comes with the modern rise of secular society,
    where man is freed from the hold of the old
    mystical, magical ways of thinking and so is
    able to venture forth on the liberating but
    dangerous path of secularization.[3]

The religious left embraced secularization because of the
conviction that:

Traditional Christianity is largely irrelevant
to the current world situation. For any religion to become and remain a vital force in the
lives of a new generation it must be remodeled
from time to time. This is especially important in times of rapid and basic social change.
Ours is such a time, and Christianity has not
kept pace.[4]

Out of these perspectives one theologian defines the
religious left when he says, "To call this church
'secular' is only to emphasize that it is concerned with
the short- and long-range possibilities of the here and
now, assuming that the best functional orientation is the
creative use of the present in relation to the past as
remembered and the future as anticipated."[5] From these
sources it is now possible to define the religious left
as this-worldly, scientifically loyal, people-oriented,
and temporally focused on the present. These characteristics help to explain why the liberal church has been
oriented toward social action.[6]

The religious right is easiest to define by suggest-
ing that it is the opposite of the religious left; this
is always their favorite way to describe themselves. Following such a lead, the right would be other-worldly,
creationist in world-view, tradition-oriented, and temporally focused on the past and the future. Documentation
of this is not difficult. For example, a prominent fundamentalist spokesperson has written:

Fundamentalists view themselves as the legitimate heirs of historical New Testament Christianity. They see themselves as the militant and

faithful defenders of biblical orthodoxy. They
oppose Liberalism, communism, and left-wing
Evangelicalism.[7]
A church historian, George Marsden, has defined fundamentalism as the:

> twentieth-century movement closely tied to reviv-
> alist traditions of mainstream Protestantism that
> militantly opposed modernist theology and the
> cultural change associated with it. . . . When
> those efforts failed they became increasingly
> separatist, often leaving major denominations
> and flourishing in independent churches and
> agencies.[8]

The fundamentalist resistance to change favored by the
left is also characteristic of the political right,
according to John Cooper, who says:

> The right attempts to retain the kinds of value
> it honors in the present, while bringing the
> future more into line with its basic values of
> economic independence and the least government-
> al influence possible in the citizen's daily
> life (especially in business life).[9]

Thus the religious right and the political right are
closely identified, and their union brought the religious
right to national attention in the 1980 elections.[10] This
political activism came as a surprise to many, as the
fundamentalists had been little involved in politics for
half a century. However, the rationale for political
activism had already been espoused as early as 1976 by
Bill Bright of Campus Crusade for Christ, in his pamphlet
entitled *Your Five Duties as a Christian Citizen*. He
wrote, "Citizenship in a free country is a blessing from
God. Our great system of self-government assures every
Christian a voice in the affairs of the nation. God wants

us to do His will in government, just as in the church
and in the home."[11]   Were it not for the political
power generated by the union of the political right and
the fundamentalists, the fundamentalists would be of
little interest beyond their own borders. However, since
this power exists, inquiries regarding fundamentalists
are increasingly frequent.

Defining secularization is more difficult than the
previous definitions, because there is no popular concept
that is readily understood with which it may be contrasted. The difficulty is increased by the fact that the
term has been used derogatorily by the religious right,
favorably by the religious left, and without precision by
academicians. Most who use the term seldom define it,
thus adding to a general vagueness regarding secularization.

> About the only thing that can be said with cer-
> tainty of the concept of secularization is that
> one can seldom be certain of exactly what is
> meant by it.[12]

Therefore, before attempting to present a working definition of secularization, a better understanding of how it
has been used should prove helpful.

Secularization has either been seen as a result of,
or accelerated by, industrialization.[13]   Thus, secularization is a rather modern phenomenon variously seen as two
to four centuries old. Howard Becker makes a key distinction between the sacred and the secular in cultures when
he says:

> Any society or part thereof that imparts to or
> elicits from its members evaluations that can be
> altered, if at all, only in the face of definite
> emotional reluctance is a sacred society. . . .
> Any society or part thereof that imparts or

elicits from its members evaluations leading to
a well-marked readiness for change is a secular
society.[14]
The industrialization of the modern world has brought
unparalleled impetus for change. The impact of modernization in religious societies is most often thought of as
secularization.[15] Therefore, one can see why Gustave H.
Todrank let the Latin root of secular, "saeculum . . .
(meaning) of this time or age . . . related to this
world," guide him when he established a definition of
"secular" as "oriented around the present world, having
to do with our own life and time."[16] However, an
etymologically sound definition does not take into consideration the ways the term is being used in differing
circles. Larry Shiner starts with the same etymology in
his article, "The Meaning of Secularization," but goes on
to list and define the five common ways the term secularization is used. He observes that secularization is
conceived as:

1. the decline of religion. (Its) doctrines,
values, and institutions . . . lose their status
and influence. . . .
2. conformity with the world. The religious
group increasingly turns its attention from the
supernatural and the next life and becomes more
and more preoccupied with and similar to the
surrounding society. . . .
3. the desacralization of the world. The world
is gradually deprived of its sacred character as
man and nature becomes the object of rational-
causal explanations and manipulation. . . .
4. the disengagement of society from religion.
Society separates itself from religious understandings which have previously informed it in

order to constitute itself an autonomous reality and consequently to limit religion to the
sphere of private lives . . . .
5. the transposition of beliefs and patterns
of behavior from the "religious" to the "secular" sphere. . . . Aspects of religious belief
or experience . . . are shifted from their
sacral context to a purely human context.[17]

These five are all related to how religious groups handle
change, and this relationship provides the needed clue to
fashion a working definition of secularization.

Secularization in its broadest understanding is the
product of the changing process brought about when the
societal context for a religious group undergoes radical
restructuring. The radical restructuring of the societal
context of American Christianity became conspicuous with
the industrial revolution. Industrialization, however,
is only a physical manifestation of the restructuring of
society that has been called modernization. Modernization
theory is an expansive theory that attempts to look at
and explain the many changes that have been experienced
and are being experienced in industrialized countries.
Thus, secularization in its most general sense is the
impact and results of modernization upon the ideological
framework of a society. For the purpose of this inquiry,
secularization is the impact and results of modernization
as it acts upon American Christianity. Therefore, to the
degree that the major characteristics of modernization are
present and observable in the religious left and right,
they have functionally experienced secularization.

CHARACTERISTICS OF
MODERNIZATION

In Wilbert Moore's *World Modernization* five characteristics of modernization are applied to the question
of the extent of secularization in a society. Those five
are the degree a society experiences (1) rationalization,
(2) commercialization, (3) differentiation, (4) technification, and (5) bureaucratization. An examination of
these five areas is adequate to reveal the degree of
permeation of secularization in the religious left and
right. To lay an adequate groundwork for the comparison
of the secularization of the religious left and right in
America, the characteristics require at least a brief
explanation.

Rationalization is the single most significant factor
in modernization generally, and in secularization particularly. Wilbert Moore said of rationalization, "By this
I mean the use of facts and logic in the choice of
instrumental behavior for the achievement of various
identified goals."[18] Elsewhere he notes that the key
characteristic of rationalization is the "instrumental
character of the process of change, . . . [or what he
calls] instrumental problem-solving."[19] Rationalization,
in its essence, is the structuring of one's thoughts
according to the mode that has led to the scientific
worldview, and by definition leaves one open to continual
change as new information affects the process of reasoning.

Commercialization has been with the human community
since the earliest exchange of material or services for
the mutual benefit of those doing the exchanging. However, when commercialization is spoken of in regard to
modernization it means, "the process of rationalization of
exchange relationships" through monetization,

because it lends itself to "careful, instrumental
calculation in the achievement of individual and
collective goals."[20] Though the religious community
seldom thinks of itself as a commercial venture, the
absence of income quickly proves beyond a doubt that it
really is such a venture. But commercialization as an
evidence of secularization would go far beyond the
necessity of money to keep the church doors open, to the
basis of exchange relationships. For commercialization
to be evidence of secularization a product/consumer
exchange relationship must be found.

"Differentiation . . . denotes the process whereby
each social sector becomes specialized. The hub is
diminished and each social function forms a distinct
specialized area,"[21] according to David Martin. Wilbert
Moore says similarly that differentiation is the rationalization of social behavior that is seen in the
division of labor and specialization of skills in
individuals and in the functional specialization of
organizations in society.[22] What Larry Shiner gives as
the disengagement definition of secularization is by his
admission really differentiation.[23] The privatizing of
religion in America is an evidence of disengagement of
differentiation, according to Shiner.   But what we must
look for as well are evidences of a marked increase in
individual specialization, a finer division of labor or
functional specialization in religious organizations as
evidence of increased differentiation and, thus, secularization in America's religious left and right.

Technification is the process of increasing technological sophistication. This is most obvious in a
modernizing society and is characterized by "deliberate
technological change."[25] The change comes about in industry as the means of production and distribution are

rationalized.[26] However technification in the religious
community may be harder to recognize until one becomes
sensitive to what may be the technical evidence of
secularization.

The final characteristic of modernization is
bureaucratization:

Bureaucratization is the process of rationaliz-
ing work organizations. The impersonal administration of specialized tasks for the achievement of clear-cut goals . . . rests on a form
of complex organization with features sufficiently common to justify the standard
designation: bureaucracy.[27]

Wilbert Moore goes on to list the features of a bureaucracy as:

(1) Purposes [or missions] are specific, limited, and ordered in terms of importance; (2)
Membership constitutes a livelihood for participants; (3) Specialized activities are governed
by explicit rules of conduct; (4) Those rules
of conduct include coordination on the basis
of differential authority.[28]

With these features in mind the question of the degree of
bureaucratization of a religious community can be approached.

These five characteristics of modernization prepare
us to examine the religious left and right in American
Christianity to determine to what degree they are permeated with these evidences of modernization and, thus, how
much they are permeated with secularization.

SECULARIZATION AND THE
RELIGIOUS LEFT

Since the religious left has never claimed to be
other than secular, the need is not to prove that it is
secular. Rather, the need to show how the left is secular
in the light of the five characteristics of secularization previously defined is the purpose of this section.
This is necessary in order to provide the information on
the secularization of the left in such a form that will
facilitate a more thorough comparison with the case of
secularization on the part of the religious right.

Rationalization is evident in Todrank's definition
of the secular church of the left. The instrumental
character of a process of change that is very goal-
oriented is clearly present. His focus upon the short-
and long-range possibilities and functional orientation
in the creative use of the present reflects rationalization.[29] Colin Williams speaks of the rise of the rationalistic approach to religion when he declares:

. . . physics [is] no longer dependent on metaphysics. The range of science now has broad-
ened until even "religious experience" itself
is understood from below by scientific analysis.
The swaddling clothes of metaphysics--of thinking from above . . .--have been cast off. The
building of human knowledge is now assumed to
have reached the point where the old ontological
scaffolding can be dismantled.[30]

Williams may have been more optimistic than the situation
warrants, but his comment demonstrates the adoption of the
scientific/rational approach that is characteristic of
rationalization.

Commercialization is somewhat less conspicuous than
rationalization, because commercialization is normally
characterized by monetized exchange relationships. These
clearly do not exist unless one pauses to ask if the
church has a product that is consumed. Little stretch
of the imagination is necessary to suspect that the
church offers a consumer product in our American pluralistic structure. What does the left offer to religious
people for which there is no extraction of a price
[normally called tithes and offerings]? At least the
religious left offers a:

> "transcendent" life [that] is no longer mystic-
> al-metaphysical. It takes shape within the
> very heart of our secular conflicts. The
> "earthly" life we put off is a narrow shrivel-
> led worldly life--the life in which we allow
> ourselves to be restricted by race, religion,
> culture and class or caste division. The life
> --in which the restrictions to human community
> are broken through and we enter into that
> truly human society in which there is full
> openness to each other.[31]

This product is the basis of the commercial success
of the religious left. The minister who offers the
"transcendent" life gets in exchange for it his/her
livelihood. The success of the venture may well be measured as accurately as any Wall Street stock fluctuation
by weekly records of attendance, income, additions of new
members, and/or building improvements. Religion on the
left is nothing less than big business. Peter Berger adds
credence to this when he suggests that the simultaneous
rise of ecumenicity and denominationalism can best be
understood, "if the denominations involved in the paradox-

ical situation are perceived as economic units which are engaged in competition within a free market."[32]

Differentiation is evident both personally and socially in the religious left when one stops to reflect that many churches now commonly have a senior minister, several associates, age group specialists, education specialists, psychologists and a support staff of secretaries and custodians. The day of the minister who single-handedly fulfills the total needs of his/her congregation is over. Even in single staff churches the minister will find numerous occasions when he/she will call upon specialists to aid in the local church endeavor. Personnel specialization of this nature is differentiation. Organizational specialization is also common in the religious left. Ross P. Scherer has demonstrated just how common is organizational specialization and complexity in the work he edited that presented a sociological view of American denominational organization. He argues, "because modern society is complex and changing, denominations too become complex and must continually face 'dilemmas' which require adjustments in goals and strategies for mission."[33] The United Methodist dual mode of organization is how one denomination has faced the complexity of modern society. "The conference system on the one hand and the episcopacy on the other hand"[34] has led to a very complex organizational structure. Other denominations have had different organizational strategies, but the end result has been to increase the organizational structure and complexity to face the "dilemmas" of modern life.

Technification is evidenced by such simple things as the telephone in the church office, the minister's electronic pager, the office machines used each week, the sound system in the sanctuary, and/or the total inability

262   RELIGION AND THE SOCIOLOGY OF KNOWLEDGE

of most churches to operate without electricity. But
these evidences are common to nearly every church. Less
common illustrations may be the larger church's use of
computer services in its membership records, accounting,
and mailings. Other examples are as plenteous as one
cares to notice. The things that have been culturally
taken for granted are, in actuality, technification.

Bureaucratization is most evident where organizational differentiation exists. This is certainly true on the
religious left. Gary P. Burkart reveals the degree of
bureaucratization in the United Methodist Church, for
example, when he says:

> The bureaucratization of Methodism has taken
> place chiefly through the elaboration of the
> agency structure and concomitant attempts to
> create a unified convention-agency-conference
> program.[35]

The same rationality that has affected Methodist ideology
has affected Methodist organizational structures as well.
This rationality has often resulted in schisms, realign-
ments, and organizational shifts which have impacted the
structures also. Thus, in this example, bureaucratization has been a developing phenomenon. Paul Harrison
has documented a similar development and rise in the
bureaucracy of the American Baptist Convention.[36]

Each of these five characteristics of modernization
reveals how the religious left has been impacted by
secularizing influences. Where these influences have
caused changes in the activities and/or structure of the
organizations of the religious left, there is evidence for
the process of secularization.

SECULARIZATION AND THE
RELIGIOUS RIGHT

The religious right would undoubtedly object to the
way secularization has been defined here by placing it in
the larger context of modernization. Such a definition
will lead to the conclusion that the religious right is
deeply modern and, thus, deeply secular. The religious
right is opposed to what they call secular humanism, a
modern ideology that starts with humanity as its primary
concern rather than God. Such a perspective, the religious right suggests, caused the fall of the Roman Empire,
is inspired by Communists, and is responsible for all
moral decline in America.[37] The religious right is
opposed to secularism as an ideology, but not to modern
technology. However, it is a risk that the religious
right takes when it embraces modern technology, for
modern technology and modernization are too entwined to
separate. Such an embrace exposes the right to the
rationalistic/scientific method of thought that is required to maintain and extend the applications of modern technology. Thus, in looking for the evidences of modernization in the religious right, it is necessary to look at
more than just the ideological realm.

Rationalization as the use of facts and logic in the
choice of instrumental behavior for the achievement of
specific goals is central to the modern scientific method.
One might suppose the religious right to be opposed to
this kind of thinking. However, persons of the right think
in the same manner as their contemporary peers; the only
difference is that they start their logic with a different
set of presuppositions. The persons of the right are
quite rational after taking a faith stance that believes:

1. The inspiration and infallibility of
scripture.
2. The deity of Christ (including His
virgin birth).
3. The substitutionary atonement of Christ's
death.
4. The literal resurrection of Christ from the
dead.
5. The literal return of Christ in the Second
Advent.[38]

Rational logic and the distinctive presuppositions of
their faith stance have produced a binding, biblical
systematic theology that is basic and foundational in
the thinking of persons of the religious right. Growing
out of this foundation are additional evidences of
rationalization. The goal-oriented method of missions
and evangelism is one. The classification of persons into categories of "lost" or "saved" is another. The
measuring of ecclesiastical success in terms of the number
of converts, the increase in one's budget or the size of
one's physical plant is a rationalistic approach to
religious life.

Commercialization is evident in the religious right
in all the ways it was evident in the religious left. But
the religious right has a much more concrete product, thus
it is much more commercial in selling its product. The
right criticizes the left because, "they placed Christian
'nurture' above confrontational evangelism and promoted
an experience of Christianity that was not dependent upon
any biblical verification."[39] Confrontational evangelism
has a measurable response: yes or no. To get the correct
response (i.e.: yes), many business techniques have been
used. An example of this was the 1975 "Here's Life,
America!" campaign that combined the persuasiveness of

motivational psychology, telephone sales techniques,
mass advertising, computer analysis and aids, and multi-
media follow-up. Every technique of commercial advertising has been used by the right, even explicit sex, however negatively it has been treated. One fund raising
effort gave examples of the moral decay threatening
Christian America

> All these perceived threats are what Madison
> Avenue would call "sexy." The discussion of
> them, especially the obligatory "horrible"
> examples, provide an opportunity for sexual
> fantasizing and titillation--for tickling the
> dirty little secret. . . . These sexy issues
> are not new, nor are the highly successful
> efforts of Right-wing religion to capitalize
> on them and their attendant guilt feelings.[41]

The misrepresentation of facts has also been suggested by
ex-Senator Thomas J. McIntyre, who accused the political
right and its associated fundamentalists of duplicity and
deceit in the successful campaign that ousted him from
office.[42] If any commercial tool or tactic is justified
by the end it produces, then the religious right is no
less commercial than any other American business enterprise. The commerciality of the right is obvious when
one realizes that Jerry Falwell and Pat Robertson take
in more money annually than do the Republican and
Democratic parties combined.[43]

Differentiation is similar to commercialization in
that it is applicable to the religious right in the same
ways previously mentioned for the religious left. The
differences are basically two. One, personnel specialization is more evident on the right. Fundamentalists have
engaged in specialization since their earliest days. The
separate ministries assigned to pastors, evangelists,

music or song leaders, educators and church executives
have some overlap, but are mutually exclusive in their
most typical expressions. More recently, specialization
has grown rapidly since fundamentalists, ". . . have
enjoyed almost complete domination of the media--
particularly radio and television."[44] Their need of
technologically sophisticated specialists has grown with
the media industry. Large independent ministries such as
Jerry Falwell's, Bill Bright's and Robert Billing's use
computers extensively.[45] This usage also necessitates
additional specialization. Also, the religious right is
largely comprised of autonomous religious bodies that
cooperate around single-issue political concerns. This
has generated a whole new area of specialization within
the ranks of the right. The rapid growth of this area
of specialization has impacted the entire political scene
in the United States. Thus, in these two broad areas
differentiation is more pronounced than was observed with
the religious left.

Technification on the part of the religious right
has been foreshadowed in the section dealing with
commercialization. Jeffery K. Hadden and Charles E. Swann
make it clear just how far technification has developed
with the right in their critical look at the religious
right called *Prime Time Preachers: The Rising Power of
Televangelism.* Satellites on the cutting edge of the
communications industry are beaming the "old-time gospel"
to every part of the globe. Certainly, not every group
on the religious right has such sophistication, but many,
if not most, accept the electronic success of the "Old-
Time Gospel Hour" and the "700 Club" as normative. That
acceptance and the American drive to be successful has
produced a situation where, "Every format of secular
television entertainment is being used in the electronic

church today, with the possible exception of comedy."⁴⁶
Televangelism is a prime evidence of technification. The
extensive use of computers is another prime example.
Computers have added a whole new dimension to fund raising. Computer-personalized letters in direct-mail
campaigns are common to every large evangelistic ministry,
all television ministries, and the successful political
activities of the religious right. A final example of
technification is the sophisticated use of public relations firms to help design everything from evangelistic
campaigns, to educational programs, to fund raising
efforts.

Bureaucratization is perhaps less obvious on the
religious right than it is on the left. However there are
several forces within the religious right that are causing real growth in this area. Single-issue political
concerns have generated much new organizational specialization which is already taking the form of bureaucratization. Even though such groups as the Moral Majority
claim not to be religious, their inherent bureaucracy is
aligned with the religious right. Armentrout even claims
that the Moral Majority is in reality a right-wing
religious body since in the media it is most frequently
listed with such groups.⁴⁷ It is a case of how a group is
functioning. The power of the Moral Majority is political,
the appeal of the Moral Majority is religious. Further,
L.J. Davis says of the organizational coalition of the
right, "It is so tight-knit, in fact, that any diagram of
its organization looks like an octopus trying to shake
hands with itself, so completely interlocked are the
directorates of its various components."⁴⁸ Thus, the
political aspects and the religious aspects of the right
are so connected as to discount the claim that such groups
as the Moral Majority are not religious. Therefore, the

organizational development of the political-religious
right must be included in an examination of bureaucratization. A second force that is causing bureaucratization
is the commitment on the part of persons of the religious
right to non-public educational alternatives. Their
commitment to such education is to perpetuate their movement, which is a bureaucratic drive:

> One of the most important requirements for the
> perpetuation of any movement is that the move-
> ment provide an opportunity for the training
> of new leaders. Any organization that fails to
> prepare and train new leadership will ultimate-
> ly deteriorate and die.[49]

Because of this type of conviction, new educational
ventures from kindergarden up are being initiated with
increasing regularity by the right. A third force, though
on a smaller scale than the previous two, is quite powerful. The democratic structures in the church organizations among the religious right have certain built-in
bureaucratic elements. This is particularly evident
among paid staff members where differentiating authority
is the context for all operation. Among unpaid church
workers the bureaucratic power of the committee is
abundantly evident. Thus, from the microcosm of the local
church to the macrocosm of national organizations, bureaucratic growth is being experienced by the religious right.

CONCLUSION

The most obvious conclusion that one can draw from
this study is that both the religious left and right show
significant evidences of functional secularization. The
study has demonstrated that the left and right manifest
about equal evidences of rationalization. The left man-

ifests greater evidences of bureaucratization. The right manifests greater evidences of commercialization, differentiation and technification. Thus in one category of characterization the religious left and the right are basically equal, in one category the left leads the right, and in three categories the right leads the left. Therefore, the religious right manifests an over-all picture of greater secularization than does the religious left.

Even though the religious left has embraced the secular, it has evidence of secularization in fewer areas than does the religious right. This makes it clear that the antisecular rhetoric of the religious right is just that--rhetoric.

NOTES

1. Donald S. Armentrout, "The New Religious Right,"
St. Luke's Journal, Vol. 25, No. 1, December 1981, p. 19.

2. Martin E. Marty, *The Modern Schism: Three Paths
to the Secular*, New York: Harper and Row, 1969, p. 117

3. Colin Williams, *Faith in a Secular Age,* New York:
Harper and Row, 1966, p. 31.

4. Gustave H. Todrank, *The Secular Search for a New
Christ*, Philadelphia: Westminster Press, 1969, p. 7.

5. Ibid., p. 75.

6. John C. Cooper, *The Turn Right*, Philadelphia:
Westminster Press, 1970, pp. 12-16.

7. Jerry Falwell with Ed Dobson and Ed Hindson, *The
Fundamentalist Phenomenon: The Resurgence of Conservative
Christianity*, Garden City, NY: Doubleday, 1981, pp. 1-2.

8. George Marsden, "Fundamentalism as an American
Phenomenon: A Comparison with English Evangelicalism,"
Church History 46, June 1977, pp. 215, 216.

9. John C. Cooper, p. 16.

10. "New Right Tops 1980 Religious News," *Christian
Century*, 31 December, 1980, p. 1283.

11. Donald S. Armentrout, p. 15.

12. Larry Shiner, "The Meanings of Secularization,"
Secularization and the Protestant Prospect, James F.
Childress and David B. Harned, eds., Philadelphia:
Westminster Press, 1970, p. 30.

13. David Martin, *A General Theory of Secularization*,
Oxford: Basil Blackwell, 1979, p. 83.

14. Howard Becker, "Current Sacred-Secular Theory and
its Development," *Modern Sociological Theory in Continuity
and Change*, Howard Becker and Alvin Boskoff, eds., New
York: Dryden Press, 1955, p. 142.

15. David Martin, pp. 83-91.

16. Gustave H. Todrank, p. 40.

17. For a detailed explanation of the five meanings of secularization see Larry Shiner, pp. 30-42.

18. Wilbert E. Moore, *World Modernization: The Limits of Convergence*, New York: Elsevier, 1979, p. 1.

19. Ibid., pp. 29, 30.

20. Ibid., pp. 33, 35.

21. David Martin, p. 69.

22. Wilbert E. Moore, pp. 46-57.

23. Larry Shiner, p. 38.

24. Ibid.

25. Wilbert E. Moore, p. 63.

26. Ibid., p. 64.

27. Ibid., p. 90.

28. Ibid., pp. 93-94.

29. Gustave H. Todrank, p. 75.

30. Colin Williams, *Faith in a Secular Age*, New York: Harper and Row, 1966, p. 42.

31. Ibid., p. 81.

32. Peter Berger, "A Market Model for the Analysis of Ecumenicity," *American Mosaic: Social Patterns of Religion in the United States*, Philip E. Hammond and Benton Johnson, eds., New York: Random House, 1970, p. 179.

33. Ross P. Scherer, *American Denominational Organization: A Sociological View*, Pasadena, CA: William Carey Library, 1980, p. 2.

34. Gary P. Burkart, "Patterns of Protestant Organization," *American Denominational Organization: A Sociological View*, Ross P. Scherer, ed., Pasadena, CA: William Carey Library, 1980, p. 65.

35. Ibid., p. 66.

36. Paul M. Harrison, *Authority and Power in the Free Church Tradition*, Princeton: Princeton University Press, 1959.

37. Homer Duncan, *Secular Humanism: The Most Dangerous Religion in America*, Lubbock, Texas: Christian Focus on Government, 1979, p. 5.

38. Falwell, Dobson and Hindson, p. 7.

39. Ibid., p. 23.

40. Donald S. Armentrout, pp. 13-14.

41. Sue Hiatt and Carter Heyward, "Right-wing Religion's 'Dirty Little Secret'," *Witness* 64, 1979, p. 10.

42. Thomas J. McIntyre with John C. Obert, *The Fear Brokers*, New York: Pilgrim Press, 1979, p. 88.

43. Falwell, Dobson and Hindson, P. 1.

44. Ibid., p. 19.

45. See Donald S. Armentrouts' article for details.

46. Jeffery K. Hadden and Charles E. Swann, *Prime Time Preachers: The Rising Power of Televangelism*, Reading, Massachusetts: Addison-Wesley, 1981, p. 19.

47. See Donald S. Armentrout's article for details, p. 22.

48. "Conservatism in America," *Harpers*, October 1980, p. 21.

49. Falwell, Dobson and Hindson, p. 20.

TUMBLED OUT OF THE UNIVERSAL EGG

Jan Sumner

In the beginning, Eurynome, the Goddess
of All Things, rose naked from Chaos, but
found nothing substantial for her feet to rest
upon, and therefore divided the sea from the
sky, dancing lonely upon its waves. She danced
toward the south, and the wind set in motion
behind her seemed something new and apart with
which to begin a work of creation. Wheeling
about, she caught hold of this north wind,
rubbed it between her hands, and behold! the
great serpent Ophion. Eurynome danced to
warm herself, wildly and more wildly, until
Ophion, grown lustful, coiled about those
divine limbs and was moved to couple with her,
. . . Eurynome was likewise got with child.

Next, she assumed the form of a dove,
brooding on the waves and, in due process of
time, laid the Universal Egg. At her bidding,
Ophion coiled seven times about this egg, until
it hatched and split in two. Out tumbled all
things that exist, her children: sun, moon,
planets, stars, the earth with its mountains
and rivers, its trees, herbs, and living
creatures.[1]

"Out tumbled all things that exist . . . ," including
women minsters. For those who are children of a rational,
practical, technological world, a Greek myth of the creation of clergywomen will have a few shortcomings. Perhaps
a more recent and "scientific" explanation of the appear-

ance of women in the ministry would be more appealing.
How might the discipline of the Sociology of Knowledge
account for the "being-in-the-world" of clergywomen?

In a book written just prior to the time when Naziism
destroyed the liberal Weimar Republic of Germany, Karl
Mannheim suggested that each individual was a product of
his or her social milieu. Each person is predetermined by
the "situation" into which she or he is born, and by the
"preformed patterns of thought and action" which surround
her/him in their culture. Mannheim asserted that a modern
theory of knowledge assumes spheres of thought in which we
cannot even conceive of a truth that would be independent
of the person's values, ". . . and unrelated to the social
context."[2]

According to Mannheim, morality, ethics, or such
fundamental concepts as duty and sin are correlatives of
"distinct social situation."[3] He writes: "We must realize
once and for all that the meanings which make up our world
are simply an historically determined and continuously
developing structure in which man develops, and are in no
sense absolute."[4] He also believed thought to be dynamic
and relational rather than static.

Mannheim's work both paralleled and contrasted with
that of another German thinker who later became known as
the father of *Wissenssoziology*, the Sociology of Knowledge.
This scholar, Max Scheler, published a classic work entitled *Problems of a Sociology of Knowledge* in 1924.
According to Kenneth Stikkers, who introduces Scheler to
the English reading public, the fundamental principle of
the Sociology of Knowledge as conceived by Scheler is
that, ". . . the forms [vis., not the contents] of mental
acts, through which knowledge is gained, are always, *by
necessity*, co-conditioned sociologically, i.e., by the
structure of society."[5]

Max Scheler was aware of the narrowness of the
positivistic sociology of his day, particularly as set
forth by August Comte. He began his analysis of groups,
therefore, with a phenomenological investigation ". . .
into those subjective, experiential, psychic bonds that
unite unique, individual *persons* in feelings of love and
sympathy."[6] Somewhat influenced by Buddhist thought,
Scheler sought to use phenomenology as a technique. He
believed that a growing, becoming tendency permeated all
of nature, not in a random or chaotic way, but in a
striving toward spiritualization. This striving would
project its own "ability-to-be" ahead of itself as a
"phantasmic image."[7] Accordingly, he

> . . . sought to show, through phenomenological
> analysis of concrete moral acts, that organic
> drive-life, in its process of be-coming and
> tendency towards increasing spiritualization,
> strives to realize itself according to an
> *absolute hierarchy of values*, which he calls
> the "ordo amoris," or order of the heart; that
> is to say, vital drive is always value-intended.[8]

Instead of tumbling out of the Universal Egg, a young
woman considering the ministry might be following her
"ordo amoris," projecting her "ability-to-be" ahead of
herself. Another possibility would be that she comes
from a family in which her mother or father is a professional minister. Wilbert E. Moore says, "A very dis-
proportionate number of professionals come from families
with professional fathers."[9] For her own reasons, the
young woman decides to enter the full-time ministry. Is
that all there is to it?

Not quite. After all, this is a man's world. Most
men are identified by the work they do rather than the
person they are. Many jobs and professions are gender-

oriented: nurses and teachers are women; doctors and
lawyers are men. The social order tells us which position is appropriate for the male, and which is suitable
for the female. Traditionally the ministry has been exclusively the domain of the male. Scheler writes, "The
political society is the beginning of the formation of
classes and the beginning of large-scale suppression of
animistic, matriarchal cults and womanhood. Religions of
founders are of express *male* and *mental* origins."[10]

A somewhat more contemporary sociologist, Richard
Hall, stated in 1969, "In light of the traditional role
expectation that the woman's place is in the home, those
who deviate from this expectation, at least to the degree
that they have outside employment, might need a higher
level of dedication to their occupation as a motivational
source."[11]   Determination will be a necessary characteristic of the woman who wishes to be a minister. Even as
mainline denominations today prepare for growing numbers
of women seminarians, the Moral Majority, Total Womanhood,
and Women Aglow movements experience increasing popularity
as movements of opposition to the feminist thrust.

Whether or not it is a man's world, a young woman
entering the ministry must prepare for the world of work.
Scheler thought the concept of work was changed when the
early Christians accepted the Jewish view of the Godhead.
He writes:

This conception brought with it a positively
creative God of "Work," who "made" the world
in seven days, and a new evaluation of work,
which first pertained only to an attitude of
the mind. . . . The twofold ordinance, "Work,
but do not enjoy," which spread from Christian
orders into the layman's world, is the origin
of the systematic *tendency to collect* riches,

the first form of the capitalist will to
acquisition.[12]

Richard Hall provides an even more interesting history of the meaning of work. Apparently the definition
has evolved over the ages. Hall cites a book by Adriano
Tilgher entitled, *Work: What It Has Meant to Men Through
the Ages*. Tilgher has discovered that manual labor was
considered a curse by the ancient Greeks, although intellectual "work" was a bit more respectable. The Romans had
a similar view. The early Hebrew people agreed, but
". . . with the additional rationale that work was drudgery
because it was the way in which man could atone for the
original sin. At the same time, work received a slightly
higher meaning in that it was a way by which spiritual
dignity could be captured." The Christian meaning of work
was essentially the same as the Hebrews, except they added
the notion that the fruits of one's labor could be shared
with those who were less fortunate. "The doctrine that
idleness was akin to sinfulness also appeared during this
era."[13]

Work in itself had no intrinsic meaning; it was simply
a means to other, loftier ends. This definition continued
through the Middle Ages, with the Reformation bringing a
slight change. "Luther saw work as a form of serving God.
Whatever a person's occupation, if the work were performed
to the best of one's ability, it had an equal spiritual
value with other forms of work." Calvin added a new notion: people should work for profits which could be invested in new ventures for more profits, and so on. "An
additional, important aspect of Calvinist doctrine was that
man had an obligation to God to attempt to achieve the
highest possible and most rewarding occupation. Thus
striving for upward mobility is morally justified."[14] The
importance of looking at this review of the history of work

lies in the possibility that some of these concepts influence motives for working within the church today. A
young woman following her heart may also find one of
these values hidden there.

If she does not, Victor Vroom offers other possibilities in *Work and Motivation*. He suggests the following
motives:

1. Wages, or financial remuneration. This, he says,
is an "indisputable source of the desire of people to
work." If we are to have bread to eat, we must pay for it.

2. Expenditure of physical and/or mental energy.
Vroom writes, ". . . good evidence suggests that some
energy expenditure is satisfying rather than dissatisfy-
ing." And, ". . . the need for activity probably has
both a physiological and learned basis, though the interplay between the two factors has not yet been examined
systematically."[15]

Other motives suggested by Vroom include (3) satisfaction derived from the production of goods and services, (4) social interaction that affords the opportunity
to have influence over others, and to be liked or controlled by others, and (5) social status. Hall states
that, ". . . occupations are perhaps the single best de-
terminant of social status."[16]

Edward Gross makes the interesting observation that
professionals are not believed to be interested in sordid
money. "While this supposition is probably unwarranted in
practice, the point is that the professional is thought to
be one who would work just for the intrinsic rewards of
his occupation."[17] This may be a prevalent myth among the
laity, but the fact is that most United Methodist ministers
who are males keep close tabs on the amount of salary
drawn by their colleagues.

The facts may be different for women. In their book
Women of the Cloth, Carroll, Hargrove, and Lummis indicate
that women clergy seem more satisfied with their salary
than men.[18] The authors speculate on the possible reasons
for the difference in salary expectations and conclude that
the difference may lie in the person's reference group.
Women in ministry do not use clergymen as their reference
group. Instead, they base their expectations on the stories and experiences of "pioneer" women clergy. The
authors write,

> With earlier women clergy as their reference
> group, the women in our study did not expect
> their rewards to be great, and therefore they
> express relative satisfaction with what they
> have found. Had they made clergymen their
> reference group (or *when* they make clergymen
> their reference group) their anger might have
> been (or *will be*) quite different.[19]

If the young woman realizes the salary situation and
still determines to strive for the ministry, her pil-
grimage will be a long one. Most churches and/or minis-
terial organizations expect an aspirant to the ministry
to complete a seminary education. Wilbert Moore asserts
that, "In most established fields the professional schools
act as the first formal gatekeepers: in setting admission
standards, standards for performance in the course of
training, and requirements for the appropriate degree."
Furthermore,

> no less a sociological observer than Max
> Weber, several decades ago, noted the success-
> ful attempts of various occupational groups
> to use diplomas and certificates as their
> claim to position and remuneration quite apart
> from useful work done. And, with quiet but

acidulous perception, Weber doubted the relative influence of a thirst for education as
compared with a "desire for restricting the
supply of these positions and their monopo-
lization by the owners of educational certifi-
cates."[20]

Of course, a young woman must meet the requirements
and standards of the seminary prior to embarking on the
educational aspects of her chosen field. She might even
possess a true "thirst for knowledge." At the same time,
she is made aware that in some denominations the supply of
churches is not as great as the supply of candidates for
the ministry. This means that not everyone will achieve
his/her goal. One way of diminishing the supply of young
hopefuls is to make the requirements for the educational
degree ever more demanding and difficult. She "girds up
her loins" and enters seminary.

What the neophyte discovers in her new environment
will depend a great deal on the institution. Some seminaries have a more formal atmosphere than others. Some
are conservative, some liberal; some highly regulated,
some relaxed; some with compulsory chapel, and others
without. Male chauvinism will be more or less conspicuous wherever she goes. The beginner is in seminary to
learn, however, so she is most interested in the class
work that will be required in order to be a good pastor.
What does she find?

According to Moore, she is likely to encounter a
somewhat irrational mixture of several components. They
include:

1. Those things which the professors have learned.
This content is necessarily a collegiate generation
earlier, "and usually a full biological generation gone
into antiquity."

2. Those things which certifying and/or qualifying
authorities believe should be known. ". . . for a variety
of not very subtle reasons, the persons serving on review
or certifying committees are likely to represent a full
biological generation--or more--in ascendancy over the
new aspirants."

3. Whatever else the professional school faculty
thinks is appropriate for the training of future professionals. "It should surprise no one that conservatism is
the norm and innovation the exception in professional
education."[21]

In his own irascible way, Moore continues:
Irrelevant knowledge abounds in every established field. It is scarcely surprising
that "abstract" and "irrelevant" should get
confused, and that those who claim professional standing command, and demand of
neophytes, irrelevant knowledge that has no
abstract, and therefore inferential, value.[22]

The clergy "neophyte," however, is convinced that she
is indeed shaped by her surroundings, and so she enters
wholeheartedly into each class that can be squeezed into
her schedule, integrating the experience to the best of
her ability. Berger and Luckmann would express it this
way: "While it is possible to say that [wo]man has a
nature, it is more significant to say that [wo]man constructs [her] own nature, or more simply that [wo]man
produces [herself]."[23]

Class work alone does not a minister make. The young
woman finds that attending seminary full-time tends to
remove her from the world of "reality." She feels insu-
lated from both the pain and the celebration of the "real
world." She hardly has time to read the daily paper, let
alone get together with friends from her "previous life."

She is sheltered, encapsulated, wrapped in a cocoon where
metamorphosis occurs. Moore believes that theological
schools, like military academies, set persons apart from
normal social activities. This "setting apart" can
happen in a variety of ways, including "the sheer burden
of work demanded of students."[24]

Moore calls this concept the "punishment-centered
theory of socialization." He writes:

> The initiate is put through a set of tasks
> and duties that are difficult, and some are un-
> pleasant. Success is accorded to most of the
> entrants, but not all; failure is a realistic
> possibility. These challenging and painful
> experiences are shared with others, who thus
> have a sort of fellowship of suffering.

> Now if we add the probability that peers
> and adult role models constitute significant
> others, and thus that relations with them are
> marked by some degree of affectivity, we are
> well on the way to comprehending how an occupa-
> tional identity gets formed.[25]

In their writing, Berger and Luckmann differentiate
between "primary" and "secondary" socialization. Emotional attachment is one of the important aspects of primary
socialization, which is ". . . the first socialization an
individual undergoes in childhood, through which he becomes
a member of society."[26] Moore affirms that this type of
affective component is an equally important part of becoming a professional.

Moore completes his argument for the theory of punishment-centered socialization by stating,

> The person who successfully learns the language
> and skills of a trade, and survives the ordeals
> that punished him and his fellows will emerge

. . . not only with an internalized occupational commitment but also with an identification with the collectivity, the brotherhood.[27] [Or with the sisterhood.]

The seminarian believes that she is acquiring a remarkable variety of skills, techniques, and even attitudes
in seminary. She applies herself vigorously, although
there are moments when she agrees with Sartre: "The
attentive pupil who wishes to *be* attentive, his eyes
riveted on the teacher, his ears open wide, so exhausts
himself in playing the attentive role that he ends up by
no longer hearing anything."[28] She finds herself so caught
up in the unceasing flow of class work that she periodi-
cally forgets why she is there. Mannheim suggests it is
easy to be so involved in one's work that ultimate, meaningful goals are lost. He quotes Nietzsche, "Ich habe
meine Gründe vergessen." (I have forgotten why I ever
began.)

The seminarian, in this respect, can be compared with
the medical student. Goffman believes they exchange their
early idealism for practicality. He notes:

Thus, students of medical schools suggest that
idealistically oriented beginners in medical
school typically lay aside their holy aspirations for a period of time. During the first
two years the students find that their interest
in medicine must be dropped that they may give
all their time to the task of learning how to
get through examinations. During the next
two years they are too busy learning about
diseases to show much concern about the persons who are diseased. It is only after their
medical schooling has ended that their original
ideals about medical service may be reasserted.[29]

The beginner in seminary may have to lay aside her "holy aspirations" until after graduation.

In the course of time, however, she will have completed the necessary number of hours and classes, and will look forward to graduation. Most seminaries mark the occasion with appropriate "pomp and circumstance." Few students miss the opportunity to take part in the ceremony which indicates to the world (and to themselves) that they are moving from one phase of their career life to another. Berger and Luckmann remark, "In most societies . . . some rituals accompany the transition from primary to secondary socialization."[30]

The seminarian may experience a variety of rituals which indicate the transition. There will be the graduation ceremony itself, climaxed by receiving the stole. There will be fond, and probably damp goodbyes exchanged with those who have, through the process, become true sisters and brothers. There will be faculty members who will insist that "now we are colleagues," and others who will mistake clumsy attempts to say "thank you" for something more, so that the young woman may have to extricate herself from an amorous embrace or two.

If she has proceeded "on schedule," the seminarian has already begun the process toward ordination prior to graduation. Each denomination has its time-table and requirements. If being admitted to seminary had its challenges, being accepted into the "brotherhood" of denominational clergy borders on "the impossible dream."

Berger and Luckmann point out that the institution can seem overwhelming to the person attempting to enter it. The institution has existed for a much longer time than the individual, and has its own structure, patterns, and expectations. The authors write:

An institutional world . . . is experienced as
an objective reality. It has a history that
antedates the individual's birth and is not
accessible to his biographic recollection.
The institution cannot be "wished away." Institutions
resist [the person's] attempts to change or
evade them. They have coercive power over him,
both in themselves, by the sheer force of
their facticity, and through the control mechanisms that are usually attached to the most
important of them.[31]

The seminarian will be given various reasons why she
must complete a myriad of requirements prior to being
accepted by the institution. Her appeals to the fact that
she has received a "calling," or that she is following her
"ordo amoris," may or may not fall on deaf ears. Much
will depend upon the denomination's current need for ministers. Since the social order has long defined ministers
as "male," she will have three strikes against her before
she begins. Moore states:

The claims of professional bodies to regulate
admission to their occupations and the performance of those in it are neither untainted nor
unchallenged. Self-regulation may serve to
preserve and even enhance standards, but may
also be used merely to enhance occupational
prestige, to control the number of authenticated
practitioners in order to reduce competition
and increase income, and, not uncommonly, to
protect a particular orthodoxy against reasonable and even superior alternatives.[32]

If the denomination is currently experiencing a demand
for pastors, and if the denomination to which the seminarian applies is United Methodist, she will be assigned a

"supervising pastor." The role of this person is to help
the applicant "properly" complete the required materials
prior to officially entering the institution. The person
of the "supervising pastor" is crucial; she/he will be
very influential with the District Committee on Ministry,
the first hurdle on the way to ordination. Furthermore,
the supervising pastor will be a repository for all the
unwritten do's and don't's of "breaking into" the institution.

 Berger and Luckmann call these do's and don't's "recipe knowledge," a term borrowed from Alfred Schutz. They
write:

> On the pretheoretical level . . . every insti-
> tution has a body of transmitted recipe knowl-
> edge, that is, knowledge that supplies the
> institutionally appropriate rules of conduct.
> Such knowledge constitutes the motivating dyna-
> mics of institutionalized conduct. . . . It
> defines and constructs the roles to be played in
> the context of the institutions in question.
> *Ipso facto*, it controls and predicts all such
> conduct. Since this knowledge is socially
> objectivated *as* knowledge, that is, as a body
> of generally valid truths about reality, any
> radical deviance from the institutional order
> appears as a departure from reality. Such
> deviance may be designated as moral depravity,
> mental disease, or just plain ignorance. . . .
> They all share an inferior cognitive status
> within the particular social world.[33]

The supervising pastor will help the aspiring minister
avoid the appearance of radical deviance from the
proscribed order.

The young person fortunate enough to grow up within
the system has the advantage of a parent as role model,
and as "transmitter" of recipe knowledge as well. This is
especially true for men. The young male will usually be
adopted by a "mentor" who has a position of power and
status within the institution. The mentor will serve as
a "transmitter" of recipe knowledge also. Berger and
Luckmann elaborate: "All transmission [of meaning] requires some sort of social apparatus. That is, some types
are designated as transmitters, other types as recipients
of the traditional knowledge." Furthermore, ". . . both
'knowing' and 'not knowing' refer to what is socially
defined as reality." And, "To put this crudely, maternal
uncles do not transmit this particular stock of knowledge
because they know it, but they know it (that is, are defined as knowers) *because* they are maternal uncles."[34]

Transmitters, mentors, or supervising pastors ("maternal uncles") can function as entree into the institution
for the woman also. If she has been brought up in a
parsonage family she will have the advantage of knowing
some of the "right" people. It is doubtful that these
people will treat her in the same way they would treat a
young man headed for ministry. They might be either
paternalistic or overly protective. But they will "know"
her, and that is a big hurdle crossed. She will also have
the advantage of having seen the role played close at hand.
Some of the ministers she observes may serve as a "negative" role model; she will decide that is not the kind of
ministry she wants. She will have few women as models
simply because they are not available. The few clergywomen who are around will serve as a positive or negative
role model, depending upon their style and personality.

There are times when the mentors or "maternal uncles"
are a hindrance more than a help. Out of their own human

need and/or weaknesses they may take advantage of the
seminarian's status by making sexual demands. If she
appeals to others in the system for help, she may be
perceived as a troublemaker. Worse yet, they may accuse
her of "asking for it." One advantage that accrues to the
neophyte minister through these painful and sometimes
wrenching processes is a bedrock commitment to her calling.
All superficiality is washed away by such experiences, if
she is able to survive them, and she emerges with a solid
foundation for her ministry. She knows exactly why she is
working in and through the church. Her male colleagues
may not be so fortunate. Erving Goffman writes:

    And so we find that clergymen give the
    impression that they have entered the church
    because of a call of felt vocation, in
    America tending to conceal their interest
    in moving up socially. . . . And again,
    clergymen tend to give the impression that
    they have chosen their current congregation
    because of what they can offer it spiritually
    and not, as may in fact be the case, because
    the elders offered a good house or full pay-
    ment of moving expenses.[35]

    If in spite of the stumbling blocks strewn across her
path the young clergywoman remains true to her be-coming,
she will eventually be ordained, enjoying an impressive
ritual that will mark her entry into another new world,
full-time work in the church. Whether she moves into a
church where she is "the" pastor, or into the role of
associate minister, she will find that certain expectations precede her. Church people "know" what a minister
is, and what a minister does. That information has come
to them as a part of their socialization process. Goffman
explains:

> . . . it is to be noted that a given social
> front tends to become institutionalized in
> terms of the abstract stereotyped expecta-
> tions to which it gives rise, and tends to
> take on a meaning and stability apart from
> the specific tasks which happen at the time
> to be performed in its name. The front
> becomes a "collective representation" and a
> fact in its own right.

He continues along the same lines:

> When an actor takes on an established social
> role, usually he finds that a particular front
> has already been established for it. Whether
> his acquisition of the role was primarily
> motivated by a desire to perform the given
> task or by a desire to maintain the corres-
> ponding front, the actor will find that he
> must do both.[36]

The young minister may discover there are advantages to being a woman in this position at this point
in history. Because few women have preceded her into the
ministry, and most likely *no* woman has occupied her pulpit
before, she has more freedom to be innovative and creative.
After all, who in the church "knows" what a *woman* minister
should do, or be like?   Who "knows" how she should dress?
Who "knows" how she should preach, or what she should say?
Of course, it helps to be "attractive," and to "look
professional." Goffman comments on appearances:

> Executives often project an air of competency
> and general grasp of the situation, blinding
> themselves and others to the fact that they
> hold their jobs partly because they look like
> executives, not because they can work like
> executives.[37]

Just as her life in the seminary served to mold and
shape the person she becomes, so does her new role as
minister. Berger and Luckmann affirm that "By playing
roles, the individual participates in a social world. By
internalizing these roles, the same world becomes sub-
jectively real to him."[38] This may well come in terms of
a revelation to the pastor. For example, if the young
minister in her first church has continued to see herself
as still a student learning to be a pastor, she might
achieve instantaneous "conversion" the first time a per-
plexed parishioner insists, "But . . . you're our *pastor*!"
Experiences of this sort help her to integrate and internalize her role. Berger and Luckmann continue:

> To learn a role it is not enough to acquire
> the routines immediately necessary for its
> "outward" performance. One must be initiated
> into the various cognitive and even affective
> layers of the body of knowledge that is
> directly *and* indirectly appropriate to this
> role.[39]

However she is perceived by her congregation, the
clergywoman will find herself confronted by a wide variety
of responses from the general public and her colleagues
in ministry. She is, after all, still a small minority
and in a new position. In many social situations she will
seem radical no matter what her politics. This in turn
will begin to shape her responses. Hall observes:

> For the minority professional status inconsis-
> tency is an obvious condition. He ranks low
> on the ascribed characteristics of race,
> religion, ethnicity, or sex and high on the
> achieved characteristics of education and
> occupation. Gerhard E. Lensky and Elton F.
> Jackson's findings suggest such a person should

experience some psychological disturbance because of the inconsistency. The response
pattern to this disturbance, when the inconsistency is in this direction, tends to be
one of political liberalism--trying to change
the system.[40]

Political liberalism is only one of the possible
responses to status inconsistency. The young minister
could also opt for perfection. She might try to become
the perfect image of the *male* minister: working sixteen
hours a day, seven days a week; limiting her friends to
influential clergymen; attending all the promising
meetings; volunteering for district and conference posi-
tions--in short, becoming completely coopted by the system.

Because of her rather unique position, the clergywoman will be watched closely by the institutional hierarchy. In the United Methodist Church system her direct
supervisor is the District Superintendent. This person is
likely to be her primary contact with the rest of the
institution. This person will also have a direct impact
on her career growth. For example, if she has served well
for a number of years in one church she should be eligible
for promotion to a larger church with its increased
salary. If she has a close relationship with her District
Superintendent, she stands a good chance of receiving a
promotion--regardless of her "gifts and graces." The
Peter Principle applies in the church as well as in other
institutions; persons are advanced to their level of incompetence. Provided the District Superintendent likes
them.

The opposite also applies. If the relationship is
poor, the minister is not likely to be promoted. So, it
is crucial, at those times when the District Superintendent visits the church, to make a good appearance. The

congregation is likely to help at these times unless they
strongly dislike the minister. Goffman points out that no
matter what the setting, at times of inspection

> . . . the audience is likely to behave itself
> in a model way so that the performers who are
> being inspected may put on an exemplary show.
> At such times, team lines are apt to shift
> slightly and momentarily so that the in-
> specting . . . guest will be faced by per-
> formers and audience who are in collusion.[41]

If the clergywoman is a "beginner," the congregation is
going to be even more thoughtful in this respect.

The research of Carroll, Hargrove, and Lummis provides
support for the assertion that career growth is highly
dependent upon the decisions of the hierarchy. Many of the
clergywomen they surveyed reported the necessity for
strong advocates. Even neutrality among church executives
acts as a negative when it comes to appointments or pro-
motions. The authors state that:

> . . . for women to be placed it is necessary
> for judicatory officials of all denominations
> to be more than pleasant but inactive in support
> of women clergy; rather, they need to be active
> advocates if women are to find jobs. One large
> United Methodist annual conference was cited
> to the researchers as a case in point. The
> conference has very few women clergy, and several
> women have transferred out in recent years.
> Neighboring conferences, in contrast, have
> significant numbers of women. The difference is
> in the attitude of the bishops.[42]

Regardless of her ability to climb the ladder of
success, the clergywoman will make every effort to continue
her growth in ministry. She will not want to grow stale,

and with good reason. Moore points out:

> . . . although greater freedom follows
> successful survival of trials, the *persis-*
> *tent* possibility of failure is character-
> istic of most professional and technical
> occupations. We are suggesting that this
> is an important ingredient of continuing
> occupational commitment. Another allegation
> then follows: persons who get into positions
> of absolute security, with no need to expose
> themselves to risk and uncertainty, in fact
> become occupationally unproductive. (We
> have discovered Calvinism by a devious route,
> but there it is.)[43]

Continuing education for the professional minister is
important in most mainline denominations. Within the
United Methodist system ministers are required by *The Book*
of Discipline to accumulate a certain number of continuing
education units each year. Even if the demands were not
made by the institution, the pastor as a "professional"
would want to remain informed.

> What is general to these fields [medicine,
> law, ministry] is the expectation of *growth*:
> in proficiency, wisdom, and recognition.
> Plateaus and declines do occur, but they do
> not correspond to ideal norms. The pro-
> fessional calling is ideally not a fixed
> position of competent service, but a career
> that shows progress. . . . The professional
> is expected to meet criteria of competence
> and performance, and to seek and recognize
> excellence. And, . . . it is precisely be-
> cause professionals enjoy a large measure of
> autonomy in their exercise of what amounts to

a form of power over their clients' welfare
that their responsible behavior is, ideally,
self-imposed.[44]
So the young pastor looks forward to enrolling in classes
at a nearby graduate school.

If she is a strong feminist, the clergywoman may want
to reject out of hand the typical male model of "climbing
the ladder of success." She may discover, however, that
she can use that model for her own purposes. After all,
how is she to serve as a good role model for other women
coming through the process unless she is serving a sizeable church? How can she help to change the system unless
she acquires some power of her own? She will probably do
what she can with integrity. It becomes even more important, therefore, that she cultivate and maintain friendships with her colleagues. Hall observes:

> [Oswald] Hall notes that factors such as
> race, religion, and ethnic background play
> a role in acceptance into the "inner frater-
> nity" of physicians who dominate the medical
> profession in the community he examined. Hall
> stresses that competence is vital to accept-
> ance, but so is the proper personality. Non-
> acceptance can lead to a situation in which the
> possibilities for financial and professional
> advancement become blocked.[45]

Even those colleagues with whom she has not built
relationships will have expectations of her, particularly
if they have not worked with a woman before and/or have
strong prejudices about women in ministry. As soon as she
is ordained, they will begin watching her behavior and
performance, and making judgments about her. Berger and
Luckmann assert,

As soon as actors are typified as role
performers, their conduct is *ipso facto*
susceptible to enforcement. Compliance
and non-compliance with socially defined
role standards ceases to be optional,
though, of course, the severity of sanctions may vary from case to case.[46]

Colleagues need not have prejudices against women in
the clergy to observe and critique the pastor's performance. Male ministers are apt to have some of the same
doubts or questions about their calling that women clergy
experience. Moore affirms this:

Professionals do not quite spend their lives
judging colleagues--after all, they do have
clients, and, mostly, families, friends,
neighbors, and the usual run of lay organizations and involvements. Yet it remains true
that they do make comparative judgments of
their nominal peers, ranking those peers in
relative competence and always anxious as they
typically are, compare themselves to ideal
and actual fellow practitioners.[47]

The clergywoman is also likely to find at least a few
"soul-mates" within the professional system. If she is
fortunate, her church will have ordained several women
with whom she has a special relationship. She is also
apt to find that personality differences arise even in a
minority group. Women as well as men suffer from insecurity, incompetence, and petty jealousies. Perhaps her
group of friends will include as many men as women. Because they share so much in common, a particular closeness
is able to evolve.

Colleagues, as it is said, share a community
of fate. In having put on the same kind of

performance, they come to know each other's
difficulties and points of view; whatever their
tongues, they come to speak the same social
language. And while colleagues who compete
for audiences may keep some strategic secrets
from one another, they cannot very well hide
from one another certain things that they hide
from the audience. The front that is maintained before others need not be maintained
among themselves; relaxation becomes possible.[48]

If the clergywoman is to maintain a healthy perspective not only on her relationships with colleagues, but on
her institutional involvements as well, she would be wise
to seek out friends from other professions and walks of
life. Moore reminds us of the hazards involved in becoming overly committed to one's profession.

The charming French phrase *déformation
professionelle* refers to the possible dis-
tortions in character that derive from
participation in the world of work--in any
occupation. One mild example is the incapacity to divest oneself of occupational
concerns in other social contexts: the in-
veterate shoptalk of professionals. . . .
Rampant and increasing specialization may
result in an excessively narrow view not only
of the world of work, but also of the world
generally.[49]

The American clergywoman does not rise unbidden from
chaos as does Eurynome, nor is she hatched from the Universal Egg. She comes, as does the clergyman, out of a
local church and parish. She has been fashioned and
formed, in large part, by the social order in which she
lives. The people, organizations, and institutions

which surround her have a vital impact on the kind of
person and minister that she becomes.

Perhaps equally important to her development as a
minister is her own motivation, ability, and calling. In
her "be-coming," in her "striving toward spiritualization,"
and in the way she projects her own possibilities ahead of
herself, "as a phantasmic image," she is a minister. She
experiences the coming into being of her self through the
doing of the calling. The call becomes the self, the self
becomes the call. Carroll, Hargrove, and Lummis point out
that some theorists speculate that "self-initiated" socialization is just as important as the socialization brought
about by others.[50]

The American clergywoman is shaped by her social
order and by her own "ordo amoris." She in her turn helps
to fashion and reform the world from which she comes,
touching its people, its organizations, and its institutions. Every worship service she conducts, every meeting
she attends, every class she teaches touches the church
and renews it. The wider her involvement at every level
(local church, District, Conference, National), the
greater will be the change. The church will never the the
same again, simply because of her be-ing in it. She and
her world are engaged in a dynamic dialectic. If she has
courage, vision, and creativity, the church may become a
new thing altogether.

298   RELIGION AND THE SOCIOLOGY OF KNOWLEDGE

NOTES

1. Robert Graves, *The Greek Myths* (Baltimore: Penguin Books, 1955), p. 27.

2. Karl Mannheim, *Ideology and Utopia* (New York: Harcourt, Brace, and Co., 1936), p. 70.

3. Ibid., p. 72.

4. Ibid., p. 74.

5. Max Scheler, *Problems of a Sociology of Knowledge* (London, Boston and Henley: Routledge and Kegan Paul, 1980), p. 23.

6. Kenneth W. Stikkers, "Introduction," to Max Scheler, *Problems of a Sociology of Knowledge* (London, Boston and Henley: Routledge and Kegan Paul, 1980), p. 7.

7. Ibid., p. 9.

8. Ibid., p. 14.

9. Wilbert E. Moore, *The Professions: Roles and Rules* (New York: Russell Sage Foundation, 1970), p. 67.

10. Scheler, p. 82.

11. Richard H. Hall, *Occupations and the Social Structure* (Englewood Cliffs, New Jersey: Prentice-Hall, 1969), p. 86.

12. Scheler, p. 162.

13. Hall, p. 16.

14. Ibid.

15. Ibid., p. 37.

16. Ibid.

17. Ibid., p. 75.

18. Jackson Carroll, Barbara Hargrove, and Adair Lummis, *Women of the Cloth: A New Opportunity for the Churches* (San Francisco: Harper & Row, 1983), p. 132.

iv class="hl

19. Ibid., pp. 134-135.

20. Moore, p. 122.

21. Ibid., p. 74.

22. Ibid., p. 75.

23. Peter L. Berger and Thomas Luckmann, *The Social Construction of Reality* (Garden City, New York: Doubleday Anchor Book, 1967), p. 49.

24. Moore, p. 76.

25. Ibid., p. 77.

26. Berger and Luckmann, p. 130.

27. Moore, p. 78.

28. Irving Goffman, *The Presentation of Self in Everyday Life* (Garden City, New York: Doubleday Anchor Book, 1959), p. 33.

29. Ibid., p. 20.

30. Berger and Luckmann, p. 140.

31. Ibid., p. 60.

32. Moore, p. 111.

33. Berger and Luckmann, p. 65.

34. Ibid., p. 79.

35. Goffman, p. 47.

36. Ibid., p. 27.

37. Ibid., p. 47.

38. Berger and Luckmann, p. 74.

39. Ibid., p. 77.

40. Hall, p. 135.

41. Goffman, p. 232.

42. Carroll et al., p. 122.

43. Moore, p. 78.

44. Ibid., p. 80.

45. Hall, p. 129.

46. Berger and Luckmann, p. 74.

47. Moore, p. 150.

48. Goffman, p. 160.

49. Moore, p. 82.

50. Carroll et al., p. 73.

SOCIOLOGY OF KNOWLEDGE AND PASTORAL PSYCHOTHERAPY

Kady Cone

INTRODUCTION

As a pastoral counselor, I am both psychologist and
practical theologian. These are two organizations of
knowledge within the social sciences that view persons
within the world. However, they select their data by
different criteria, organize it according to different
conceptual worlds, with different problems to address or
different ways of viewing the same problems. They have
different ways of perceiving value and value systems
and different ranges of usefulness. Even within each
discipline the ways of viewing themselves and each other
will vary widely from strictly reductionist (each subsumes
the other under its own aegis, denying the separate identity of the other) to strictly exclusionist (denying the
validity or existence of the other). In between are
varying interactional or interrelational models.[1] In
these models the different disciplines are perceived as
informing, complementing, supplementing and/or illumining
each other in helpful ways. No one of these disciplines
alone is adequate to deal with the complexity of the human condition, in spite of the claims of reductionist or
exclusionist models to do so. Each discipline will
reflect its own particular bias as it utilizes common
data, but will also reflect particular insight and expertise in areas of its own particular bias.

What is a consideration of the relationship between
psychology and theology is true of the other social
sciences. Sociology is particularly relevant to both, and
there is a close interrelationship among the three disciplines. Sociology is interested in groups, and also in
the social sources of all human knowledge and individual-
ity. However, within this field different weights and
understandings are given to the role of the individual in
the shaping of society or social groups. Sociological
determinism is strongly implied simply by the focus in
this discipline upon group structures and the social
sources of knowledge. The individual *per se* and the ways
in which the individual might impact social systems is
generally a peripheral concern. I agree enthusiastically
with the basic premise of the sociology of knowledge--
that all human knowledge is social in its origin, its
preservation, its expansion and its transmission. It is
social in the language and thought forms that carry and
shape it. Further, no such thing as human personality is
possible without social origins and a social context of
some sort.

Therapy is necessarily a social process. It is
socially defined and would be meaningless without social
outcomes. Pastoral psychotherapy is in addition a theological process. It adds a theological dimension to the
therapeutic tasks and goals. But therapy is also rooted
most deeply in psychology, in a concern for help and healing at an intrapsychic level. The integral relationship of the three disciplines becomes apparent as we
realize that the pain and pathology responsible for a person's seeking help have social sources and social implications as well as theological and normative implications in
terms of meaning and value.

The questions that this chapter will address are the following:

1. What structures and organizations of knowledge are operating in the task of pastoral therapy and how do they interrelate?

2. How does the sociology of knowledge inform this understanding of the therapeutic practice?

Concluding remarks will be concerned with the implications of a sociology of knowledge for pastoral therapy, and some problems it raises.

WHAT STRUCTURES AND ORGANIZATIONS OF KNOWLEDGE ARE OPERATING IN THE TASK OF PASTORAL THERAPY, AND HOW DO THEY INTERRELATE?

The individual, as client, the pastoral therapist, and the society or societies to which they belong form structural centers for the organization of knowledge. Each of these may be considered as structural wholes and viewed as autonomous, or each may be considered as interacting with the others and with other relevant systems. The "client" may even be a group, such as a family or a family subsystem (for instance, the marital couple, or siblings), in which case the client will also comprise a set of structures or systems. Each will represent a variety of organizations of knowledge--about personality, about self-identity, about purpose and meaning and value. Each will be in interaction with the others in the therapeutic process, sharing information which the others will receive or block (whether by negation or by not comprehending). This information and the way it is received may be verbal, behavioral, or emotional.

The therapeutic process is often enhanced (or hindered) by the particular permeability between therapist and client as the therapeutic relationship develops in the transference phenomenon. Behind the participants in the therapeutic process are the various social structures that they represent, including religious or faith structures. The therapist and the individual or individuals involved in treatment are all subject to perceive values, styles, and structures of the society which they may identify as normative, or by reification may give to them an absolute quality. These social structures may interpret themselves in terms of absolutes. This will affect expectations of therapy and therapeutic goals from the side of the client or the side of the therapist.

Organizations of knowledge that each participant brings to the interaction that is therapy include those having to do with the permeability of the systems (locus of control and open and closed systems), those that are practical (having to do with the therapeutic process and the classification of mental disorders), and those that are theoretical (personality theory and theology).

The social systems that are formative and that impact the individual participants in the therapeutic process can be highly structured, such as a denominational church, or highly amorphous, as a cultural group or identity. In a pluralistic society, there will be many such groups that are overtly or covertly influential--a prayer group, a class in parenting, a counter-culture group, a social services department politically imbedded in a country's social philosophy. Persons will integrate some of this, keep some in logic-tight compartments of mental processes, and live with ambiguity with some. Some they will actively resist or reject even when it sets them against a group that is important to them. Individuals take from their

groups and from their own developmental processes a
perception of the locus of control and of the relative
openness or closedness of systems. Both the reifying
tendencies and the legitimating tendencies of the groups
are evident in the way these are interpreted and understood. Both will tend to germinate expectancies which
act as self-fulfilling prophecies in regard to goals,
attitude about moving toward those goals, as well as
motivation to expend energy required to work toward them.

Perception of the locus of control relates to a
person's expectancies of control as residing within the
self (internal) or outside the self (external). In the
latter case control may be seen to be in the indomitable
forces of nature, or society, or in economics or bureaucracy, or in a leader or significant other. It may be
projected transcendentally onto God or Fate. With an
internal locus of control a person believes that he or
she has the power to act within the conditions of a
situation to shape his or her own fate. [2]

Extremism in either direction can lead to a need for
therapy. However, those with pathology in the realm of
internal locus of control are less apt to seek it and more
apt to be constrained by a society, due to the underlying
gradiosity. Persons with a pathological range of external
locus of control can function well if the society endorses
that by accepting the dependency and giving it a transcendent context of meaning. This was done by Hitler in a
political context, and by the Franciscans in an ecclesiastical context. (More recently, the Jonestown fiasco
represents this dynamic of the utilization by a religious
leader of the external locus of control of a large group
of people.) The therapist, too, can legitimate acceptance
of things that are not perceived as changeable. The therapist can also help persons with an external locus of

control to perceive options about which they do have
control, thus opening the possibility of the expectancy of
"no control" being changed. The therapist may also need
to deal with the impact on the client of legitimating
social institutions, including the state and the church,
and their political or theological rationales. If the
client's rootedness in these groups is great, therapy
intended to reduce this dependency will either fail or
leave the client marginated from his or her significant
groups. Evaluating this potential is an important ethical task for the pastoral therapist, with consequences in
regard to the client's belonging in his or her community.

Open or closed systems are those belief or attitude
systems which are accepting or rejecting of people, ideas,
or authority,[3] and which concern willingness to change
or resistance to change. Whenever the individual is
limited in behavioral options by particularly closed
systems leading to discomfort in interpersonal or social
relations, therapy may be sought, with possible diagnoses
of obsessive-compulsive or depressive disorders. Therapists with relatively closed systems may be theoretically and operationally rigid, but may also convey through
this a sense of stability and dependability of self and
environment. Where persons are struggling with the over-
availability of options, the clash of world views, the
relativity value crises common in modern society, and
where the person feels isolated and unsure, to be able to
borrow ego-support from a therapist's closed system may
legitimate a more or less unified life-world.[4] Again, the
therapist may help to provide boundaries and skills for
prioritizing so that an open system is manageable and not
overwhelming or immobilizing. The therapist, however, is
not the most likely source of this grounding. Social
groups or their representatives may serve this function
also. Persons who need to reach for absolutes to give

their lives meaning are ripe for such closed settings as
most cults, ideologies, or utopian mentalities and their
movements. They may embrace them with religious fervor--
the dynamic is "religious," even if the content is not.

Perception of systems as open or closed, and expectancies including locus of control, are socially defined
learnings derived from a social context such as family,
church, school, ethnic group, or other important group.
Locus of control helps to define what is possible, and
information will move back and forth between the client
and the therapist, and from there to and from the social
groups of both according to the relative openness or
closedness of the particular systems involved. The ghost
voices present and influential in the therapy session are
many and varied, and represent both sides of the therapeutic process.

Practical organizations of knowledge have to do with
how the therapeutic process is understood and structured.

The relationship between the individual and social
groups is marked by a continuous process, and any attempt
to define priority is probably tautological. According
to Berger and Luckmann, "Psychological status is relative
to the social definitions of reality in general and is
itself socially defined."[5] However, it could as easily be
said that the social definition of reality is relative to
the psychological status of persons, and is itself individ-
ually defined. Or it could be said that in spite of the
implied determinisms involved in the social sciences,
particularly psychology and sociology, transcendence does
sometimes take place and change is sometimes introduced.
The individual is inescapably social from fetal times.
Society is inescapably composed of individuals and has no
existence apart from them. Persons are necessarily religious, structuring their existence around centers of mean-

ing and value. Persons and societies too, sometimes find
themselves going beyond self-maintenance and self-interest
to serve larger concerns. In terms of the structures of
knowledge of individuals and of social groups, it would
seem important to determine how each is impacting the
other mutually and interactionally, rather than to attempt to define either totally from the psychological,
sociological, or theological perspective.

Various disciplines within the human sciences tend
toward particularistic (and reductionist) biases. Psychology may focus so exclusively upon the intrapsychic
or individual behavioral aspects that it loses sight of
the interactions of larger structures. Theology may
focus on ideal and abstract matters and lose sight of
praxis. Sociology makes acknowledgement of individual
contribution difficult or awkward. The very language and
constructs used focus on larger systems and so define this
to a minimal role. For Mannheim, elites or intellectuals
may be unattached, which gives them some freedom of movement to join other groups, but he wants us to know that
the individual must not be overestimated. Even in the
utopian mentality the group must empower what first is an
individual's wish-fantasy.[6] While there are individual
thinkers and knowers, most human knowing is in the context
of the social aspect of human life. What is new is built
on existing knowledge foundations.[7] For Marx, individuals
are either perceived as enslaved by class consciousness,
thus in need of a levelling of classes, or as those whose
interests are reinforcing the dominant ideas of the ruling
class.[8] "Man" is unique, but also "the whole," and "his"
life is manifested socially. Marx appears to blur distinctions of boundaries between person and society by class-
levelling values and by the idea of consciousness, which
gives a sense of identity and belonging on a unified

level. "The nature of man is the totality of social
relations."[9] Scheler, on the other hand, gives somewhat
more significance to the individual role in a change
process as the "lonely thinker" or metaphysician (who
needs an independent living in order to function), and
through the religious founder (who needs a bonded group
ready).[10]

While these sociologically weighted understandings
limit the way in which persons are perceived as structuring their own experience and reality in a structured
social world, they do enlighten ways in which the level
of society impacts the individual reality. The question
arises, "What society?" Is it the dominant society, or
a counter-culture, or a belonging in several diverse but
significant groups? Does the person perceive himself or
herself to be an integral part of that society, or to
what extent and in what way is he or she self-perceived
(or perceived by the society) as marginal? Is there some
support group or family that provides a "home-world"
where emotional and personal needs are met and a sense of
belonging fostered in a setting of meaning and value
affirmations and endorsement?[11]

Society (or societies) can supply more or less
official definitions of reality and symbolic universes to
legitimate them to help persons locate themselves in life.
However, individuals also have their own structuring to
do based upon their own experience, their needs, their
developed values, their conscious reflection, their
emotional and relational deficits, and the systems available around them. From these they may choose, accept
unquestioningly, or reject all or a part. It is in this
way, too, that identity is formed, but in a way that is
heavily dependent upon socially-transmitted options,
perceptions and values. Such identity is actually a

multitude of identities--of work or function, of effec-
tiveness or competence, or physical appearance and
acceptability, of sexuality and relationality; all of
these and many more are derived from interactions between
persons and society. Both positive information and negative feedback are mirrored. All of this helps persons
to locate themselves in society and to know "Who they are,
and what the Lord requires of them," as in Fiddler on the
Roof. It is difficult for an individual to conceive of
options not offered by society. Pluralism makes more
possibilities available, but persons who do entertain
unusual or unheard-of options are electing almost certain
social margination.

    Berger, et al, speak of identity as a plan, open,
unfinished, and individual, in the context of the family
unit. This life-plan, then, also organizes for the individual and in the individual the expectancies and knowledge of society.[12] Roles, identities, meaning-systems
(symbolic universes), relational interaction patterns, all
may be socially mediated and may become inadequate, no
longer viable, or threatened by competing or conflicting
values or options. The therapist stands in a position of
clarification, of interpretation and mediation. Options
not previously seen may be offered, that circumvent the
difficulty. Ways of re-interpreting an event or relationship or feeling or attitude may put what was ego-dystonic
into a trajectory that is ego-syntonic. New myths may be
found that locate a new sense of identity in the dominant
society or in an available social option. Mediation can
take place between clashing life-worlds, or more satisfactory private meanings may be developed. Re-decision may
be encouraged about choices made in the past concerning
identity and relationships. And life-planning may be
made more satisfying and more intentional. All of these

are forms of therapy that are decidedly socialization processes. In addition, they are counseling situations that may not be clearly delineated by diagnostic standards. Loss of meaning may not be a psychiatric category, but it has a decided effect upon the person in terms of painful symptoms or functional impairment. Stress and burnout are epidemic due to multiple expectations, loss of support systems, with resulting senses of isolation, overresponsibility, vulnerability, and loss of meaning. Theology offers a framework to do this work. It can begin with experience and work toward a perspective that makes sense at the level of meaning and value. It can show how life is, and can be, blessed in spite of personal or social failures or tragedies. It can offer solutions (resolutions) to guilt, resentment, loss of meaning, and alienation. It can begin with the socially transmitted and interpreted traditions and reframe them to account for new occasions. In this case the work is most often performed by experts trained in the tradition who frame canon and interpret it. In the former cases the work is done by persons in pain who struggle with or without other experts (this time, experts in both the tradition and its interpretation and the way it can be set in the context of the marginal cases, the boundary experiences of life). The task of the pastor counselor includes exegesis of the tradition *and* of the present situation of those seeking therapy in a pastoral setting.

Organization of knowledge that is basically practical relates to the therapeutic process. Berger and Luckmann state that therapy requires a body of knowledge which includes a theory of pathology or of deviance, a diagnostic apparatus or symptomatology, and a conceptual system of treatment which is the curative process.[13] The normative diagnostic apparatus, at least for this culture and this

time, is the descriptive symptomatology prepared by the
American Psychiatric Association and published in 1980,
the Diagnostic and Statistical Manual III, (DSM III).
It defines a mental disorder as a "clinically significant
behavioral or psychological syndrome or pattern that
occurs in an individual" and which has a painful symptom
or functional impairment. It is inferred that there is
a behavioral, psychological, or biological dysfunction,
and that the disturbance is not only in the relationship
between the individual and society (in which case it
would be social deviance, not necessarily a mental disorder).[14] Thus treatment in therapy deals with painful
symptoms of functional impairment. The DSM III does
include diagnostic categories that are suitable foci for
treatment when not due to a mental disorder as well.
These include crisis adjustment problems, family, interpersonal, or job related problems, etc. It does not
include therapy as a growth and enrichment process, or as
preventive experience, nor does it, of course, preclude
this. It does allow for a multi-axial evaluation to be
able to include in the profile other factors such as
pertinent physical conditions, recent adaptive functioning,
and outside stressors. While the categories of the DSM
III provide standardized categories of diagnosis, the
theory of pathology, and thus also of the curative process, must come out of the theoretical structures of the
therapist.

          Theology also offers theories of diagnosis, although
the variations of theoretical framework are extensive.
Categories are sin, alienation, guilt, pride, idolatry,
faithlessness--to name a few. They are derived from an
understanding of human nature, the human situation and
the holy. They may be translated into concrete "rules
for living" or left as principles to be applied con-

cretely. This understanding also presents a context for living faithfully, and is the matrix for ethics and values. It provides a context for intimacy and belonging in a primary group. It identifies the person in relation to the cosmos and to God.

An alternative practical organization of knowledge to that of the DSM III would be the classification of the mental disorders included in the DSM III around the social etiology of the problem. (This would be in direct contrast to the intent of the DSM III, which was to avoid etiology and stick to descriptive categories. Since it is an artificial relocation of categories from another system, it is necessarily tentative, loose, and over-lapping.)

1. Relationship problems:
   a. Disorders deriving from relational losses or dysfunction in childhood. This could include developmental disorders or disorders of child-hood, and in adulthood the pervasive and chronic personality disorders.
   b. Psychotic disorders. This could include paranoia, schizophrenia, etc. Psychosis is a break with reality, including relational reality. Schizophrenia particularly is currently considered to be based in family interactional patterns.
   c. Defenses against intimate relationships. This could include conduct disorders, avoid-ance, distancing, projections as defense mechanisms.
2. Intrapsychic problems:
   a. Disorders of impulse control, as anti-social personality structures.

    b. Disorders in adjustment following crises
       or stress.
    c. Affective disorders, such as depression,
       mood swings, anxiety, panic, manic states,
       pathological grief.
    d. Internalized defenses and controlling
       mechanisms.
 3. Problems of identity (ordinarily a conflict
    between perceived identity and socially trans-
    mitted identity).
 4. Problems with organic (biochemical) components:
    a. Substance-induced disorders.
    b. Mental retardation and degenerative dementias.
    c. Adjustment to problems of illness, physical
       disability, etc.

The reclassification obviously has no value as a
diagnostic tool, but in considering treatment strategy or
in identifying some causal factors, to review them according to the personality theory of choice would give options
for the treatment process. Where the appropriate social
interactions have been lacking or inadequate in early
development at the optimal time for these experiences, the
developmental process may be enacted or re-enacted at a
later time. It is apt to take a long time, and may never
be completed. It is important to assess these developmental factors.

    Organization of knowledge that is basically theoret-
ical relates to the personality theory and the theology
of the pastoral therapist, and to a less "expert" extent
ordinarily, that also of the client. Because of the
theoretical variety of therapists, the DSM III provides
intentionally descriptive, clinically useful categories.

Even this is under fire by systems theorists, who prefer
to see interactional patterns rather than symptoms or
descriptions that imply a medical model. Therapists who
embrace a cybernetics epistemology tend to downplay
linear causation in favor of a broader way of interpreting
the interactions of systems with each other, thus the
impact of larger social systems upon individuals and upon
families or couples.

A question raised by the sociology of knowledge to
the DSM III is that of the degree to which the categories
of pathology are defined by a particular experience, that
of the white male. Some of the categories are descriptive
of the approved roles culturally endorsed for women, such
as dependent personality disorder. Additionally, the
category of hystrionic personality disorder can be applied
to persons whose behavior is quite appropriate to the
black cultural endorsement of open affective styles.

A rather gross implication for the goal of therapy
relates to the criteria of "painful" and "interfering with
functioning." A general objective of therapy would be
the removal of such symptoms, and better and more comfortable functioning. This objective is implied within the
standards themselves. Significant biases will be introduced with the goals of therapy, the conceptualization
of "what went wrong," or pathology, and the treatment
strategy. The theoretical system may even modify the
definition of "therapy."

Generally, personality theory is categorized as
cognitive, psychoanalytic, or behavioral, or there may
be mixed theories. The newer cybernetic theories are
generally behavioral at the present. Therapy may be
supportive, aimed at the symptoms, and designed as short
term, or it may be psychoanalysis, which is an intense
process of re-orienting the self-understanding, going back

to the earliest interactions with the help of a therapist.
In this case, through the transference phenomenon
(dynamic identification of the therapist with the early
social nurturing process), there is actually a re-work-
ing of the process of bonding, separation and individuation. This is always a long term process. It contains
the presupposition that change is slow and difficult and
requires a certain level of insight (and it does). The
more radical behaviorisms contain the presupposition
that behavior is determined, but that one can change the
conditions under which change has been impossible (and
this happens). Psychoanalytic theory has spawned numerous developmental offspring such as ego psychology, the
cognitive/moral/social/faith constructs, transactional
analysis, and many of the recent self-theories. Most of
these recognize in some form a developmental process that
is social in nature (as well as having physical components), and which is the basis for all later adjustment.
Thus the roots of problems presented in therapy are
sought in an examination of this process (and found there).
     Within limits, the expectancies of the therapeutic
process function to fulfill themselves. The fulfillment
of these expectancies will also be related to a reasonable
functional relationship between theory and situation.
Treatment of symptoms only and not of underlying problems
may mean that other symptoms will appear (or secondary
growth or better coping skills may reduce or eliminate
the underlying problems). Fulfillment of expectancies
relates also to trust level between therapist and client
and how that trust is used in therapy (transference), and
some congruence of values among person, therapist, and
society, so that the therapeutic goals are perceived as
ego-syntonic. Ideally, they should be syntonic with the
self-identity of the faith group to which the client be-

longs also, but in some cases the problem with which the
client is struggling is related to a dystonic dynamic
between client and church.

Since the early socialization process is by far the
most significant event in the life of a person, theory
relating to separation-individuation and to the cognitive/
moral/social/faith development must be considered here.
Most personality theory retains some roots in psychoanalytic theory, but has moved in a variety of directions since
Freud. As was previously mentioned, fetal existence is
social, and is characterized by responsivity. With birth
certain sensory stimulations become crucial, along with
their social context--eye contact, labyrinthine and skin
stimulation, cuddling, etc. Without these there will be
neurological deficits that can result in permanent
irreversible brain damage and even death. The first
bonding, too, is important for all later attachments,
beginning with a symbiosis stage at about three months,
when the infant perceives that needs are met. Gratifica-
tion of needs at this stage is also essential to development. Failure of symbiosis may result in regression to
autism or childhood psychosis, or if this is avoided, a
borderline personality structure may result. Lasting
consequences of the lack of a good symbiotic stage may
be failure to attain object constancy and the splitting
of the object world into good and bad. (Such persons
tend to cluster theologically around dualistic views of
God and the world). The first bonding means attachment to
one figure, usually the mother, and becomes strong enough
and discriminating enough by four to six months that it
attains an exclusive quality, so that strangers make the
infant anxious--in fact, anyone but this one figure. The
bonding has nothing to do with worthiness of the one
attachment figure, which means that children abused

physically by their mothers have no place to go for
comfort except to the mothers who abused them. Those
who were not nurtured or who were over-nurtured and
suffer imbalances of entitlement tend to seek social
structures (such as the church) to provide it. But it
will never seem enough to them, and they will blame these
groups as inadequate.

Separation and individuation take place as the child
becomes psychologically aware of his or her separateness.
The responses of the mother to cues from the child during
this period help to mirror a frame of reference and to
provide support for practicing independent excursions.
Gender identity and self image have roots here, as does
the ability later to relate to mother without being en-
gulfed back into the symbiotic relationship, such as
trust, self-worth, and self-confidence (in which locus of
control issues and open or closed systems have their
genesis).

When a therapist is faced with personality disorders,
particularly those having borderline features, the difficulty of the therapeutic process ahead is assured. These
people are psychologically marginal. These people are
lacking the early patterns by which later relationships
can be shaped. Social relationships in their environments
are apt to be shaky or based on reciprocal need-meeting
rather than real caring or concern. Both as children and
adults they are apt to be "hollow" in respect to very basic
structures necessary to relate to others. Failure of the
socialization process at this level is something that
virtually can never be replaced, since the optimal time
for it has passed; but choice of treatment is probably to
try to help it happen anyway, and to hope for slightly
improved functioning. Persons with borderline personality
syndrome or other related personality disorders may become

more comfortable in life with a lot of help, but the
prognosis for great results of therapy are not good.
They tend to drain off resources from social agencies
to contribute marginally and with a lot of pain. They
are vulnerable to absolutist solutions and leaders.
There are limits to the prospect for resocialization in
these cases.

Developmental issues also figure in the organization
of knowledge in personality theory as an interactional
process with social, physical, and cognitive components.
It is useful to consider them, particularly in viewing
the interdisciplinary relationship. The best researched
and the most integrated developmental model is the
cognitive/moral/social/faith developmental model.

According to this theory, persons are developing
organisms, and maturation is both a physical process and
an interactional process with a cognitive-developmental
base. Persons experience increasing numbers of others
in their social world and meet with increasingly complex
cognitive problems. When the existing level of thinking
is inadequate, being pushed by conflict, they may
restructure their thinking along more adequate lines.
Generally, higher states are characterized by more
adequacy according to maturational criteria of inclusivity
and generality, thus "better" by these standards. Since
it has a cognitive base, it has to do with structures of
thinking and judgment. Since it also has to do with
social perspective, increasing social worlds will introduce cognitive conflict when existing ranges of solutions
are inadequate, with the possibility of restructuring and
a more adequate stage of thought. Through the sets of
transformations, continuity is maintained by cores that
remain stable. At the later stages the concepts of
welfare and justice emerge, justice eventually taking over
from love, as justice is a more absolute form of partiality.

This developmental model has to do with structures
of thinking rather than content of thought, so it can be
identified across many cultures and faiths. Decision-
making based upon a particular structure of thought will
include such important value-loaded issues as law,
authority, value of human life, property, truth, society,
and roles. It is out of this matrix, and in accordance
with cognitive and moral structures available to a person,
that the data for a religious view of life are drawn and
an overarching symbolic universe is created. The *content*
of that religious life-view and symbolic universe, of
course, is drawn from the social world. The *structure*
is drawn from the developmental process. The way it is
interpreted and its values organized and understood will
be in line with a particular developmental stage.

Since therapy deals with discomfort or dysfunction
in life, persons will seek therapy when their life-
problems are not adequately handled by the kinds of
solutions available to them. These problems may arise
from the conflict resulting from inadequate solutions of
a stage, and a readiness to move to a more adequate
moral judgment; or, they may be a conflict between one's
own interpretation of the meaning of the world and that
of one's community or other social groups or societies
impinging upon it. The problems will involve one's
management of interpersonal and social issues. They may
result from the margination that occurs when one moves
past the prevailing stages of thought of one's community
or begins to question its validity. Obviously, theology
must be reinterpreted by persons as they move to more
inclusive and abstract thinking and away from the concrete.
When persons fail to see that their tradition can provide
this upgraded view and be understood in more adequate
interpretation (and most of them apparently can accom-

modate most levels of thinking) they may assume that the
tradition is inadequate and withdraw from the faith
community. The church as conservator and transmitter of
the tradition has the challenge of providing its young
and those in crisis with continuing resocialization at
their growing edges. Berger and Luckmann put a sociological organization of the same data base in terms of
symbolic universes, which serve to integrate all realms
of reality and meanings to encompass every area of everyday and institutional life, and include the marginal life-
situations. It is a map for locating roles and relations
and priorities and practices, plus the frame of reference
for death and disaster and loss of meaning.[15]

Whether this phenomenon is considered psychologically, sociologically, or theologically, it can operate to
open or close options. In the developmental theory,
options may be closed because they are cognitively unavailable to persons according to the structure of their
thought, as well as being unavailable to them because
their knowledge base does not contain the possibility or
provide the foundation from which the new possibility
could emerge, or because an authority prohibits new alternatives. In the Berger and Luckmann conceptualization,
more emphasis is placed on the social sources and functions of the symbolic universe, and less on the responsibility of the person to construct it, apply it, and hold
it together when the ends split, as in either growth or
crisis. By whatever construct one uses, a therapy around
issues of the adequacy of the meaning and value of clients
may be appropriate. For this, a pastoral therapist has
knowledge to help him or her move in the client's faith
structure and symbolic system, as well as world view and
support community.

HOW DOES THE SOCIOLOGY OF
KNOWLEDGE INFORM THIS
UNDERSTANDING OF THE
THERAPEUTIC SITUATION?

According to Berger and Luckmann, therapy applies to
individual cases the legitimating apparatus of a particular symbolic universe in order to keep these individuals
with the institutionally defined reality and to prevent
them from deviating or straying.[16] Successful therapy
establishes "a symmetry between the conceptual machinery
and its subjective appropriation in the individual's
consciousness; it resocializes the deviant into the
objective reality of the symbolic universe of the
society."[17]

Where realities are widely discrepant, prognosis for
therapy is not good. The cohesive function of therapy
complements another universe-maintaining conceptual enterprise, nihilation, which negates everything outside the
symbolic universe. The two have a challenge in pluralistic societies, where subuniverses of meaning clash or
compete or raise contradictions and challenges to the
dominant society, and result in varying degrees of alienation and margination.

For these authors, therapy is a large and sociological construct. It does have specific institutional
arrangements and a therapeutic process involving a theory
of deviation, diagnosis, and curative process. When
negation, or the fear of chaos outside the symbolic
universe, or guilt arising from moving away from social
norms, bring persons back to the symbolic universe of
society, therapy may be sought for re-engagement. Thus
meaning systems, undergirded by mythological symbolic
systems, must cover these and other boundary situations

in life, and bring persons back into the system, a task
of theology,[18] but also of therapy. Both are concerned with plausibility structures to maintain community. The role of the therapist in such a situation is
intriguing. Civil courts, justice systems, and
exorcists would fit this description. In addition, the
one applying the therapeutic process is apt to be a
marginal type, an "expert," or an "intellectual," so
marginal by definition.[19] "Individualism" as such is
also a partially unsocialized situation, and individual-
ists are more mobile socially, vocationally, and physically. In a pluralistic society the therapist is theoretically a crucial institutional cog to maintain social
cohesion.

Berger, Berger, and Kellner give another perspective
on the conditions that might require therapy, although
they do not speak of therapy as directly as does the
earlier book. They speak of "consciousness" from a
sociological framework as shared views of the world, along
with roles and patterns suitable to that world and meanings involved. Where other life worlds are seen as
having viable political and religious integrations,
socialization and legitimation acquire a relativity that
becomes uncomfortable as monolithic authorizing structures
give way. Additionally, the consciousnesses associated
with the bureaucratic state and with science and technological production raise the sense of anonymity, alienation,
and discontent. Persons are thrown back upon the need to
develop more individuated life plans and meanings as
individuals and in families. This, too, is isolating, and
raises anxiety about belonging and about personal responsibility. The sense of homelessness, along with meaning
and value issues in modern consciousness, appears to make
the therapeutic process need to include ministry, or to be

contained in the concept of ministry and the function of
organized religion. Because of the different tasks set
for the works involved, somewhat different roles are
assigned to the therapist, both within a sociological
perspective.

Similarly, there is no one psychological understanding of the therapeutic process. The DSM III provides a
reference for diagnosis of mental disorders based upon
general criteria of painfulness or dysfunction, and involving more than the relationship between individual and
society. Yet the treatment of mental disorders does not
contain the whole of the meaning of therapy even within
a psychological model. Growth and prevention issues,
along with crisis issues, are only nominally referred to
in the manual as separately coded diagnoses not defined
as mental illness but requiring treatment. Individualism,
margination, or alienation may be only threatening in a
social perspective, but may be quite functional for the
person involved. A case in point might be gender identity
disorders, dealing with incongruence between anatomical
sex and gender identity. "Gender identity is defined as
private experience of the gender role, and gender role as
public expression of gender identity."[20] Disorders in the
DSM III have to do with discomfort in the roles and the
social life-world rather than in disturbance in gender
identity, which is rare. Gender identity is, of course,
based upon the interplay between social definitions and
the infant/child's self-perceptions and identifications.
However, it is established powerfully at a very early age
and is not apt to change after this. Continuing social
definitions of reality may make a person feel marginal--
rejected or "different"--but they are not apt to change
gender identity once it is set. Persons may, however,

be helped to live more comfortably in society, which is
a subtle form of socialization.

Within the definitions of mental disorders by the
relatively atheoretical DSM III, any number of psychological theories may be applied with different consequences
for the understanding of origins and the treatment process.
The varying sources of social knowledge for the individual
will be perceived differently by these theoretical bases,
and treatment defined accordingly. For a behaviorist it
will not matter much what social learnings or experiences
may have been missing in the past, and for a psycho-
analyst it may not matter much (for some time) what is
happening dysfunctionally in the present, due to dif-
erences in weightings of what needs to happen in the
curative process. Most therapy falls somewhere between
these extremes, and takes some cognizance of history,
present behavior, and goals of life (as well as of therapy). A model for assessment might follow the lines of
identifying the particular sources of the social knowledge
that is causing the pathology or impacting it.

There is no one theological understanding of the
therapeutic process. Perspectives on pastoral counseling
by the various theologically endorsing groups range from
purely exclusionist (spiritual well-being is separate from
psychological and situational well-being) or reductionist
(spiritual well-being is identical to psychological
functionality) to ways of trying to integrate theology and
psychology in practical matters. This has been until
recently an underrated area in seminary education, and one
that is of vital importance in the role of pastor in a
parish. In this case, a pastor is dealing with a relatively confined range of theological variation. In the case of
a pastoral psychotherapist working in a pastoral counseling center or offering counseling services to a wider

theological range in clients, the theological task is
harder. It includes "getting inside" the world view of
the client to understand the functioning and the integration of that system. The therapist, outside of exclusionist and reductionist models, has a primary responsibility not to change the client's beliefs and faith
system, but to help the client to a more mature theological perspective. "Mature" in this case would be
according to the criteria of more adequate and more
broadly applicable faith. It would include the ability
of the client to think more theologically about his or
her own life and goals.

CONCLUSIONS

     The importance of a sociology of knowledge for pastor-
al therapy:
     Sociology of knowledge allows different organizations
of what is known. In this chapter, and in respect to
therapy, knowledge has been seen as pertaining to that of
the therapist, the client, and the society or societies
involved. It has been seen as organizing theoretical
material around a number of human science disciplines, and
within disciplines as different theories and constructs.
Whether this organization is according to a particular
discipline, or according to different theoretical perspectives within a discipline, it will reflect a particular
framework, presuppositions, and biases, and will use the
data base selectively, based upon particular values. Each
is partial and perspectival, and will have a particular
range of usefulness, and equally important, a particular
range of invalidity. The organization of knowledge, as a
starting point for viewing the background context for
therapy, is helpful--what organizations are involved at

the level of discipline and theoretical base for therapy?
Some flexibility in working with these may prove to be
both clarifying of the process and enabling of successful therapy.

Problems raised, and new insights gained in consideration of the sociology of knowledge in relation to therapy:

In spite of my psychological bias, I have found
sociology helpful in elaborating and clarifying some of
the social sources of pathology. Insights from my consideration of the sociology of knowledge include the need
for the person to have a social home and an adequate
symbolic universe, the need to consider both place in
society (in terms of self-worth, role, fulfillment, belonging, etc.) and individual need-meeting, the need to
identify the particular social context of pathology, and
beyond these, insights from sociology of knowledge that
can inform the therapeutic process as it treats problematic social learning.

However, I do not find any possibility of doing without my own grounding in psychological theory as a basis for
therapy, and I have begun to formulate a new way of
perceiving the relationship between disciplines in the
human sciences. Each discipline is apt to consider itself
to the exclusion of the others. This has been brought out
sharply for me in the relation between psychology and
theology. None of the varying methods is problem-free.
Both attempt to describe the whole person. Therefore, to
divide up turf is as unacceptable as to reduce one to the
other. Possibly any method of dealing with them is
inappropriate. Each, and sociology similarly, attempts to
describe a symbolic universe which is a whole. Since it
begins with a particular perspective from which it views
reality, it will contain limitations and biases that are

necessary and unavoidable. Where it deals with areas
of prime concern to another discipline, each will do so
inadequately, but it also will challenge the other
discipline to be broader and more adequate at the same
time that it is challenged. If each can be perceived as
relative to certain ranges of usefulness, and with
limitations accordingly related to validity within those
ranges, each may complement the other in a helpful way.
The DSM III neglects many sociologically based problems,
particularly the social aspects of alienation, margination, threats to symbolic universes, pluralistic values,
and the pressures arising from these. Sociological theory
is apt to leave out the individual pain, creativity, the
need to grow, leadership and psychosis. Neither is sure
what to do with grounding meaning and value, and with
transcendence. But theology in turn needs to be grounded
in praxis--aware of the needs and situations of persons
and of its own sociological embodiment. Data from all
these areas is important to reflect accurately the human
situation in relation to the perspective of each, but
each will by its very presuppositions be limited as to the
extent or method by which data for the other fields can be
handled.

It is important to know the dimensions of the knowledge fields we are operating within, so that we do not
give them undue ultimacy nor see them as the only possible
constructs. Matching the range of usefulness with theoretical constructions does not seem like an unreasonable
task, but it appears lacking in the past, hidden by
territorialism. We need all the constructs of human
sciences--history, philosophy, anthropology, theology,
sociology, psychology, ethics, political science. Each
will on occasion subsume some portions of others, but
there is also an advantage in maintaining a tension and

not reducing one to the other. If the dimensions within
which they function are clear, along with presuppositions
and limitations, the total advantage will be significant.

A large question remains relating to therapy, but
also by implication to the human science disciplines as
well--the question of normativity. What is good and what
is better, and how is that validated? Sociology, because
of its particular perspective, tends to have to deal with
normativity in social terms, and ends up with problems of
conservation and conformity as determining. Psychology,
on the other hand, has to struggle against continuing
implications that individual need-meeting is the norm, and
ends up with problems of isolation and egocentrism. I do
not mean to imply that these are never overcome, only that
they are always present as concerns, due to the theoretical bias. Theology, on the other hand, has problems
relating forms of transcendence to real life, or even
defining it without help from other disciplines. Within
the limited area of therapy, the question of norms will
affect the therapist's location of pathology and strategy
and goals for the curative process, as well as the client's
own perception of the process and what he or she values
as an outcome of therapy. How therapist or client deal
with prevailing social norms when theirs differ significantly is also an issue.

The sociology of knowledge gives a perspective for
viewing the complementarity of different disciplines within the range of the human sciences, which may illumine
psychological theories of perceiving various sources of
knowledge in the developmental and socialization process.
This in turn may provide insight for defining strategy
and treatment goals in the definition of mental disorders
or other therapy, and indicated treatment.

NOTES

1. H. Richard Niebuhr provides an insightful discussion of the styles of relationships that exist between theological and social issues in *Christ and Culture* (New York: Harper & Row, 1951). This model can be adapted to the relationship between psychology and/or sociology and theology.

2. Herbert M. Lefcourt, *Locus of Control: Current Trends in Theory and Research* (New Jersey: Lawrence Erlbaum Associates, 1976).

3. Milton Rokeach, *The Open and Closed Mind* (New York: Basic Books, 1960).

4. Peter Berger, Brigitte Berger, and Hansfried Kellner, *The Homeless Mind* (New York: Vintage Books, 1974), p. 64.

5. Peter L. Berger and Thomas Luckmann, *The Social Construction of Reality* (Garden City, New York: Anchor Books, 1967), p. 176.

6. Karl Mannheim, *Ideology and Utopia* (New York: Harvest/HBJ Book, Harcourt, Brace, Jovanovich, 1936), p. 206.

7. Ibid., p. 268.

8. Karl Marx, *Selected Writings in Sociology and Social Psychology*, translated by T. B. Bottomore (New York: McGraw Hill, 1950), p. 79.

9. Ibid., p. 77.

10. Max Scheler, *Problems of a Sociology of Knowledge*, translated by Manfred S. Frings (London, Boston, and Henley: Routledge & Kegan Paul, 1980), p. 81.

11. Berger, et al., *The Homeless Mind*, p. 66.

12. Ibid., pp. 72 ff.

13. Berger and Luckmann, *The Social Construction of Reality*, pp. 113 ff.

14. American Psychiatric Association, Diagnostic and Statistical Manual III (Washington, D. C.: 1980, p. 6.

    15. Berger and Luckmann, *The Social Construction of Reality*, pp. 95-104.

    16. Ibid., pp. 112-114.

    17. Ibid., p. 114.

    18. Ibid., pp. 104-116.

    19. Ibid., p. 126.

    20. DSM III, p. 261.

PART IV

SOCIOLOGY OF KNOWLEDGE AND NEW RELIGIOUS
AND SOCIAL MOVEMENTS

TOWARD A CRITIQUE OF MODERNITY

Peter L. Berger

As so often, the problem begins with language. In
this instance the very term "modernity" has been given a
significance both normative and distortive by the myth of
progress which has crucially shaped Western thought since
the Enlightenment. It is a normative significance because
modernity is understood as intrinsically superior to whatever preceded it--the opposite of being modern is being
backward, and it is difficult to entertain the notion
that backwardness may have something to say for itself.
And, ipso facto, it is a distortive significance because
such a perspective makes it very hard to see modernity
for what it is--*a historical phenomenon,* in principle
like any other, with an empirically discernible beginning
and set of causes, and therefore with a predictable end.
Minimally, a critique of modernity must begin with a
bracketing of the normative assumptions about it.

Marion Levy has defined modernization as "the ratio
of inanimate to animate sources of power." This is not an
altogether satisfactory definition, but it is useful in
pointing to the core of the phenomenon, namely, the transformation of the world brought about by the technological
innovations of the last few centuries, first in Europe and
then with increasing rapidity all over the world. This
transformation has had economic, social, and political
dimensions, all immense in scope. It has also brought on
a revolution on the level of human consciousness,
fundamentally uprooting beliefs, values, and even the
emotional texture of life. A transformation of such vast-
ness could not have taken place without profound anguish,

first of all material (due to the exploitation and
oppression that have accompanied modernization virtually
everywhere), but also cultural and psychological. It
should not be surprising, therefore, that from the
beginning modernization has been in a seesaw dynamic with
forces opposing it.

In the contemporary world this dynamic of moderniza-
tion/countermodernization is readily visible. There
continue to be aggressive ideologies of modernity, con-
fidently asserting that the transformations of our age
are the birth pangs of a better life for humanity. These
modernizing ideologies span the great political divide;
there are capitalist as well as socialist versions. There
also exist a variety of countermodern ideologies, both in
the so-called advanced industrial societies (as in the
counterculture and in segments of the ecology movement--
I need only refer here to the debate over the limits of
growth) and in the countries where modernization is a
more recent event (as in miscellaneous blends of neotradi-
tionalism, nationalism, and indigenous modifications of
the socialist vision). A critique of modernity requires
further an act of deliberate detachment from these
polemical positions, at least on an ad hoc basis. A
critique is not an attack, but rather an effort to
perceive clearly and to weigh the human costs. It should
be stressed that such a critical attitude *in no way*
precludes the existential possibility of other attitudes
as well, including the attitudes of moral judgment and
political engagement.

Only the barest outline of such a critique can be
offered here. The focus will be on five dilemmas that
modernity has imposed on human life. Each of these
dilemmas can be studied (and, I believe, to a degree
explained) by historical and social-scientific methods.

Each of them touches on profound philosophical questions
as well as on very practical questions.

The first dilemma is brought on by the *abstraction*
that is one of the basic characteristics of modernity.
It is also, perhaps, the most intensely studied aspect
of the phenomenon, especially by sociologists. Georg
Simmel put it at the center of his analysis of modern
society, an emphasis that has recently been reiterated by
Anton Zijderveld. But, in the guise of different ter-
minologies, most of the classical theorists in the
sociological tradition have attempted to grasp this aspect
of the phenomenon--Karl Marx (capitalism as the source of
"alienation" and "reification"), Emile Durkheim (the relation between "organic solidarity" and *anomie*), Max Weber
(the discontents of "rationalization"), and others.

The abstraction of modernity is rooted in the underlying institutional processes on which modernity rests--
the capitalist market, the bureaucratized state (as well
as the numerous nonstate bureaucracies of more recent
origin), the technologized economy (as well as the
domination by technology of noneconomic sectors of society), the large city with its heterogenous agglomeration
of people, and the media of mass communication. On the
level of social life, this abstraction has entailed the
progressive weakening, if not destruction, of the concrete
and relatively cohesive communities in which human beings
have found solidarity and meaning throughout most of
history. On the level of consciousness, the same abstraction has established forms of thought and patterns of
emotionality that are profoundly inimical (if you will,
"repressive")with regard to broad sectors of human
experience. Specifically, a quantifying and atomizing
cognitive style, originally at home in the calculations
of entrepeneurs and engineers, has invaded other areas

(from the theory of political ethics to the praxis of
the bedroom) in which that style has produced severe
discontents. In the highly modernized Western countries
the process of abstraction has gone so far that a great
effort is required to wrench free of it, even in a simple
act of perception (let alone in actual living). In the
countries of the Third World the collision between modernizing abstraction and older, more concrete forms of
human thought and experience can be observed every day,
often in dramatic situations.

It is certainly too much to say that all the facets
of this process of abstraction are fully understood, although all are "empirically available" and especially
accessible to the methods of the social sciences. In
any case, the process is sufficiently understood, I think,
to permit a passage from description to critique. Philosophically, the critique will have to face a deceptively
simple question: To what extent is the cognitive style
of abstraction adequate for an understanding of the world
and of human experience? This question has repeatedly
been asked in various ways from within Western philosophy;
it seems to me that today it may be asked in a much richer
way as a result of the encounter with non-Western traditions of thought. Practically and politically, the
question is once more deceptively simple: Given the fact
that modern man must live in a number of inevitably abstract structures (notably those given with technology
and bureaucracy), how can there also be room in society
for the rich concreteness of human life? Once more, the
scope of this question ranges from the constructions of
political order to the way in which men and women go to
bed together. And let me make just one slightly polemical
observation here: Contrary to current intellectual fashion, the question cannot be resolved by a critique of

capitalism alone. To date, in any event, socialist
societies have exchanged the "alienations" of the market
for the "alienations" of bureaucracy (leaving aside
whatever else may be the gains or costs of socialism).
In this matter, it is still timely to recall what H. L.
Mencken said some fifty years ago: "To believe that
Russia has got rid of the evils of capitalism takes a
special kind of mind. It is the same kind that believes
that a Holy Roller has got rid of sin."

The second dilemma is that of *futurity*--a profound
change in the temporal structure of human experience, in
which the future becomes a primary orientation for both
imagination and activity. Of all the simplifications
one may commit in describing the process of modernization, perhaps the least misleading is to say that
modernization is a transformation in the experience of
time. John Mbiti asserts that he knows of not a single
African myth that deals with the future. I cannot evaluate this assertion, but it is clear that modernization
everywhere (not just in Africa) means a powerful shift
in attention from past and present to the future. What
is more, the temporality within which this future is
conceived is of a very peculiar kind--it is precise,
measurable, and, at least in principle, subject to human
control. In short, it is time to be mastered. This
temporal transformation takes place on three levels. On
the level of everyday life, clocks and watches become
dominant (it is no accident that the wristwatch is a prime
symbol of being modern in many Third World countries,
and what a potent symbol it is--a machine strapped onto
the naked skin, machine time superimposed upon the organic
rhythms of the body). On the level of biography, the
individual's life is perceived and actively planned as a
"career" (say, in mobility). On the level of an entire

society, national governments or other large-scale
institutions map out projects in terms of a "plan" (say,
a five-year plan, a seven-year plan, or even more long-
range scenarios such as "stages of economic growth" or
the "transition to communism"). On all three levels, this
new temporality is in sharp conflict with the way in which
human beings have experienced time before the advent of
modernity.

In premodern China the clock was a harmless toy; in
Europe it became what Baudelaire called *"un Dieu sinistre,
effrayant, impossible."* The same institutional forces
that produced Western abstraction gave birth to this
sinister divinity in the West. The clock as well as the
calendar come to dominate human life as the latter is
technologized and bureaucratized. Within the spheres of
technology and bureaucracy there is little chance of
escaping this domination. But this peculiar temporality
has gone far beyond these limited spheres. To a remarkable degree we have become engineers and functionaries
even in the most intimate aspects of our lives. There is
a powerful nexus between "time engineering" in industry
and in the nursery, as there is among the "planning" of
military strategists, guidance counselors, and sex
therapists.

The philosophical questions that must be addressed to
modern futurity are, I think fairly obvious (though I'm
not at all sure that they are easily answered). The
practical and political questions are no less important.
There is no reason to doubt what battalions of psychologists have been telling us for decades, namely, that the
pace of modern living is detrimental to mental well-being
and may also be harmful to physical health. Futurity
means endless striving, restlessness, and a mounting
incapacity for repose. It is precisely this aspect of

modernization that is perceived as dehumanizing in many
non-Western cultures. There have also been strong
rebellions against it within Western societies--a good
deal of both youth culture and counter-culture can, I
think, be understood as insurrections against the
tyranny of modern futurity, not to mention the current
vogue of "transcendental-meditation" and similar mystical
aspirations toward a liberating, timeless "now." I would
contend that these movements are to be taken very seriously. To be sure, there is no alternative to the
dominance of futurity in certain areas of social life. To
bring this point home, one has only to imagine public
utilities operated by hippies and government agencies by
contemplative monks. (Sometimes it seems that such take-
overs have in fact taken place. But that's another
story.) A romantic rejection of futurity may be aesthet-
ically attractive, but it has little practical value. The
critical task is rather a painstaking analysis of the
possible *limits* of this particular temporal mode. Put
simply, the question is how and in what areas of social
life it may be possible to do without clocks and calendars.

The political component of such a critique must, above
all, deal with the human costs of every long-range project
or plan that bases itself on an allegedly certain future.
The world is full of people (most of them intellectuals,
bureaucrats, and politicians) who claim to know the future
by this or that allegedly scientific method--and who
impose enormous sacrifices on the putative beneficiaries
of their wonderful programs. These people (latter-day
secularized proponents of Biblical eschatology) range from
left to right on the political spectrum. Their claims
regarding the future must be subjected to ruthless

342   RELIGION AND THE SOCIOLOGY OF KNOWLEDGE

scrutiny. It seems to me that sociology, with its habits
of irreverence and debunking, is particularly suited for
this critical task.

The dilemma is that posed by the modern process of
individuation. Modernization has entailed a progressive
separation of the individual from collective entities,
and as a result has brought about a historically unprecedented counterposition of individual and society. This
individuation is, as it were, the other side of the coin
of the aforementioned abstraction, and it relates to the
latter in a paradoxical way. The external, social-
structural causes are the same--to wit, the weakening of
the all-embracing, all-containing communities that used
to sustain the individual in premodern societies. The
paradox is that, at the same time as these concrete
communities have been replaced by the abstract mega-
structures of modern society, the individual self has
come to be experienced as both distinct and greatly
complicated--and, by that very fact, in greater need of
the personal belonging which is difficult in abstract
institutions. It is likely that this paradox has taken
a particularly virulent form in Western societies because
of some factors that are not intrinsic to the modernizing
processes as such--for example, the factor of the Christian tradition in the West, which made possible the
development of a highly sophisticated conception of
individual rights, and the factor of what (following
Philippe Aries) one may call the "invention of childhood"
by the rising bourgeoisie of Europe, which resulted in
peculiarly individuating patterns of socialization. If
that is so, one may conceive of modernization *without*
Western-type individuation in societies lacking these
factors in their history (Japan is an instructive case in
point; China may turn out to be another). Even in such

societies, however, there is the problem of mediating
between the new megastructure and the communities which
order individual life. Thus it is relatively easy to
teach people with (let us say) a medieval self-image
to fly jet planes; it is more difficult to build medieval notions of personal loyalty and obligations into
bureaucratic institutions (both the Japanese and the
Chinese have had interesting problems of this kind).

Be this as it may, modernity, by simultaneously
making institutions more abstract and the people in them
more individuated, has enormously aggravated the threat
of what sociologists call *anomie*. Once again this dilemma
has both philosophical and practical-political dimensions.
The current debate over the meaning of equality at least
has the merit of having made more people aware of the
philosophical dimension. It may also serve to uncover an
underlying ambiguity of people wanting *both* individual
autonomy (often pushed to an extreme libertarian pole)
and communal solidarity. Only by understanding this
dilemma of individuation can one understand the recurring
propensity of Western intellectuals (who, for reasons that
cannot be elaborated here, experience the anomic threat
more sharply than other people) to be fiercely committed
to individual rights and at the same time to be uncrit-
ically admiring of totalitarian societies that deprive
the individual of all rights in the name of the collectivity. There are vital questions here of philosophical
anthropology and of political ethics: Is the modern
conception of the individual a great step forward in the
story of human self-realization (as liberal thought since
the Enlightment has maintained), or is it, on the
contrary, a dehumanizing aberration (as it would appear
to be in the perspective of most non-Western traditional

cultures)? These questions, as should be clear, also
have a practical side in public policy and in the way
people manage their personal lives.

Those who view modern individuation as an aberration
have no real problem. They just have to decide which
system of collectivism appeals to them most. Those who
value the rights and liberties of the individual, despite
the high price in *anomie* and occasional anarchy, face
practical and political problems of staggering scope.
The overriding problem is the search for social arrangements that will at least partially satisfy the yearning
for community without dismantling the achievements of
individuation. Such a search will take different forms in
different countries, and it is by no means limited to the
West or necessarily dependent on a Western-type political
order (as ethnocentric Western social scientists continue
to maintain). Thus this search is at the heart of what
has been called "socialism with a human face" in Eastern
Europe. In parts of the Third World there is the problem
of the still powerful presence of those who want to opt
out of much or most of modernization, including modern
individuation. In all of this there is ample room for
that combination of theoretical questioning and practicality which has always been the hallmark of the "sociological imagination" at its best.

The fourth dilemma is that of *liberation*. An essential element of modernization is that large areas of human
life, previously considered to be dominated by fate, now
come to be perceived as occasions for choice--by the
individual, or by collectivities, or by both. This is
the, if you will, Promethean element in modernity, which
has always been seen by the adherents of traditional
religious world views as a fundamental rebellion against
the divinely instituted human condition. Modernization

entails a multiplication of options. One of the most
seductive maxims of modernity is that *things could be
other than what they have been*. This is the turbulent
dynamism of modernity, its deeply rooted thirst for
innovation and revolution. Tradition is no longer
binding; the status quo can be changed; the future is
an open horizon. This dynamism can be traced back to
early developments in Western history, but there are
more proximate institutional causes. Today it is not so
much that individuals become convinced of their capacity
and right to choose new ways of life, but rather that
tradition is weakened to the point where they *must* choose
between alternatives whether they wish it or not. The
existentialist dictum of freedom as a condemnation is
peculiarly and revealingly modern. The sociological
theories of Arnold Gehlen have gone furthest, in my
opinion, in shedding light on this transition from fate
to choice. Gehlen also makes understandable why this
change produces tensions and discontents of great severity. He has shown persuasively that one of the most
archaic functions of society is to take away from
individuals the burden of choice. With modernization,
this "unburdening" function becomes progressively weak-
ened--fate is challenged, the social order ceases to be
taken for granted, and both individual and collective
life come to be more and more uncertain. To be sure,
there is an exhilarating quality to this liberation.
There is also the terror of chaos.

The philosophical question, of course, concerns the
limits, if any, of human liberation. It is once more the
classical question of discerning between what may and what
may not be changed in the human condition--but it is a
question that looks very different today than it did in
the time of the Stoics, because today we have a vastly

different view both of the relativity and the manip-
ulability of the human world. The practical question is
how to sustain (or, for that matter, to construct *de
novo*) social arrangements that provide at least a modicum
of stability in an age of dynamic uncertainties. This
is a problem for the revolutionary no less than for the
conservative; indeed, it could be argued that the problem
is even graver for the revolutionary, because the social
arrangements that he constructs do not have even the
remnants of traditional taken-for-grantedness still
available to the conservative, and are therefore all the
more precarious in a world in which fate has been abol-
ished.

The liberation from all bonds that limit choice (be
it individual or collective) continues to be one of the
most powerful inspirations of modernity. Its price is
precisely that "anguish of choice" which existentialists
have described so well. The latter phenomenon has brought
about that peculiarly modern paradox that Erich Fromm has
called the "escape from freedom"--an escape which actually
views *itself* as a liberation. This may not be very
logical, but it makes much sense psychologically. Thus
there are two quite contradictory notions of liberation
in the world today (not only in the West): liberation of
the individual from fate of any kind (social, political,
even biological), and liberation of the individual from
the *anomie* of a condition without fate. Put simply, there
is the ideal of liberation *as* choice and the ideal of
liberation *from* choice. The two ideals crisscross contemporary values and ideologies, and it is of great importance that their social and psychological presuppositions
be clearly understood; otherwise, all becomes confusion.

Finally, there is the dilemma of *secularization*.
Modernization has brought with it a massive threat to the

plausibility of religious belief and experience. Put
differently, modernity, at least thus far, has been
antagonistic to the dimension of transcendence in the
human condition. Again one may ask whether the distinctive cultural conditions of the Western culture that
served as the matrix of modernity have led to this result;
conversely, one may ask whether modernization *without*
secularization is possible in different cultural contexts.
But even in Third World countries, where traditional
religion has shown great resilience and even the capacity
for strong resurgences (for instance, in the Islamic
world), the secularizing effects of modernization have
been felt. The reasons for this are not at all mysterious. The common explanation of secularization in terms
of the impact of modern science and technology undoubtedly has much merit; I think that equally important are
the consequences of the pluralizing and ipso facto rel-
ativizing forces of modernization. Secularization, of
course, has not meant that religious belief and practice
have disappeared, and not even the most thorough proponents of so-called secularization theory regard such
disappearance as a likely outcome in the foreseeable
future (the reappearance of strong religious impulses in
the Soviet Union, after half a century of intense anti-
religious propaganda backed up by repressive actions of
all kinds, is very suggestive on this point). But
secularization *has* meant a weakening of the plausibility
of religious perceptions of reality among large numbers
of people, especially as the world view of secularity has
come to be "established" by the intellectual elites and
in the educational institutions of modern societies.

Obviously, religious and nonreligious observers will
differ in the assessment of this phenomenon. For those
who see transcendence as a necessary (because true)

constituent of the human condition, secularization is an
aberration, distortive of reality and dehumanizing. For
them, the critique of modernity will have a crucially
important theological dimension; indeed, their critique
will probably both begin and end with theological prop-
ositions. But those who do not have such religious
commitments (say, agnostic sociologists, or even atheistic ones) can also see the dilemma posed by secularization. The dilemma comes from the fact (an empirically
"available" fact, *not* a theological proposition) that
secularization frustrates deeply grounded human aspira-
tions--most important among these, the aspiration to
exist in a meaningful and ultimately hopeful cosmos.
This dilemma is closely related to what Max Weber called
the need for "theodicies," that is, for satisfactory
ways of explaining and coping with the experiences of
suffering and evil in human life. There are, of course,
secular "theodicies," and they clearly work for some
people. It appears, however, that they are much weaker
than the religious "theodicies" in offering both meaning
and consolation to individuals in pain, sorrow, or doubt.

This last dilemma, more than the preceding four,
raises more philosophical than practical problems, although it, too, has its practical side. The question here
is, quite simply, that of the rights of religion in a
modern society. I think it is no accident that counter-
modernizing trends and movements have frequently been
characterized by powerful reaffirmations of transcendence.
The experiential realities of mystery, awe and transcendent hope are hard to eradicate from human consciousness. Yet, even in Western countries with strong legal
safeguards for religious liberty, there is an Enlightenment tradition of "delegitimating" these experiences;
the tradition, of course, is strongest in the cultural

and educational elites. For very sociological (that is
non-theological, *non*-philosophical) reasons, I doubt that
this is a viable state of affairs. It goes without saying that there are issues of public policy involved in
this (in the United States, most of these relate to the
question of how the constitutional separation of church
and state is to be interpreted).

   I believe that the critique of modernity will be one
of the great intellectual tasks of the future, be it as a
comprehensive exercise or in separate parts. The scope is
broadly cross-cultural. It will be a task that, by its
very nature, will have to be interdisciplinary; I'm
enough of a parochialist to believe that sociology has a
uniquely useful contribution to make. It will also be a
task linking theory and praxis, touching, as it does,
certain fundamental philosophical as well as highly
concrete practical-political questions. The task is also
of human and moral urgency. For what it is finally all
about is the question of how we, and our children can live
in a humanly tolerable way in the world created by modernization.

THE SIXTIES GENERATION: A FISSION
TRIP TO THE PAST

Marilyn Hauck

INTRODUCTION

A world view doubling as an understanding of the
source and creation of the physical universe, and, as an
explanation of the logic and purpose of such a reality,
has historically been a combination product of theological/
philosophical inspiration and scientific observation. Such
understandings have moved from the static and detailed
theological frameworks of traditional societies to the
wide-ranging speculative theories of modern scientific
method. Where once rationalism tried to fit itself into
a world view set by revelation, now religion struggles to
stay relevant in the world according to mathematical
formula.

In the ancient world, cosmology did not change much,
for that was part of cosmological understanding. Even by
the Middle Ages, when Aquinas systematized theology and
cosmology, he went to classical philosophy, mainly that of
Aristotle, for a basic structure. Since physical creation
was understood as a completed and stable structure evoked
directly from the mind of God, the social structure was
likewise regarded as fixed into the feudal estates of
Church, Nobility, and Commoners. History was a pre-
ordained and repeating drama. But even this slow drip of
time could erode the institutional stalagmites as it
shaped the economic viability of a middle class of trades-
men, artisans and craftsmen. Ownership of land as the

basis of wealth was called into question. With the
breath of the Renaissance came a revival of interest in
empiricism and applied cognition as set forth by classical
thinkers. Attempts to explain reality moved from "Explanation by Purpose" to "Experiment and Theory."[1] Copernicus
and Galileo pioneered the new methodology and were per-
secuted by the Church. It took Newton (1642-1727) to
bring the revolution in scientific outlook to its fruition
with the postulation of the law of gravity.[2] Newtonian
physics initiated a whole new world model. Instead of a
hierarchical system of personalities, with God as Puppet
Master, creation was a reliable mechanism which could be
understood. It was thought to be rather like a watch--
wound, set and left by its Maker to function on its own.
Rationalism with its emphasis on cause and effect flour-
ished in the political philosophy of John Locke, and in the
economic justifications of the stirring industrial revolution. With the passing of the medieval sense of God's
presence expressed in intervention and revelation, life's
meaning became a more pragmatic matter of human management.
Scientific proof replaced faith as a prevailing standard.
Protestantism and American national philosophy grew
directly on the roots of scientific rationalism. Since
life's meaning was a practical, here-and-now matter,
theology applied to the everyday life of middle class
effort. Rational believers "did well by doing good."
The two were connected by God's reward to the efficient
faithful. The fruits of industry and thrift were rein-
vested in still larger business holdings and tithed to
religious institutions which raised up larger buildings
and increased the missionary movements sent out to evangelize the heathen.

With the publication of *Origin of the Species* in 1859,
Darwin added the idea of progressive betterment to rational

scientific structure. The thrust of evolution came to be
applied institutionally and socially, as well as biologically. This interpretation of human destiny could imply a
humanly achieved Eden in the future. Such an idea countered conservative despair centered on the past garden and
humankind's banishment from perfection. American philosophy, sometimes called the "American Dream" or liberal
Protestantism, invested heavily in social, economic and
political manifestations of Newtonian and Darwinian world
models. We have swept along well into this century rely-
ing on the old mechanism, although newer postulations
point to different, or at least wider realities.

    This century has Einstein's addition of "relativity"
to scientific speculation. Troubled by the seeming lack
of order and reliability in macro- and microcosm, he
formulated the traits of molecules in relational terms.
Again a parallel process can apply scientific theory to
other fields and disciplines. For instance, historical
relativism notes that "although specific historical content is existential, it is experienced and its aspects are
grasped by various historical vantage points of the
mind."[3] Sociology of knowledge builds its understanding
of the variety of human social structures upon such
moorings.

    In this essay, I have chosen to use a scientific
model that only slightly preceded the social phenomenon
discussed here. Nuclear fission was an outgrowth of
Einstein's molecular investigation. I postulate that
something like social fission was manifested in the dis-
ruptive causes and effects around the postwar generation
of children--the youth of the sixties. They were the
first of our species to start out in a nuclear world.
I am not so much interested in describing exhaustively the
sociological causes and effects of that generation, as in

applying some of their interactions to a nuclear or
fission model. This is simply an attempt to develop a way
to think about the meaning of these notorious and well-
described youngsters.

The analogy will be made that this marker generation,
for some of the reasons mentioned here, acted as a trigger
to the "fissionable material" of surrounding society. Not
only was the generation split in the very nucleus of its
social/theological grounding, but the environment around
it reflected and reacted to this inner split. In numerous
ways the revolt of the sixties was comparable to other
attempts of the young to deny the mainstream world view.
For instance, the sixties generation shares many similar-
ities with the Romantic Movement of 1780-1840. Both
reacted to aspects of modernization: the Romantic Movement
to the Industrial Revolution with its concomitant trends
of urbanization and depersonalization; the Sixties Movement to high tech industry and to the rootless life style
that bloomed in the decade following World War II. Both
revolts were demodernizing.[4] They looked back to (different) times in an idealized past. The predecessors spent
much artistic energy in creating stories and poems around
the Middle Ages and Gothic themes,[5] while this century's
time travelers pursued rural and frontier America in
their dress and life styles.[6] Karl Mannheim, in *Ideology
and Utopia*, defines the conservative mind as one that
looks backward into the past for its utopia: ". . . the
conservative mode of experiencing time found the best
corroboration of its sense of determinateness in discovering the significance of the past, in the discovery of time
as the creator of value."[7] The children of the sixties
resembled other youthful rebels, but they were different,
too. They were aided by the very technology they sought
to discount. They were given weight by their numbers and

position in the social framework. Their very existence--
who they were and where they were--was closely shaped by
the aftermath of great global upheaval and destruction.

SPLITTING THE NUCLEI

Nuclear fission is the process of bombarding the
nuclei of heavy atoms with neutrons, so that they (the
nuclei) split. This process releases a great deal of
energy (mostly in the form of heat) and provides the ex-
plosive power for bombs.[8]

The factors (neutrons) that bombarded the children of
the postwar generation and succeeded in "splitting" a good
many of them are multiple and complex. Only a few causes
will be listed here.[9] Of first mention is the theological/
mythological deprivation which marked this generation
from previous ones. Modernization was closely linked to
liberal mainstream theology which tended to shun explicit
creed and biblical reference. Many of the parents of
these children had come from more fundamental backgrounds,
and in their embrace of modernity and urban living, had
turned away from the demands of particularistic belief.
God talk was embarrassing and was likely to uncover
individual differences in the newly-formed neighborhoods
of suburbia. Even social gospel with its updated view of
Christian ministry was watered down by the affluence of
suburban churches. Civil religion, closely enmeshed with
the American dream of progressive prosperity, was alive
and well in this new environment. The assumption was that
the younger generation implicitly understood this.

Shut away from biblical reference, the young were
also deprived of the legends and myth, even the history of
their ancestors. No longer were King Arthur and Robin
Hood a part of early educational experience, nor was

Western mythology cited. The fairy tales and nursery
rhymes that figured in the childhood of the parents were
not echoed in the new generation's ethos. In *The Uses of
Enchantment*, Bruno Bettelheim addresses some of this. Unlike the expectations of modern rationalism, the child is
not rational. Genuine fairy tales (as opposed to modern
cleaned-up and prettified versions) start exactly where
the child is emotionally. By means of a story, the child
is told where she/he needs to go (in the developmental
business of growing up), and how to accomplish this. The
message is implied by the use of fantasy material that the
child may adapt to his or her own condition.[10] If human
beings are innately religious and symbol oriented ("homo
religioso"), then some such expression can be expected
to manifest itself at some time in life. If developmental
tasks are not completed in the young child's id, the
adolescent may project fantasy material into his or her
current task of identifying the self. There is much about
the life styles and drug culture of the sixties revolt
that could support an assumption of delayed development,
acted out in ways more dangerous and destructive than the
earlier, culturally-shaped process around fantasy.

        Fundamental to liberal thought is the tenet that the
human baby is born without important inherited or innate
character traits--that in the expression of John Locke,
the personality is a "rasatabula" (blank tablet), waiting
to absorb any message written upon it. To this end, the
parental generation invested in books of child rearing--
child raising as a science, as it were. Never before had
such conscious effort been so widely expended in shaping
children in a new style. They were to be the leaders of
the as yet unknowable future. Taught to view their task
in this way, the young often reacted as though this

prospect was more fantastic than any of the stories con-
jured up by J. R. R. Tolkien.[11]

Another element of this generational splitting was
the experience of great change by the parents' generation.
Many of the parental group had grown up in depression and
fought (in some manner) in a global war. Many had come
from small towns or farming communities. After the war
they found themselves part of the rapidly growing suburban
scene. War had not only given impetus to technological
advancement, but through the G.I. Bill, had trained its
participants to become part of the boom of new products
and new life styles. The raw new communities were popu-
lated with families from other places. Generally they
were affluent, and oriented to consumption with the knowledge that the purchase of new products acted to guarantee
their own continued employment and advancement. The new
suburbanite was typically dependent upon "the job" and
"the company." Family members (other than the nuclear
family) were not in the immediate geographic picture, and
there was no capability of self support from the land or
from the familial commitment implied in traditional cultures. Work was "downtown" and separate from the home.
Increasingly the home was privatized and was seen as a
refuge from the "jungle" of business and the "dog-eat-dog"
world of competition.[12] That world could be entered only
after the due process of an education in increasingly
technical and specialized disciplines. Sophisticated
technology demands well-trained acolytes who must devote
adolescence and young adulthood to attending a program or
institution of formal learning. Children immured in these
institutions or in private homes seldom saw adults at work
or engaged in any serious decision-making process. Home
life and parental interaction with the young were reserved
for play and "togetherness," which was touted as being

"fun." The institution of the home began to appear
trivial and outside the scope of real meaning and action.
    A third bombardment on that period's youth was the
lack of a physical frontier at a time when there was the
capital, personnel and energy to take on such a challenge.
The parental group had been highly active in the broil of
war and war's aftermath attempting to create new Edens out
of the old. There was little understanding or involvement
of the young in this enterprise. Also, there was no wild
new land waiting to absorb the energy of these self-
disenfranchised. The modern adventures of space exploration, medicine, and physics all required motivation for a
disciplined level of education that many middle class
households seemed not to supply. With affluence, adolescence and young adulthood was promoted as a time for prolonged exploration of the "options" and "fit" of youth to
individuated occupations and life styles. There was
little to stimulate autonomy, self-knowledge and competence. Private suburbs began to be perceived as closed
and limiting, perhaps rather like the fission chamber in
a nuclear pile. The walls seemed monolithic and imprison-
ing.
    Uniformity and numbers were part of the suburban equa-
tion. Uniformity was more apparent than real among the
new settlers. There was a kind of gloss of recent experience (of war-related dislocations and occupations), but
there were none of the assumptions implicit in traditional
societies. Suburban dwellers were of many different
nationalities and from many different places, circumstances and background. Not only were cultural expectations altered in the newly urban setting, they were
different in individual homes in the same neighborhood.
Equality of economic status was more prevalent than more
profound cultural factors. Housing developments were

planned and defined by a given price range, and this
tended to allow the assumption that ability to pay that
price was the primary cultural factor.

The sheer size of the population relocation was unprecedented.   Subdivisions appeared almost overnight and
shopping centers proliferated in the wake of residences.
Schools, churches and libraries materialized where
horses had grazed the previous season.   Growth begat
statistics, norms and a "componential" view of social
relevance.[13]   Statistical data with mathematically drawn
norms tend to de-individuate.   One number is much like
another without an implicit history of ethical struggles
or personal experience.   A norm is an unrecognizable
amalgamation of averaged facts.   Who or what is a norm?

Berger mentions the factor of "componentiality" as a
kind of segmentation or assembly-line understanding of
human life.   One unit of life (or person) is deemed inter-
changeable with another, and will fit a slot or situation
equally well.   With such an understanding comes impersonal
labeling.   One is a "worker" of the "working class" or a
"housewife" in the "suburban household," and defines oneself as such.   This is "self-anonymization in a high
degree."[14]   Also, for the first time, children were regarded as the "primary products of the home."   Success on the
home front (or in the private sector) revolved around the
viability of these "products,"[15] who were expected to excel
in the structured and competitive arena of high tech industry.   The young resisted with what they had--themselves.
They declared themselves visibly different from the general
population in their hair styles and clothing.   They ate
different foods and listened to different music.   Thus
separated, they sought wholeness--with nature and with the
oppressed and their peers.   Wholeness did not include

larger society. It was defined over and against modern
social construction.

Finally, a word about speed is in order. Bombarding
neutrons are propelled at fantastic speeds. Society has
been transforming itself with increasing momentum since
World War II. Children born in a world of satellite
communications, television, computers and the threat of
nuclear destruction have no real knowledge of the rural
time and place of their immediate ancestors. "Today,
everyone born and bred before World War II is such an
immigrant in time--as his forebears were in space--strug-
gling to grapple with the unfamiliar condition of life in
a new era," says Margaret Mead.[16] Disappointed in the
present, youth in the sixties floundered toward a self-
created world of the past to go home to.

Nor does the pace slow. A few years may mark differences that were once generational. Siblings in the same
family may live in very different times and places.

THE CHAIN REACTION OF
THE CRITICAL MASS

As mentioned before, the fact of generational revolt
in the face of pervasive change is not unprecedented. What
is noteworthy in the latest round is the extent of the
effect--the chain reaction. "Critical mass" denotes the
volume necessary to sustain a chain reaction. To quote:
"The release of two or more neutrons by uranium fission
allows the process to multiply into a 'chain reaction,'"
that is, the neutrons produced cause the uranium^{235} nuclei
to fission and produce more neutrons, and so on."[17]

Chain reaction and fallout occurred with the sixties
rebellion. In the presence of critical mass, causes
quickly became effects, which then changed into somewhat

transformed causes again. Such spiraling suggests the
circle in Berger and Luckmann's *The Social Construction
of Reality*. This is described as a inward-outward cycle
of social and institutional creation in which the individual externalizes and objectifies an idea and is in turn
shaped and affected by the objectification. This new
interaction must then be internalized and re-understood
so that it can be objectified in its altered form.[18] Some
such process went on in the chain reaction of society, in
which the projections of the rebelling generation were
quickly objectified again by surrounding society. Very
quickly some of the outward signs of revolt were taken up
by the imitators--beards on men did not necessarily pin-
point age, and jeans became ubiquitous. Causes such as
preservation of the environment or physical fitness also
resonated in the surrounding society. The reasons and
goals for such adherence were changed by the new supporters, so that the objectification tilted toward a new
reality.

The middle class was its own Pygmalion. Tuned by
larger events, it created its suburban environment. Unlike the Watchmaker of rationality's understanding, the
middle class did not withdraw but stayed to live in its
own creation. It comprised the critical mass, available
for chain reaction. Members of this mass were as numerous
as were their baby-boom progeny. They had a superficial
kind of uniformity, born of their recent concentration
into an urban environment. But most important, they *were*
middle class, and as such, formed the normative center of
society. This was not a disaffection of some fringe of
the social order--some elite in education or experience--
some group with little influence or impact. The rebellion
came from the children of *the* American class--the traditional sustainers and definers of the country.

Further, this was not class warfare. It was generational conflict. The predictions of Marx about inevitable
class clash became obsolete in the newer generational
schism.[19] Differences between the socialization of generations of the same class formed the cutting edge of this
rebellion. Middle class American family rooms were the
laboratories that tested current problems of a sociology
of knowledge. As social programming has revolved around
class issues, there now is a similar thrust around
generational differences. Children's rights are being
buttressed with legal representation. Laws on child
abuse and state responsibility in domestic issues are
being reviewed and rewritten. There are even recent cases
in which children have sued parents for "inadequate upbringing."

Rationalization is easier and trauma is less when an
incongruity of socialization (disbelief or heresy) can be
ascribed to some "outsider." Otherness can be blamed on
race, nationality, differing religious faith, or class.
But domestic warfare is the worst kind, and two elements
of the sixties uprising were particularly galling. First,
in line with modern rationality,[20] the rebel generation
had been raised with great conscious effort by their
parents to fulfill a new and largely unknown destiny.
Americans have long been doing this in keeping with their
immigrant/pioneer heritage. Foreign families, newly
arrived in this country, often encouraged their offspring
to put aside their inherited old world culture for the
language and culture of the adopted country.[21] The
importance of continued upward mobility has conditioned
Americans to abet and tolerate children who "leave home
and can't return" except to visit. Disjunction between
age groups is persistent in a modern society.[22] The
trouble with this generation was that it went the "wrong

way," backwards into the sunset instead of forward towards
a new dawn. It wanted to dismantle modernity. And there
was an answering echo rumbling in the larger society.

I have characterized the milieu that produced the
young rebels as predominately white, middle-class and
liberal. Liberal mind sets must suffer particular *angst*
when their children drop out, for the liberal utopia in-
habits future time. Cooperative progeny are necessary to
such a belief of progressive evolvement. These children
are not measured against ancestral standards or by personal
comparison, but against the needs of a future incohate in
the present. The concrete nature of childhood thinking is
almost certainly not well tuned to these future abstrac-
tions, and a socialization process that ignores the dis-
parity between the nature of childhood and future requirements is bound to fail in intent.

In addition to the above anomolies, the media did
their share in assuring the existence of "critical mass."
What is a more ubiquitous witness to modernity than television and floods of printed materials--newspapers,
periodicals, books, and the like? No one who was able to
read or watch a television set could escape media impact.
The disaffection of the young was news. Their issues and
opinions were discussed, promoted, quoted, and sometimes
created. Chain reaction did not happen in an atmosphere
of sensory deprivation. The air was full of sights and
sounds.[23]

There is a double irony in the marriage of media to
the youthful refusal of modernization. State of the art
communication needed news. The war experience had
established a market for current events--the more dramatic
and ominous, the better. Public displays of polarities
were the stuff of ratings, never mind their basis of
rationale. The crusaders to the past were using, and being

used by, space-age technology. To dramatize their point
they were helping to assure the success of "the enemy,"
and incidentally invoking the pragmatic modernism that
"ends justify the means."

Finally, there was a high degree and incidence of
"marginality" in the critical mass of larger society itself.[24] That is to say that much of the subjective reality that the parental generation had internalized in its
premodern youth did not match the reality of the modern
present. Further, there was schism between their primary
and secondary socializations. Primary socialization takes
place in the child's experience of family life and is
(traditionally, at least) the most important and lasting
influence. Every subsequent socialization experience,
such as school and work, that further introduces the
social being into other objective realities is secondary
socialization.[25] Values and world views that the parental
generation had learned in childhood often did not mesh
with the educational and occupational assumptions of their
ongoing experience. The contrasting inputs frequently
remained mutually undigested, and fostered the compartmentalization of constructed public and private spheres.
Church and home formed the private sphere, separated from
all other daily experience which went on in the public
sphere of life. It is worth noting that divided minds
projected divided everyday realities.

To sum up, there was a response in larger society to
the youthful revolt. If there was not agreement in full,
there was further stripping of traditional assumptions
from many who were not of the specific generation. There
may have been some predisposition to follow the young
voices because of this society's history of generational
change. Also, the voices came from the valued children
of the leading class. They could not easily be thrown

away or sent into exile. So was the chain reaction set
into motion.

ATOMIZED SOCIETY

What characterizes a society which manifests chain
reaction to nuclear fission? One has the image of tiny
particles whirling about in search of stability and
weight, or some promise of wholeness.

In his sacred-secular theory, Howard Becker gives
such a description. He depicts a nearly formless aggregate of anonymous fragments--equalitarianism by non-
distinguishability rather than by adherence to principles
or "rights."

> Mental accessibility leading toward norm-
> lessness is widely prevalent and usually is
> non-rational. . . . The society is also fully
> open to scientific developments, even though
> these may clearly be detrimental to the re-
> maining vestiges of once operative value
> systems.[26]

In *Problems of a Sociology of Knowledge*, Max Scheler
constructs a tentative hierarchy of five value spheres,
from the bottom criterion of "sense values," to a top or
fifth sphere of "the Absolute." He defines the lower
values as being more dependent on material goods, more
divisible and quantifiable in content. This atomistic
level of the mass or herd has values that yield only
fleeting pleasure, and leaves the individual longing for
deeper satisfaction.[27] At this level the novel is
accepted as a matter of course. "Change for change sake"
trivializes any ultimate view of life. An objective observer can find much in these descriptions that fit the
picture of contemporary society.

To further the analogy of atomized society, we need
to consider the matter of pluralism as a consequence of
modernization. Production and advertising provide a wide
variety of choices in the marketplace. Part of the chain
reaction of the sixties was about the translation of super-
market variety into the most sacred and intimate areas of
human consciousness and theological grounding. Questions
of "What went wrong?" became anguished searches for individual wholeness and meaning in some tenable belief.

That fractured social atoms will pick up new consti-
tuents from random offerings (and as readily drop them)
can be illustrated in the growing number of independent
voters and the amorphus quality of the voting constituency.
There are fewer and fewer straight party-liners even in
elected office. Both major parties adapt with multiple
wings of choice--right, left, moderate, and every possible
hyphenated combination of labels. But this eclecticism is
much more specific than any party groupings. Individual
loyalties are inconsistent with the larger ideological
frameworks. A person may support liberal positions on
women's rights and aid to dependent children and yet be
conservative in matters of defense and foreign policy.
Historical assumptions fail and labels become meaningless
or too complicated to explain. First hand and largely
individual experience is the criterion.

Atomized society will radically shift political
programs in a single presidential term, as our last two
presidential elections illustrate. Scientific methodology
tries alternatives to solve specific problems. If an
alternative does not "prove out," it is quickly discarded.
It can be questioned whether the social process with its
commitment to organizational structure is well served by
tactics suitable for developing a new vaccine.

And what of matters *more* changeless and holy? American tradition marked its beginnings with God talk. God is
trusted on coinage and invoked before congressional ses-
sions. Protestantism has marched with representative
democracy to form a kind of mainstream concensus that has
allowed for growth in the acceptance of a new country.
Freedom of choice has carried into religious matters the
axiom "if you don't like it, found a new one!" The result
has been a veritable mall for those shopping for the best
and most suitable bargain in religious faith.

Steven Tipton, in *Getting Saved From the Sixties*,
lists three general alternatives for a generation burned
out on drugs, ideology, and communal experiments. Broadly
they are conservative fundamentalism, adaptions of Eastern
traditional religions, and psychological self-salvation
such as *est* and the like. Certainly, a feature of the
1970s was its "open and explicit religiosity," which surprised social observers.[28]

Eastern and Middle-Eastern additions to the American
scene include Eastern sects such as Hare Krisna and Zen, a
revival of Islam expressed in the Black Nation of Islam
and in Sufism and such hybrids of Eastern and Western
fundamentalism as the Unification Church founded by
Reverend Sun Myung Moon (the Moonies). In fact, the last
ten or fifteen years have seen Eastern religions return
the compliment of conversionary missionary work to this
country.[29] Just as Judaism and Catholicism have become
secularized or protestantized by modernism, Eastern
religions likewise tend to lose much of their ethnic
character, and adapt to the environment. Followers of
Krisna work the airports for donations, and the racial
politics of America are central to Black Islam.

It has long been a popular assumption that this
country's door was open to many kinds of immigrants and

their faiths. Now it would seem that almost every religious variety, home-grown or imported, is present. Not
surprisingly, this comes at a time when the factors of
modernity (pluralism, marginality, rationality, scientific
method, componentiality, disjunct generations, etc.)
guarantee discomfort with and disbelief in the old faiths.
In addition, the availability of literature, television,
and a mostly literate public make religous choice market-
able. The newly developed electronic church shapes its
service and message to the nature of the medium and its
ratings. Church membership is redefined as the passive
watchers of production numbers similar to variety show
entertainment. The religious ratings game is like any
other anonymous aggregate of mass statistics. Facts derived from such statistics have an economic bias.

In a world where every message must be short, simple
and, if at all possible, visual, the act of thinking about
theology and the ultimates is religious. Against a background of Protestant theological history, Peter Berger
argues in *The Heretical Imperative* that the contemporary
world is remarkable, "not so much for its secularity but
rather (for) its hunger for redemption and transcendence."[30] It becomes a survival issue to use the heretical imperative--the individual power of choice to select
religiously. Berger favors an inductive method of constructing religious belief. This inductive process is one
of three categories the sociologist describes. There is
also the deductive view that looks back and brings forward
traditional theology into the current setting. The re-
ductive rationale reduces all matters to what can be
proved scientifically. The inductive mind explores the
unknown, in that it seeks to determine its own belief
based on experience, and a knowledge of many theological
systems. The availability of information about the full

range of world religions allows inductive types to explore
almost every faith alternative. Berger recommends a contestation of Eastern and Christian elements as timely and
needed to "break through the impasse of contemporary
Christian theology."[31]

Scheler also speaks to a meeting of Eastern and
Western theology/philosophy. He praises the desirability
of complementing the scientific and technological advances
of the West with the psychic techniques (control of self
through inner life) of Asian cultures.[32] Contestation can
avoid confrontation and can become complementary in a
climate of totality, such as defined by Karl Mannheim:

> A total view (totality) implies both the
> assimilation and transcendence of the limit-
> ations of particular points of view. It re-
> presents the continuous process of the expan-
> sion of knowledge, and has as its goal not
> achievement of super-temporarily valid con-
> clusion but the broadest possible extension
> of our horizon of vision.[33]

The openness of modern individuated society coupled
with the availability of numerous choices would seem to
point to the possibility of a total view. Such a view
may operate in a survival capacity.

Times of religious and social confusion are marked by
increased supernaturalism and charismatic emphasis. In
the breakdown of institutionalism and authority, everyone
may seek the divine. In an odd way, this-worldly, pragmatic science has promoted the cause of religious revelation, not just in its role as promoter of social dis-ease,
but in its own history of inspiration and discovery. As
stated in the introduction, there is an intimate relationship between scientific discovery and the philosophical
and theological attempts to explain what such discovery

means in relation to human life. Experience suggests
that each new construct should have an allowance for
change, expansion, and growth. The relativity theory is
already somewhat superseded by the larger considerations
of quantum physics.

The overall message seems to be that revelation and
discovery cannot be successfully institutionalized into
"A Finished Chapter." Varying scientific breakthroughs
with their concomitant world view, *by their own appearances*
speak to the necessity of ongoing revelation and theological movement. Assimilation and choice-making go on in the
broader creation experience until they must be witnessed
in personal life styles and beliefs. It appears that
truth in time and space must be refreshed and reshaped
with constant application of ongoing life situations.
Made static or doctrinal, it withers and blocks the birth
of further revelation. Bryan Wilson, lecturing on the
change of faith, says that "religious institutions belated-
ly acknowledge changes that have already occurred, and have
caught a glimpse of themselves frozen in what, for modern
man seemed to be absurd postures."[34]

Ironically, the generation that triggered so much
awareness of absurd postures was not immune to its own
stereotypical statuary. In stripping the presuppositions
from surrounding consciousness, they may have opened up
the possibilities for more diversity and rapid change than
they imagined or intended. Marilyn Ferguson touches this
when in *The Aquarian Conspiracy* she writes:

A funny thing happened on the way to the
Revolution. There we were, beating our
breasts for social change, when it slowly
began to dawn on us that our big deal social-
political struggle was only one parochial
engagement for a revolution in consciousness

so large that it has been hard to bring it
into focus in our reality.[35]

FUSION BY CHOICE?

Societies exist by some kind of consensus, even if
it is a consensus to honor and explore pluralism, review
the givens regularly, and to institutionalize change. The
genius of this country has been its ability to maintain a
broad liberal umbrella of synthesis over a diversity of
interests, while baiting the goal with the American dream
of material betterment. The old idea has served its time,
and some new synthesis, distilled of the possibilities of
totality, needs to develop. With the elements in place
for inductive choice, a synthesis could go on at many
levels and yet be manifested in a coordinated and functional world view. Such a process could present a real
ground of being inherent in the very process of its
creation. "Ground of being" has a comfortable sound. It
is a place where one can stand while taking new bearings
and sighting the horizon. Unlike the umbrella, it does
not shut out the sight of the stars.

Once our givens were more numerous, determined heavily by the circumstances of birth and geography. Modernity
has provided much more latitutde for personal determination. It has truly made all of us time travelers. There
is a cemetery in my grandmother's Nebraska town that
contains the graves of six children, all of one family,
who died within a two-week period in the bad winter of
1888. Diptheria was the killer. Now choice can prevent
such tragedy. We may die of some defect or side effect
of technology, but we will have died by *some* conscious
choice of our own, knowing that choice involves risk.

In a consciousness switching from fate to choice, the function of God may seem to be displaced to other agencies--government, business, political ideology, or science. However, a democratic system and heritage work against the hardening of such institutional dependency, in part through the guarantee of the accessibility of information and by the power of popular election. The focus of responsibility is within the rich resource of the general population, to be used.

I have mentioned that quantum theory speculates beyond the narrow field of molecular relativity. These speculations suggest that our physical reality is just the tip of a much larger universe of material beyond our sensory scope.[36] This is a wild country, indeed, where known physical "laws" are unreliable and resist being proved by, at least, present scientific capabilities. Theory can run that this unseen universe may serve as a "possibility reservoir" for the conversion of some part of the unseen into some new aspect of our reality. Thus, new creation could constantly be going on. If there is truth here, then a "God of Fate" is not nearly so meaningful as a "God of Choice." An understanding of God as co-creator with human will may be a theological necessity in the new "Age of Choice" which we begin to discern between the fingers over our eyes.

The children of the sixties were a marker generation. In their televised dramatics, all their likes and dislikes, their mood changes, excuses and dodges, their kickings and screamings about change, are our own ditherings made manifest. Our dependencies are before us. Our disorientations are overt. How do we grow up to face the new choices upon us?

Again I return to scientific description: "Fusion is a process in which two nuclei of light chemical elements

combine at high temperature to form a heavier nucleus to
release energy. This process is the reverse of nuclear
fission and . . . releases several times the amount of
energy . . . as does fission.[37]

Notably the practicality of fusion is not established.
High temperatures indigenous to and resulting from the
process cannot yet be managed in an economical way. Perhaps there is a parallel here with social fusion. The
heat produced might melt down the containing environment.
In the interests of affecting insightful synthesis, we may
fear that social fusion would produce more heat than
light! The intensity might be better diffused in many
small transactions over a wide area. Perhaps the nuclear
analogy stops here so that fusion, the mirror twin of
fission, will not happen in society. The many individual
choices may shape some quite different synthesis out of
current experience and the knowledge of many traditional
systems. Science may have uncovered the very evidence of
its own limitations--namely, that most of creation is not
amenable to proof by scientific method. It would seem
that there is more to the human creature and the universe
than what is knowable by rational process. An adequate
belief base would need to acknowledge this "new universe"
even as it admits the necessity for methods and talents
other than strictly scientific.

Many individual choice-decisions require scope and
time duration. This duration becomes a "time between"
which collectively is a limbo, no matter how sustaining
individual faiths may be. Passage of time also implies
movement in space. Time is given to create a new world
and new personal relevance. Time is taken to construct
new ideas within and without, and to accustom the eyes to
new bearings and the ears to new messages. We are
challenged on a conscious level to grow up--to integrate

our experiences with theory, our longings with reality--
to knowingly project and objectify living syntheses. In
co-creative process the stargazer is made new with the
world, and the stars are newly accessible with meaning.

NOTES

1.   Ian G. Barbour, *Issues in Science and Religion*
(Englewood Cliffs, New Jersey: Prentice-Hall, 1966), p. 50.
Barbour gives a much more complete development of the
relationship between religion and science.

2.   Barbour, p. 36.

3.   Max Scheler, *Problems of a Sociology of Knowledge*
(Boston: Routledge and Kegan Paul, 1980), p. 152.

4.   Peter Berger, Brigitte Berger and Hansfried Keller,
The Homeless Mind (New York: Vintage Books, 1974), p. 205.

5.   The themes of Sir Walter Scott's *Ivanhoe* and
Byron's *Childe Harold* are medieval. Mary Shelley dealt
with Gothic in *Dr. Frankenstein*.

6.   *The Foxfire Books* and *Mother Earth Catalog* readily
illustrate the interest in frontier and rural life.   In
The Homeless Mind (p. 205), the ecological movement is tied
to nature worship. The same thread runs through many works
of Romantic poets as in Wordsworth's "Ode: Intimations of
Immortality from Recollections of Early Childhood".

7.   Karl Mannheim, *Ideology and Utopia* (New York:
Harcourt, Brace, Jovanovich, Inc., 1936), p. 235.

8.   Rolf Eliassen, "Nuclear Fission"; *Colliers Encyclopedia* (Crowell-Collier Publishing Company, 1962), Volume 17,
p. 712.

9.   For a much more complete account of the causes of
alienation in the young, read *Religion for a Dislocated
Generation* by Barbara Hargrove. Margaret Mead in *Culture
and Commitment* also speaks to the dynamics of cultural
schism, but in a more anthropological framework.

10.   Bruno Bettelheim, *The Uses of Enchantment* (New
York: Knopf; distributed by Random House, 1977), p. 122.

11.   J.R.R. Tolkein (1902-1973) wrote modern fantasy
or fairy tales. He was widely read and admired by the
children of the sixties who read him as teenagers and young
adults. Three of his books form *The Ring Trilogy*. They
are *The Fellowship of the Ring, The Two Towers,* and *The*

Return of the King. One might say that his work replaced the fairy tales and religious myths denied this generation.

12. Barbara Hargrove, *Religion for a Dislocated Generation* (Valley Forge, Pennsylvania: Judson Press, 1981), p. 29.

13. Mannheim, pp. 221-222.

14. Berger et al., p. 712.

15. Hargrove, p. 26.

16. Margaret Mead, *Culture and Commitment* (New York: Columbia University Press, 1978), p. 72.

17. Eliassen, p. 712.

18. Peter Berger and Thomas Luckmann, *The Social Construction of Reality* (Garden City: Anchor Books, 1967), pp. 129-130.

19. Karl Mannheim (*Ideology and Utopia*, p. 276), addressed this "dogmatic type of Marxism" by listing groups other than classes that are socially disjunct. In this list he includes generational conflict.

20. Berger et al. (*The Homeless Mind*, p. 35) speak of the "technological engineering" of character as consistent with modernity.

21. Mead, p. 81.

22. Robert Wuthnow, "Recent Patterns of Secularization: A Problem of Generations?", *American Sociological Review*, 1976, Volume 41, (October), p. 851.

23. The rebellious children of the sixties did not accept the socialization offered by such television shows as "Leave it to Beaver" and "Father Knows Best" where suburban family life was portrayed favorably. They were more convinced and convincing when their own exploits were televised.

24. Berger and Luckmann, pp. 96-98.

25. Ibid., p. 165 ff.

26. Howard Becker, *Modern Sociological Theory in Continuity and Change* (New York: Dryden Press, 1957), pp. 172-173.

27. Scheler, p. 15 ff.

28. Barbara Hargrove, "Integrative and Transformative Religions"; Jacob Needleman and George Baker, eds., *Understanding the New Religions* (New York: Seabury Press, 1978), p. 258.

29. Peter Berger, *The Heretical Imperative* (Garden City, New York: Anchor Press, 1979), pp. 59-60.

30. Ibid., p. 184.

31. Ibid., p. 185.

32. Scheler, p. 139 ff.

33. Mannheim, p. 106.

34. Bryan Wilson, "The Changing Faith and the Changing Churches", in *Contemporary Transformation of Religion* (New York and London: Oxford University Press, 1976), pp. 18-19.

35. Marilyn Ferguson, *The Aquarian Conspiracy* (Los Angeles: J.P. Tarcher; New York: distributed by St. Martin's Press, 1980), p. 58.

36. Leonard I. Schiff, "Quantum Mechanics", *Colliers Encyclopedia* (Crowell-Collier Publishing Company, 1962), Volume 19, p. 551 ff.

37. J.D. Dukes, "Nuclear Fusion", *Colliers Encyclopedia* (Crowell-Collier Publishing Company, 1962), Volume 17, p. 725.

CULTURE, POWER AND THE QUEST
FOR A JUST ORDER

Sheila Greeve Davaney

The last several centuries have been marked by the
growing recognition of the socially circumscribed character
of all human thought and action. It has become almost
axiomatic in the disciplines of sociology and psychology,
as well as history, philosophy, and theology, that to be
human is to exist within a matrix of socially derived meanings, values, and symbols that determine both the possibilities and limitations for human experience within that given
context and without which human beings could be neither
truly conscious of their world nor of themselves.

Exploration of this relationship between human consciousness and social existence has, however, never been
solely the concern of academics. From Karl Marx on, such
examination has been the focus of those groups and individuals who seek not only to understand but to transform the
social order and who, in their pursuit of liberation, have
utilized these insights as tools for interpreting the
dynamics of oppression. In this essay, I would like first
to set forth, in brief, what I take to be the central claims
that are asserted in social theories of human existence, and
second to examine the ways in which such claims illuminate
situations of oppression. Having put forth this material
in synopsis form, I then want to focus this presentation on
a central issue that arises at the point where social
theories and liberation concerns meet. This issue concerns

what might be termed the "where do we go from here?"
question; that is, recognizing the intimate relation between social reality and human experience, what are the
repercussions of such insights for attempts to overcome
oppression? In all these areas I will be working out of
the insights I have developed as a feminist primarily concerned with the transformation of women's experience.
However, in my presentation I have chosen to apply these
claims to the dynamics of oppression on a broader scale.

Underlying theories of the central importance of society and culture for all human experience and thought is
a basic assumption concerning the "incomplete" or "unfinished" character of the human person. Anthropologist
Clifford Geertz has been one of the most compelling articu-
lators of this interpretation of the human as an unfinished
creature in need of societal and cultural completion.[1] In
his work, *The Interpretation of Cultures,* Geertz argues
that, contra to the long-held belief, human physical evolution was *not* complete prior to the emergence of human
cultural development but rather the final physiological
make-up of *homo sapiens* is a product of the emergence of
culture and language. In Geertz's view, culture was not
added on to a finished human animal but was integral to
the evolution of the animal itself.[2]

For Geertz, one of the central results of this symbiotic relationship between the human physiological structure and human culture is that human beings receive only
diffuse and general instructions from their bodies. For
their part, other animals receive, from their genetic
programming, all the instructions necessary for environ-
mental adaptation and accommodation. That is, their
physiological make-up provides an adequate instinctual
basis for survival and reproductive success. In contrast,
humans, according to Geertz, would not only *not* be

conscious agents without culture, but would probably fail
to survive at all. Geertz argues that the human brain is
"thoroughly dependent upon cultural resources for its operations"[3] and that as a result, "a cultureless human being
would probably turn out to be not an intrinsically talented,
though unfulfilled ape, but a wholly mindless and consequently unworkable monstrosity."[4] Feminist anthropologists
Michele Zimbalist Rosaldo and Louise Lamphere, concurring
with Geertz's convictions, state " . . . human biology requires human culture," and conclude that " . . . human
activities and feelings are organized, not by biology directly, but by the interaction of biological propensities
and those various and culture-specific expectations, plans,
and symbols that coordinate our actions and so permit our
species to survive."[5]

     Thus, in this view, human beings do not depend solely
nor even primarily upon biologically specific instructions,
but upon culturally derived linguistic and symbolic resources
by and through which they experience and interpret reality.
This incomplete quality of human persons and the resultant
necessity of culture and society have far-reaching implications for understanding the relationship between social
determination and human existence. The first and most basic
implication that follows from this claim is that without
the linguistic and symbolic resources provided by society,
human beings would be incapable of any real consciousness
at all. Without the culturally constructed perceptual
lenses through which human experience is defined, ordered,
and understood, all that human beings would be capable of
would be a diffuse animal awareness, not clear consciousness.

     These culturally provided perceptual lenses function
in two directions. In the one direction, they provide the
ordering and interpreting categories by which we encounter

and know the natural and social world. Knowledge of the
natural and social milieus is thus never given directly,
but is mediated through the culturally derived differentiating and ordering mechanisms of language and symbol.
Hence, in a very real way, knowledge of our external environments is a cultural product. In social theorist Peter
Berger's words "on the foundation of language and by means
of it, is built up the cognitive and normative edifice that
passes for 'knowledge' in a society."[6]

This cultural foundation for knowledge functions, however, not only as the ground for consciousness of the "objective" world but equally importantly provides the basis
for *self*-consciousness and identity as well. That is, the
subjective structuring of human consciousness is also dependent upon cultural and societal resources. Individuals'
identities, roles, possible modes of behavior *and* the interpretation of such behavior are all determined by the
linguistic and symbolic developments within any given human
community. The possible ways humans can enact their humanity, the roles they can adopt, the forms of activities open
to them are all made possible only by and through the cultural visions any society has created. *There is no identity
or role which is not a cultural artifact*. Or stated differently, self-consciousness is a form of social consciousness.
In the words of Max Horkheimer, the architect of Critical
Theory, ". . . the individual is *real* only as part of the
whole to which he belongs. His essential determination,
his character and inclination, his avocation and view of
the world all have their origin in society and in his destiny within society."[7] Hence, not only does society shape
our perception of the external world, it equally influences
our self-understanding and circumscribes our ways of being
in that world.

It cannot, however, be stated that society merely provides the resources for interpreting and ordering objective and subjective experience. This way of expressing the situation implies too much of an optional quality to the relationship between society and the individual. Rather, there is a coercive character to this relationship; society not only *enables* certain ways of knowing and being but also *compels*, demands particular modes of interpretation of both the self and the world. In Berger's words, once again, "society directs, sanctions, controls, and punishes individual conduct."[8] Sometimes such social determination manifests itself in the forms of overt and brute societal tyranny. But underlying such overt manipulation is a mode of social determination that is far more subtle and more basic. Berger is instructive here. He suggests that social determination is so far-reaching because the cognitive and interpretive options available in any given society are not recognized as precisely that-- as competing options for understanding self and world, but they rather are taken to be reflective of reality itself. Berger states that ". . . the fundamental coerciveness of society lies not in its machineries of social control, but in its power to constitute and to impose itself as reality."[9] It is precisely this ability of human cultural constructions to have the semblance of "objective reality" that gives them their quality of inevitableness and necessity. Interpretive frameworks have about them, to use a phrase of Geertz's, the "aura of facticity" and culturally derived roles and identities appear in the guise of "nature." Their character as cultural artifacts is rarely evident. And given this appearance of necessity, it is understandable that any rebellion against or challenge toward such interpretive frameworks takes on the quality of rejecting reality itself.

But there is another factor that complicates this
process of social enabling and determination, and it is
this dimension of the process that persons working from
perspectives of oppression have focused upon most intently.
That factor is the relation between power distribution and
the control of cultural visions. This relation is of utmost
importance because interpretive frameworks are not *neutral*
lenses through which we encounter reality. Rather, they
embody fundamental, albeit mostly unconscious, decisions
concerning values. All interpretive frameworks are normative at heart. But not all members of society contribute
equally to the creation of such normative visions. Rather,
cultural visions and the possibilities and limitations made
available by them, are shaped, indeed controlled, in a primary manner by those who hold power in a society or in an
age. That is, the powerful control not only external
institutions and structures, but also our perceptions of
those external realities and of our roles and identities
in relation to them. And liberation thinkers have been
quick to point out that in situations of unjust distribution
of power, the interpretive frameworks through which we
encounter, define, and order reality function as legiti-
mations of the unjust social order. The socially-provided
interpretations of reality act as apologies for oppression
and the very appropriation of the roles available becomes,
for the oppressed, the internalization of the commands and
values of the oppressor. Thus, in situations of unjust
power distribution, the process of social determination
functions not as an enabler of human possibility and freedom
but as the mechanism by which the powerful control those
without power and the means through which unjust social
institutions, structures, and relationships are given the
status of the "natural" and the "good." In contexts of
oppression, social determination takes the form of what
Mary Daly labels the "colonization" of the human spirit.[10]

And such colonization, in turn, supports the very oppressive structure that caused it. That is, the appropriation and internalization of the oppressors' vision contributes to the ongoing credulity and, hence, maintenance of unjust social arrangements. Through the mechanisms of social determination, the powerless become unwitting allies to those who deny them power.

Thus we can see that the dynamics of oppression are profoundly interconnected with the very social processes by which human experience, knowledge, and action are made possible. Human beings, as unfinished creatures, require social and cultural resources for both consciousness of world and of the self. But in contexts characterized by oppression, these resources become the weapons of the oppressor, which serve to maintain the position and the prerogatives of the powerful.

Given that social determination is the ground for all human knowledge and action, and that in contexts of unjust power distribution, this process of determination functions to legitimate and to perpetuate inequitable social arrangements, the central question for oppressed individuals and groups becomes: how is such an insidious, self-perpetuating dynamic broken? Upon what grounds can the oppressed seek to transform the standing order? There are several possible responses to this query and at this juncture I would like to unpack these options and examine the repercussions entailed in each way of proceeding.

One mode of response to the dilemma of oppressive social determination has been the assertion of some form of transcendent truth and action. While this claim has taken several forms, including the assertion of a Platonic-like realm of timeless truth (e.g. Max Scheler), the one most interesting for our present context is the appeal of liberation theologians to transcendent revelation and divine

activity. A number of liberation theologians, mostly working from Latin American and Black North American Christian
perspectives, have clearly recognized the profound inter-
connection between power configurations and social determination; they are fully aware that the ways individuals
and groups think and the modes of behavior permitted them
are closely aligned to the degree of power and privilege
they hold or fail to hold. And it is precisely *because* of
this intimate relationship between power and social determination that many liberation thinkers insist appeal must
be made to that which transcends the social process. Without such a force that literally breaks into the socio-historical process, the cyclical dynamic of oppression would
be endless. If brute power is the final and only arbitrator
of the social process, then those without power are inevitable losers in any struggle. Black theologian James Cone
is an eloquent spokesperson for this perspective. In his
work *God of the Oppressed* he states,

> Black people knew that they could not trust
> the power of their own strength to break the
> chains of slavery. People get tired of
> fighting for justice and the political power
> of oppressors often creates fear in the hearts
> of the oppressed. What could a small band of
> slaves do against the armed might of a nation?
> Indeed, what can the oppressed blacks today do
> in order to break the power of the Pentagon?
> Of course, we may "play" revolutionary and
> delude ourselves that we can do battle against
> the atomic bomb. Usually when the reality of
> the political situation dawns upon the op-
> pressed, those who have no vision from another
> world tend to give up in despair.[11]

Hence Cone and others argue that without a transcendent ground, the options for the oppressed are, in the face of the oppressor's power, narrowed to blind acceptance, helpless resignation, or finally despair. Without a transcendent, indeed divine, perspective on reality, the oppressors' account of the situation, supportive of their own self-interests, is the only version of the truth. But, these liberation theologians argue, *with* such a transcendent ground, embodied in God's revelation in Jesus Christ, there is the hope that brute force is not ultimate, and that power and truth are not identical, and hence the oppressed can have confidence that, in Cone's words, "their fight for freedom is not futile."[12]

Given the dynamics of social determination *and* the reality of inequitable power distribution, there is much in this appeal to the transcendent that is attractive and even compelling. However, I would argue, there are major problems with this approach that finally render it highly problematic for oppressed individuals and groups, and especially women, in the form the argument has taken in current liberation theologies.

First and foremost, the argument for revelation-based transcendent truth is ultimately a case of special pleading that depends upon its proponents ignoring their earlier voiced insight into the social character of all knowledge and action. While repudiating the oppressors' version of reality by claiming it is solely an apology for self-interest, they argue that their own perspective has greater validity and finally, effective force, because it is based upon a transhistorical ground. Yet the bases for dehistoricizing the social process are ambiguous and unclear and remain ultimately unacceptable to those, like myself, who view appeals to revelation as socially determined viewpoints clothed in the terminology of the transcendent and

non-historical. It is finally impossible to begin with the
presupposition of the socio-historical character of all
knowledge and action and end with an appeal to that which
transcends the social process.

Second, many liberation theologians respond to this
type of criticism by stating that they clearly recognize
that what they term transcendent truth manifests itself in
historical guise; that is, that revelation takes place in
history and is embodied in the forms made possible by history. However, having said this, inevitably liberation
theologians, working from revelation perspectives, go on
to argue that there resides in such historical and socially
determined forms, a transcendent truth which is not to be
reduced to its time and place-conditioned manifestations.
Unfortunately, however, these thinkers fail to provide the
means by which to separate the transcendent truth from its
socially-determined forms. And inevitably the claims to
have isolated transcendent revelation have the appearance
of an arbitrary selectivity that serves the interests of
its proponents.

Thus, it can be argued that claims to revelation-based
truth present profound problems from the perspective of
social interpretations of knowledge and action--the very
perspective many liberationists start from. However, there
is another, and in this context quite relevant, perspective
for raising questions concerning the appeal to the transcendent, and that is the perspective of those for whom this
trans-historical vision is not liberating, but to whom it
represents a renewed version of the oppressor's age-old
trap; this perspective is that of women. While it must be
acknowledged that many women find the visions of transformation expressed by male Christian liberation thinkers
freeing, and other women are, with hope and integrity,
forging their own versions of this revelation-based position,

CULTURE, POWER AND THE QUEST FOR A JUST ORDER 389

it must also be stated that increasing numbers of us find
this approach not only problematic but ultimately self-
defeating in our quest for liberation. On the one hand,
women have been oppressed equally, if not more, on the
basis of a supposedly divinely revealed and ordained order
of reality than we have when appeal has been made to "nature"
or merely to the superior power of men. On the other hand,
the very resource to which most liberation theologians
appeal, that is, scripture, finally must fail as an adequate
basis for the transformation of the oppression of women.
For once the societal ground of *all* ideas is acknowledged,
then it must be recognized that the biblical materials, no
less than any other interpretations of reality, are socially
conditioned and reflect the power configurations of their
time and place of origination and development. And while
the social arrangements of ancient Israel and of the early
Christian era were highly complex and ever-evolving, they
certainly did not include the full freedom of women, and
neither did the scriptural material that witnessed to their
histories. Thus, while biblical sources may be at certain
points welcomed historical *resources* for the envisioning of
a non-oppressive future, they are highly problematic and
inadequate as the authoritative basis for the liberation of
women.

From the above analysis it should be clear that the
appeal to transcendent truth in the form of divine revelation is beset with inherent difficulties that render this
solution to the dilemma of oppressive social determination
problematic. Its failure, however, does not alter the pre-
dicament but only serves to focus our questions more sharply.
Is social determination so intensive as well as extensive
(Werner Stark) that there is no escape from it? In situations of inequitable distribution of power do the victors
claim not only the spoils in the sense of material resources

and institutional control, but also the very consciousness-
directing mechanisms of society? Is the only arbitrator of
the adequacy of cultural visions finally power? Is freedom
ultimately a social fiction masking a deeper and far more
fundamental lack of choice? There is much in the theory
of social interpretation that points in this direction and
there are many thinkers who do draw the conclusion that all
of our interpretations of reality and of our selves are
merely the embodiment of power configurations or, utilizing
a more physiological model, the result of biological or
psychological functionings. But while the very tenacity,
the incredible stubbornness of oppressive structures and
consciousness lends support to this mechanistic-type conclusion, it is an approach which is fraught with dangers
of the most ominous kind, especially for those who are
oppressed. On the one hand, such acceptance can only
promote either ignorant acquiescence or self-defeating
despair on the part of the oppressed. Those without power
are condemned to accept their state or to do endless and
finally fruitless battle with enemies who control all the
weapons. On the other hand, those who hold power are also
condemned in their own way; they, too, are prisoners of
their oppressors' consciousness and role, and are sentenced
to live out identities that can only contribute to the
maintenance of oppressive structures. In either case, a
kind of despairing moral license prevails, and the ultimately nihilistic spector that confronts humanity is that
of an endless war of conflicting and irreconcilable interests.

       Such a causalistic/mechanistic model is unacceptable,
indeed repugnant, for those of us who hold a vision of
liberation that seeks to move beyond the nightmare and the
madness of endless conflict. On this point of rejection,
persons such as James Cone and Juan Luis Segundo and I are

one. However, it is, as I have argued, impossible for me
and for many others to appeal to a transcendent revelation
as our basis for rejecting a model of strict and total
determinism. Instead, I would suggest, the ground for our
rejection must be found in the social process itself.

In arguing in this direction, I must state at the out-
set that I *do* understand our lives and our identities to be
significantly determined and shaped by the social milieu in
which we exist. The basic presupposition of this paper has
been that human beings cannot step outside of social reality.
However, to claim this does not entail concluding that
humans cannot be creative and transforming in relation to
that social matrix. The view of the social process presented so far is too static a picture of the process, too
reified a version of what, in fact, is a dynamic, constructive, ongoing, dialectical movement.

To begin with, we must remember that the social interpretive frameworks through and by which we encounter reality,
and the roles and identities that shape our self-understand-
ings are all human constructions. They may appear to us in
the guise of objective reality, of "nature," but in fact,
they are only the reified form of our own creations. Hence,
while it is clear that society is the creator of individuals,
it is also certain that it is humans who produce society and
the cultural resources that are found therein. We are, in
the end, products of *our own* social imaginations.

Second, while humans are indeed circumscribed by both
the internal and external options made available by their
social context, they do not simply reiterate in individual
form those social possibilities. Individual humans are not
merely microcosmic caricatures of the social macrocosm; that
is, society writ small. Instead, individuals *appropriate*
social visions and options and, I would argue, such appropriation always entails the possibility of creative and

critical transformation. The very incorporation of society's visions results in the modification of those visions;
the internalization of roles transforms them. Humans *are*,
in a very real way, determined and constituted by their
environment, but they are so shaped in a creative, dynamic
interplay with their social world. The model for social
influence should not be that of one way mechanistic determinism, but rather that of creative dialogue. This is not
to say that creativity is always present to a high degree;
it is to claim that the recognition of social determination
does not rule out *de facto* the possibility of creative
freedom in relation to and within the social matrix. If
social determination is real and ever present, it is not,
by necessity, absolute. In the ongoing social process,
determination and creativity interact to bring forth new
possibilities both for individuals and for society at
large.

And finally, if individuals are conditioned by society,
they, in their turn, contribute to the ongoing process of
shaping that societal context. Society's structures and
values *do* change and they do so on the basis of the transforming input of individuals. The creative appropriation
of societal options is eventually translated into the
creative transformation of society's values and institutions.

Thus, when the social process is interpreted in dynamic
dialectical terms, creativity can be seen to be as ingredient,
at least as a possibility, as determination is to that process. This combination of determination and creativity provides, I would argue, a more intelligible explanation for
the fact that change *does* take place, institutions *are*
modified, while at the same time it allows us to see why
the cultural artifacts of ideas, institutions, and identities are so intractable and why, therefore, change is so
often slow and painful. What this introduction of creativity

does *not* fully clarify, however, is that problematic issue
of the role of self-interest and power that was seen earlier to be so important for perspectives concerned with the
transformation of oppression. Is creativity merely another
servant of narrowly-circumscribed self-interest; that is,
do modification and transformation indeed take place, but
for the purpose of consolidating and furthering the power
and interests of individuals or groups?

This question of power and self-interest is the one I
find myself continually coming up against both in my intellectual efforts at analysis and, more seriously, in my
concrete attempts to forge a liberating vision for myself
and other women. And I must confess, as I begin to draw
this essay to a close, that I have found no satisfactory
answer to these questions. Often when I examine the insidious dynamic of oppression in its myriad forms, and
when I experience the overwhelming reality of patriarchy
as it destructively impinges on my body and my mind and
my spirit, I am tempted to conclude that the interpretation
that sees human reality as primarily and finally a series
of power struggles is correct; that power is never relin-
quished without struggle; that ultimately the oppressors
share little in common with the oppressed; our task, indeed
our only possibility, is to pursue those interests defined
by our class, sex, and race. But when I seek some ground
for *hope*, this vision simply will not suffice; it offers
no basis for liberation but is only the embodiment of
extreme cynicism, and finally a confession of defeat.
Instead, I must assert that while I am convinced that humans
often act according to the narrowest of interests and that
those interests are frequently perceived as exclusive of
the needs and concerns of others, I must also state that I
do not believe such exclusivity and narrowness are the only
possibilities. My reasons for proclaiming this lie not

only in my desire for a ground of hope, but also in my
interpretation of the *social* character of human existence.
These reasons can be divided into what might be termed the
ability of transcending narrow self-interest and the *necessity*, for truly social beings, of such transcendence. Let
me turn to the question of ability first.

To be human is, as this essay has argued, to be imaginative creators of the webs of meaning and value within
which we exist. But this human imaginative capacity need
not be only the vehicle of spinning narrow visions of
interest and concern. It can also be that basis upon which
we sympathetically expand our viewpoint to include the
perspectives of others; it can be the means by which we
move from insular preoccupations toward more universal
concerns. It can be finally the foundation for recognizing that those categories of isolated selfhood, family,
race, sex, class, nation--according to which we have defined our self-interests--are neither natural nor necessary,
but are cultural artifacts and as such are open to transformation and radical revision. The very social process
that has narrowed our concerns, that has divided the world
into power groups, can provide the ground upon which the
human community might seek reunion and the dismantling of
oppressive structures, institutions and roles. To fail to
recognize this and instead insist on a solely-power-deline-
ated-determinism is to renege on one of the basic insights
of a social interpretation of reality.

There is, I think, a correlated reason why a vision
of narrow determinism can and must be rejected. And that
has to do with the social/relational character of human
life itself. It seems to me that those who argue for a
strict determinism do so on the basis of a vision of human
selves and groups understood as isolated, self-enclosed

realities seeking to be immune to the influence of others.
In this view, separation is assumed and therefore, connection is envisioned in terms of confrontation and competition. The mode of relation is presupposed to be conflictual. This assumption of the conflictual character of
relation flows, I would argue, from the failure to recognize the truly social nature of humans, or put otherwise,
to carry through the insights of the social interpretation
worked out so far. If humans are conceived of as autonomous and self-enclosed, then influence can only be interpreted as threat; the well-being of one person or group is
always at the expense of another. However, I would contend,
that a truly social view, while acknowledging that conflict
is real and indeed, pervasive, suggests that this is not
the only possible mode of interaction. In a world which
is intrinsically and fundamentally interdependent, the line
between self-interest and the interests of others is not so
clearly drawn. Precisely as *social beings*, dependent upon
one another and the networks of meaning and value we commonly create, it is in our self-interest to take into
consideration the concerns, needs, and rights of others.
Without such consideration, the social matrix is harmed,
and with it the possibilities for all of us. In a social
universe, myopic self-interest leads to the diminution and
perhaps destruction of all.

I am not saying in this that self-interest does not
play a significant part. The realities of oppression witness clearly to this. I am arguing, however, that as
social beings we need not--indeed cannot--accept this as
the final word. We can, if we choose, nourish the connections instead of the disconnections. We can see our futures
as tied to the destiny of others and see that interconnec-
tion as a ground of hope rather than threat. I believe
that this way of proceeding is finally the only one

compatible with a thoroughly social interpretation of human history and interaction. I also believe that it is finally the only one compatible with the experience and insights of women seeking liberation for ourselves as well as a world in which conflictual power relations no longer reign. Carol Gilligan, in her new book, *In a Different Voice*, summarizes this position well when she argues that a social/ relational vision of reality is finally not tied to "the belief in the efficacy of aggression, but to the recognition of the need of connection."[13]

This recognition of connection provides no guarantee of victory. It does, I think, provide a ground of hope. It avoids, I would argue, both the pitfalls of an appeal to transcendent truth and the dangers of a strict determinism. And it suggests that finally, if there is hope, it lies precisely in that social process that can both oppress and liberate us. This may not be much, but I am convinced that it is all we have.

NOTES

1. Sociologist Peter L. Berger also argues strongly for the unfinished character of human beings. *Vide.* Peter L. Berger, *The Sacred Canopy* (New York: Anchor Books, 1969), p. 5.

2. Clifford Geertz, *The Interpretation of Cultures* (New York: Basic Books, Inc., Publishers, 1973), pp. 47-49, 68.

3. Ibid., p. 76.

4. Ibid., p. 68.

5. Michelle Zimbalist Rosaldo and Louise Lamphere, eds., *Woman, Culture and Society* (Stanford: Stanford University Press, 1974), p. 5.

6. Berger, p. 20.

7. Max Horkheimer, *Critique of Instrumental Reason* (New York: The Seabury Press, 1974), pp. 9-10.

8. Berger, p. 11.

9. Ibid., p. 12.

10. Mary Daly, *Gyn/ecology, The Metaethics of Radical Feminism* (Boston: Beacon Press, 1978), p. 1.

11. James Cone, *God of the Oppressed* (New York: The Seabury Press, 1975), p. 132.

12. Ibid., p. 17.

13. Carol Gilligan, *In A Different Voice* (Cambridge: Harvard University Press, 1982), p. 49.

ABOUT THE CONTRIBUTORS

Excerpts from the works of Max Scheler, Max Weber, and Peter Berger were considered "classics" against which the following authors played out their ideas. For the un-initiated, more information on these authors is contained in several of the articles published here.

Nancy T. Ammerman received her Ph.D. in Sociology from Yale University in 1983. The wife of a Southern Baptist pastor, she is the author of a number of articles in professional journals.

Peter Beyer is presently lecturing in the Department of Religious Studies at the University of Toronto. He has recently spent two years in Montreal studying the history of the Catholic Church in Quebec. Although of Lutheran background, he did his graduate work at the Roman Catholic St. Michael's College in Toronto where his studies concen-trated on the sociology of religion.

Kady Cone is Assistant Pastor of Grace United Presby-terian Church of Littleton, Colorado. She also serves as a pastoral counselor at the Bethesda Pastoral Counseling Center, and as Visiting Lecturer in Field Education at The Iliff School of Theology. She is a candidate for the Th.D. degree in pastoral counseling at The Iliff School of Theology.

Sheila Greeve Davaney is Assistant Professor of Theology at The Iliff School of Theology. She earned her M.A. and Ph.D. at Harvard Divinity School, and is the editor of *Feminism and Process Thought*.

D. Kerry Edwards is a Ph.D. candidate in Theology and Philosophy of Religion in the joint program of the Univer-sity of Denver and The Iliff School of Theology, currently

working on his dissertation. He received a B.A. in
Religion and Philosophy from Roberts Wesleyan College, and
an M.Rel. from the Toronto School of Theology of the University of Toronto.

Howard S. Fuller is pastor in the United Church of
Christ Community Congregational Church of Benicia, Cali-
fornia. He received his B.A. from Dartmouth College, an
M.Div. from Union Theological Seminary in New York City,
and an M.A. and Ph.D. from the State University of New
York at Buffalo.

Barbara Hargrove is Professor of Sociology of Religion
at The Iliff School of Theology in Denver. Her primary
areas of interest in that field have been in the relation
of religion to social change, including research on new
religious movements and the rising tide of clergywomen.
She is the author of *Reformation of the Holy*, *Sociology of
Religion: Classical and Contemporary Approaches*, and
Religion for a Dislocated Generation; co-author (with
Jackson Carroll and Adair Lummis) of *Women of the Cloth*
and (with Stephen D. Jones) of *Reaching Youth Today: Heirs
to the Whirlwind*. A Presbyterian laywoman, she has parti-
cipated in various working groups and commissions for that
denomination, for the United Methodist Church, and the
National Council of Churches.

Marilyn Hauck is the Assistant to the Executive
Director of the Center for Creative Living in Lakewood,
Colorado. She returned to higher education, studying
counseling and sociology of religion at The Iliff School
of Theology, at the same time her daughters were seeking
advanced degrees, and she retains an interest in the events
that shaped the lives of that generation.

Kenneth E. Merrick-Webb is an American Baptist clergy-
person pursuing his last year of class work on the Ph.D.
degree in American Relgiion and Culture in the joint Ph.D.

of The Iliff School of Theology and the University of
Denver.

Harold Remus is Associate Professor, Department of
Religion and Culture, Wilfrid Laurier University, Waterloo,
Ontario, where he teaches in the area of Christian origins.
He serves as the Executive Officer of the Council on the
Study of Religion, Managing Editor of the *Religious Studies
Review*, and Director of the Wilfrid Laurier University
Press. He is the author of *Pagan-Christian Conflict in
the Second Century* (Cambridge, MA, 1983) and of articles
treating the subjects of miracle and "magic" in the Greco-
Roman world, with special attention to the social and
cultural matrices of such phenomena.

Elizabeth Schmidt has completed her M.A.R. degree at
The Iliff School of Theology, with a primary focus on
theology and a secondary interest in the sociology of
religion. A member of the General Conference Mennonite
Church, she was at the time of this writing awaiting professional employment, piecing comforters, and "dinking
around on the hammered dulcimer."

Steven W. Stall is pastor of the Mt. Carmel/Brookland
United Methodist Church in Jonesboro, Arkansas. He has
also served the East Denver Church of God. He is a Ph.D.
candidate in Theology and Philosophy of Religion in the
joint Ph.D. program of the University of Denver and The
Iliff School of Theology.

John Stanley is Assistant Professor of Religion,
Warner Pacific College, Portland, Oregon. He served as
a Church of God (Anderson) pastor for twelve years before
seeking advanced education, expects by the time this book
is published to have been awarded the Ph.D. in Biblical
Interpretation from the joint Ph.D. program of the University of Denver and The Iliff School of Theology.

Jan Sumner is minister of the Thornton United Methodist Church, Thornton, Colorado, where she has served for the past six years. She is also working on a Ph.D. degree in American Religion and Culture through the joint Ph.D. program of the University of Denver and The Iliff School of Theology.

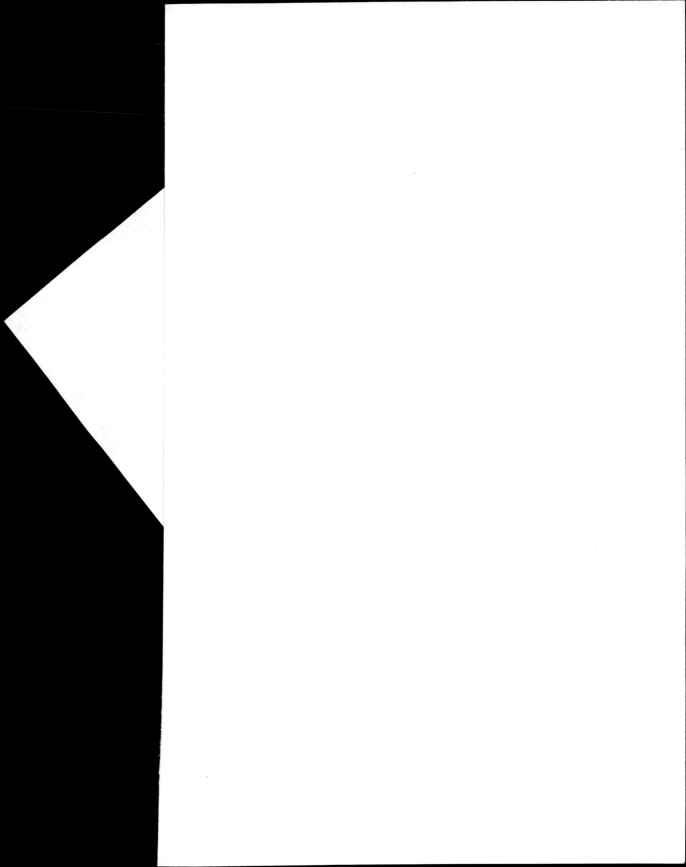

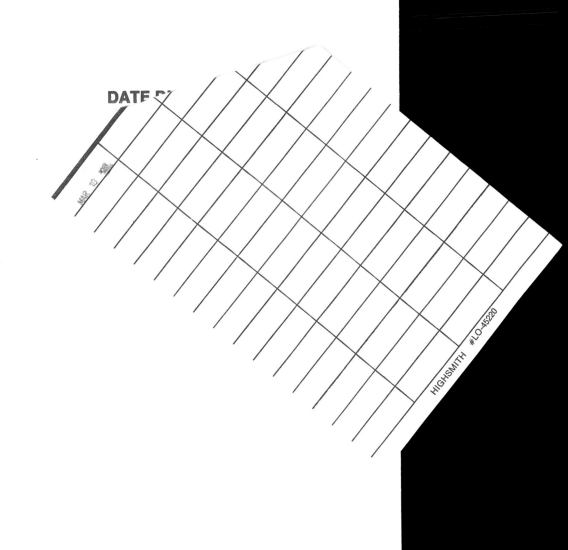

DATE D

MAR 03

HIGHSMITH #LO-45220